Contents

Publisher: Tredition, Hamburg, Germany

ISBN
Paperback: 978-3-7323-8563-8
Hardcover: 978-3-7323-9062-5
e-Book: 978-3-7323-8565-2

TAILS

of

SHEPHERDS

Ken Robson

Illustrations by

Ben Robson

For Mum and Dad, both keen dog lovers,

I think of you often.

For my wife and children, I love you all dearly.

Acknowledgements

Thank you...

Jo, my dear wife, for enduring all the insane ventures I have exposed you to, and for believing in me and for always being by my side. Also, for always smiling at that joke I have cracked countless times when people remark to me "I think you love those dogs more than your wife" and I reply "It's not true, I love them all the same".

Gill Collins for nagging me time and time again to write a book, you just don't quit do you, I like that. It's because of you that this whole thing found feet.

Chris Beeley for taking on the daunting task of first edit at a difficult time. For educating me and guiding me through this literary minefield.

Julia Hobson for subsequent edits and for adding a little colour to the whole project, and of course your efforts towards publishing, your assistance was timely indeed.

Richard Evans for your time and expertise in designing the book cover.

Inspector Annie Reavley of Nottinghamshire police for being so accommodating, allowing me access to trainings days for the purposes of book research.

Kay Greenwood for providing comfort at an emotional time.

Jon Coupe for looking after my dogs like your own, you are an amazing vet.

Tom and Elaine Edgar for being there, trusting me, and for being ready to drop everything if help was needed.

Contributions

Thanks to those who have contributed to this book, Julia Hobson, Mark Robson, Ricky Wright, Chris and Vicky Burch, and Emzy Bryan.

Sources

Mech, L David & Boitani, Luigi - "Wolves: Behaviour, Ecology, and Conservation", February 2007, published by the University of Chicago Press, ISBN 978-0226516974

Special Mention

I would like to make special mention of all the people I have met in rescue that have inspired and educated me. There are dozens of names here that I fear to document should I inadvertently leave one out.

TAILS of SHEPHERDS

INTRODUCTION

This is a story of a growing relationship between humans and dogs, that is, my wife Jo, and me, and our pack of rescue German Shepherds, which at the time of writing has numbered ten over six years. This is a story of discovery, commitment, joy and sadness all bound together with a very special kind of love. It has proved a steep learning curve, and there is still such a long way to go as I find myself becoming totally immersed in the amazing character of the majestic, noble, intelligent and often totally daft German Shepherd Dog (GSD).

I had not had a dog since I was a child, a black Labrador called Alex and he was my best friend by a long way. Alex was one of a kind, as indeed they all are, and we had a very special relationship. Alex left this world while I was in my mid-teens, and since then I have wandered in that dog-less wilderness of life. I forgot many things. I forgot about that very special bond that can form between man and dog; this bond can often be found in young men when they go to war. You may fall out from time to time, you may get upset with each other now and again, but when the time comes you will stand shoulder to shoulder, prepared to die for each other. Now that may sound a little extreme to feel that way about a dog, but trust me, that is where I am with my dogs, and I have seen many others in the same place. Certainly I have met many dog owners that have not found this connection, they care little for their canine "companions". If every dog owner found this special connection then there would be no dogs in rescue. If you are thinking "But it's only a dog" then, please, read on with an open mind and an open heart. Come with me on this journey and be prepared to learn.

I want to state early on that I am no dog expert, I have no qualifications in dog training, dog behaviour, diet, etc. I have been asked for advice many times and I always make this clear. I tell people what I think, and often suggest professional advice. So the things you may read about here are a product of the aforementioned learning curve. There may be parts of this story that you don't agree with or that don't chime with your own experiences. If I could go back to the beginning I would change quite a few things, especially in the early days and definitely on the diet front. In some cases we may need to agree to disagree, so please don't judge me, just read and enjoy. Along the way I hope to make you smile, perhaps shed the odd tear, maybe learn something, and possibly be inspired.

If you are inspired to rescue dogs then don't do anything rash. There are many ways you can help with a rescue organisation, but acquiring a pack is one of the hardest things you can do. It will bring many rewards but be under no illusion... it's hard. If you want a pack of dogs make sure you will still be feeling that way in 12 years or so from now. Understand it will be a massive money sink, your house will be covered in dust and you will constantly be picking up fur balls, blowing slowly like tumble weed across your living room floor. You will have little time to yourself and sitting on the toilet on your own will become a thing of the past. My passport has expired and I don't need another one; we take the dogs camping now. If, after all this, you decide to rescue dogs, then fantastic! Start with one and take it from there.

SO WHY EXACTLY AM I WRITING A BOOK?

Well, I was bullied into it! We got our third dog Kiera from a German Shepherd Rescue, which is where we acquired most of our dogs. Early on, Jo and I became involved with the rescue as volunteers. It's been an interesting experience and we have met some amazing people along the way. I have often posted about my dogs on the rescue social page on Facebook and, it seemed people enjoyed what I wrote, so I have been nagged by a number of people, especially Gill Collins to get this book done.

Although my Facebook posts were very popular, this is my first time putting together a whole book. I'm writing this book in the hope that I can reach more people and provide a more satisfying narrative through all of the trials and tribulations Jo and I experienced putting together our pack. Writing this book has really helped me to think through some important issues relating to GSDs and, I hope, has made me a better dog owner (which means a better human being!). Sales of the book will raise money for dog rescues nationwide and enable them to help more dogs.

I DON'T HAVE ANY ALSATIANS

This is a commonly asked question I get, "what is the difference between an Alsatian and a German Shepherd" I have also heard many times "Sorry, but my dog is afraid of Alsatians because he was attacked by one". I think to myself "Well... that's OK, because I don't have any". So we can clear this up before we start.

The German Shepherd's popularity was greatly due to the soldiers of WW1 recognising the dog's agility, power, intelligence and trainability as used by the military, (on the German side, where the dogs belonged), although the dogs were present and bred outside of Germany as well. However, towards the end of the war and for a few years after, especially leading up to WW2, there was a universal rise in anti-German sentiment. In the UK It was felt that the word 'German' in the dog's name could damage the breed's popularity. So, the breed was renamed *Alsatian*, after the French-German border city of Alsace-Lorraine. This was immediately towards the end of the First World War.

Around 1925 or so, the Alsace club, reinstated the old name, *German Shepherd Dog.* However, the Kennel Club of UK retained 'Alsatian' as the primary breed name, with 'German Shepherd' in brackets. This was reversed in 1977, when the breed became *German Shepherd Dog (Alsatian).* Finally, in 2010, the name 'Alsatian' was completely eliminated.

The breed is now simply "German Shepherd" throughout the world.

DISCLAMER

All the usual stuff- names and places have been changed to protect the innocent, and the not so innocent. If I do use a real name and you recognise yourself it's because I have your permission... remember? Outside of that, don't even think about suing me or I will come and visit you and bring Saxon with me and tell him to eat you. On a more serious note, sometimes relationships change. For most of the time of writing Jo and I were part of a rescue organisation that we have since chosen to detach ourselves from. I will refer to that rescue simply as "the rescue". We now help with another rescue which although smaller, we find more suitable.

ROXY

(The Diva Dog)

SPRING/SUMMER 2010

My wife Jo and I had often talked of getting a dog. We had been married for one year, and living in a four bedroom Victorian semi, with a very large garden, we had plenty of room. Jo has two girls from a previous marriage with shared contact and I have four children from two previous marriages. I was hoping Jo was to be my third time lucky, and so far so good.

My children were all grown up, apart from Ben, who was fourteen. Ben spent three days a week with me, he is autistic and was absolutely TERRIFIED of dogs. This was problem number one. Our second problem was our working hours, which are quite long. Jo and I own and run a full time Martial Arts School; we have between 250 to 300 students at any time from age four up. The school is open six days a week, we start work at midday and get home about 9:30 pm. Not great for a dog. The final problem was I didn't like walking. I keep fit, admittedly, but I was the kind of guy that would happily get in the car to visit our next door neighbour.

Having said all that, I've always believed that if you want something badly enough, you will find a way. The working hours were easily overcome- we would simply take the dog to work with us. Our school is only a ten minute walk from home so if we were worried about how the dog behaved around young children, I could easily pop the dog home for a bit. We had two full time staff and a few part timers so I didn't have to be there all the time. As for me walking, well I would just have to suck it up. If we had a dog, then I would be walking every day come-what-may. But... what to do about Ben? Well, we thought we would visit the local RSPCA shelter with Ben and see how things went. Ben did not react well to the visit, and we thought maybe this wasn't going to work out so the idea was put on a back burner for a while.

Some months later, Ben's Mum bought a cat and it appeared Ben had grown to really like it. This was promising because he was also afraid of cats. I mentioned to Jo that maybe we should pop back to the shelter and have another look. I remember Jo looking at me and saying "If we are going, we are getting a dog today". I guess she got her hopes built up last time and ended up being disappointed. A feeling of "Oh shit, today we will be making a commitment" washed over me as we walked to the car. We took Ben and Leigh (Jo's eldest daughter) along with us.

When we arrived at the shelter, the noise of barking was overwhelming, dogs were bouncing around in cages, and it was all a bit frantic. A Labrador caught my eye, this could be a possible. My childhood dog had been a Labrador and I had very fond memories of him. Jo and Leigh however, were focused on a Rottweiler/GSD cross. She was the only dog not barking, she just leaned against her cage with a mournful look on her face. At first I was not keen, she looked a bit weird, her head seemed too large for her body, and I was still hankering after the Labrador. We talked to the shelter staff about the two dogs and it seemed the Labrador was a stray and it was not known how he was with children. This would be a problem if we were to take the dog to work. The Rottweiler/GSD cross called Roxy had some history and they suggested for our needs this would be a better choice. That was it then, it was done. Roxy was to be ours and life was going to take a significant change... forever. Arrangements were made, we were told we would have to have a home check but Roxy would be set aside for us on successful completion of the check.

Ben was much better this time, he was still a bit nervous and when I asked him about Roxy coming to live with us he said "Errm that's OK, the lady will look after her". So he was still not won over on the idea but we had made progress. I was sure this would work out. Later Ben and Roxy would become very good friends and she really helped him overcome his fear.

A few days later I went back to the shelter to visit Roxy on my own. I fell madly in love with her, and it seems the feeling was mutual. It turned out that the reason Roxy's head was apparently too big for her body was because she was considerably underweight. We were told she came into rescue because she was destructive in the house (which gave us pause for thought!) but aside from that, no known problems. One thing I did notice was her focus and attention, very much like my son Ben's. It almost seemed like she was autistic. This was due to the way she interacted and the way she would be drawn to one thing and be mesmerised by it to the exclusion of all else. She did seem very interested in the small animals around the shelter. The pictures don't capture it but things were a bit odd here. No matter, she was going to be ours and we would work through whatever issues we found.

Prior to our home check, Jo and I could be found happily perusing the wares of various pet shops, buying all kinds of things- beds, dog food (I will come back to that shortly), toys and a massive three foot long rawhide bone. We were as excited as a young couple expecting their first child and shopping in Mothercare. We bought all kinds of crap that we didn't need and Roxy wouldn't want, but we had fun.

The home check went well. The garden was secure and they were happy with the condition of our two pet rabbits. The rabbits were the result of a request from our children- they desperately wanted a pet... and yes of course, they would care for it forever. I am sure you know where the story goes from there. The promises didn't last long, leaving me to feed said rabbits and muck them out for the rest of their lives. They lived in a play shed with a secure balcony that was elevated off the floor on three foot stilts. It was quite the little bunny palace! The home check lady suggested that maybe we should give the rabbits free run of the garden more often than we did. I wasn't keen as the foxes around here have balls the size of melons, they are not as afraid of humans as you imagine they should be, and they range through city gardens during the day. Already one of our rabbits had been rendered headless by one. The fox didn't eat the rabbit, it just wanted to kill it. However, the foxes would soon be striking our garden off their list of territories. All said and done though, the home check was a pass. FANTASTIC!! We were on the phone straight away.

3

OHH YES... I SAID I WOULD GET BACK TO YOU ABOUT DOG FOOD

This is my view which is based on research I have done. Remember I am not a canine dietician. We started feeding Roxy on an expensive well known kibble, the stuff written on the packaging suggested that the contents were the elixir of the gods, which is why I bought it. It was all bullshit I am afraid. In fact, had it been bullshit it may have been more nutritious! I got my hands on an independent report written on this kibble and the report ended with the statement "unfit for canine consumption". So, what should I feed my sweet princess on then? I did a lot of research to find that basically nearly all commercial food was roughly the same, including wet food. You can understand from a commercial point of view they are in this for the profit, of course. So cheap, and in many cases, unnecessary ingredients are used to bulk out the food and keep production costs down. Chemicals are added to increase shelf life, thereby increasing profits. It all makes sense. These companies have to make a profit, and then your dog dies in your arms of cancer. I am sure there is commercial food out there that is good, I just haven't found it, and since the regulations surrounding package labelling for dog food leaves a lot of room for creativity, I decided to go raw, feeding them with human grade food. Wolves don't eat kibble (or, as I like to call it, kill-ble), and I wanted to feed my dogs pretty much what wolves eat. I would know exactly what was in their food and there would be no chemicals. They would be on what is known as a prey model diet. There is loads of information on-line about this diet, it's very worthwhile reading up on it. A good resource I have used is dogsdinner2.web.com. It will take up a lot more of your time, both sourcing and preparing the food but it's no more expensive than kill-ble. "I don't have time for that" I hear you cry. In which case I suggest you make time. Find a way. Having said all that, the police kennels I do volunteer work for, and many rescue organisations do use kibble. Often rescues get it donated so there is no choice really, kibble is better than starving to death. People gamble with their own health all the time by smoking etc. and that's fine, it's your gamble and it's your health. However, as a dog owner I for one will not gamble with my dog's health. I may get it wrong from time to time, I may make mistakes here and there but to the best of my knowledge, which I am constantly expanding, I am doing my very best.

Now THAT'S a dog's dinner.

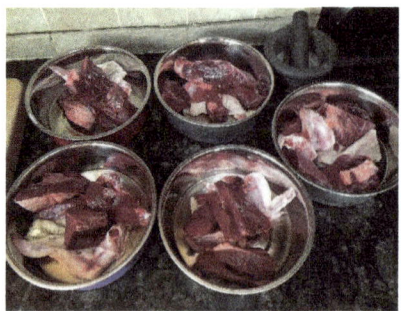

Right... I am done with the soapbox, I will put that away for now.

22nd OCTOBER 2010

With our home check successfully out of the way, Jo and I jumped in the car to get our Roxy. We arrived at the shelter to be told that she had just come into season and if we wanted we could leave her at the shelter and collect her when her season had finished. Err... NO...- have you seen all that crap we have just bought for her, we will take her now thanks if that's OK? We borrowed a blanket to keep the back seat of the car clean and we were off home, to introduce our beautiful Roxy to her new life. Jo and I were grinning like Cheshire cats feeling very happy about our new arrival.

We got Roxy home, took her inside and unclipped the lead. BOOM! She was everywhere at once, she ran upstairs and I yelled "Roxy, NO, we are not allowed up there, we need to talk about some rules." Roxy wasn't listening, we would discuss rules with her later after she calmed down a bit. She was like a whirling dervish. I opened the back door and she raced into the garden. She was sniffing everything then she found the bunny stilt palace, and... stillness. She spent the next three months staring at the rabbits. Every time we let her out into the garden she would make a beeline for the stilt house and just sit, and stare, and wait, and not move. Her dog version of autism just kept her transfixed.

In the first picture are the two rabbits that held Roxy's attention. In the second picture is the pose Roxy struck and held for three months whenever she was out in the garden.

Roxy's first night was spent on her bed placed in the living room, which is where she spent most of the evening with us. When we went to bed we made sure she had been to the toilet and we shut the living room door to restrict her access to the rest of the house during the night. In the morning there was dog poop everywhere. Not a problem, we were kind of expecting this. Bless her, she must have been very stressed in a strange place with strange people where she couldn't get away. It quickly became apparent that Roxy did not trust or really even like humans. This would manifest itself by her running away every chance she got. On day two she cleared our "secure" fence and got into a neighbour's garden. What a panic we had when we discovered she was not on guard duty outside bunny stilt house. Soon it was time for me to have a discussion with her about house rules, I was determined to be a strict but fair pack leader to her. What I say goes and all that.

RULE 1 Thou shall not lie on a human bed.

RULE 2 Thou shall not even venture upstairs.

RULE 3 Thou shall not settle upon human chairs or sofas

...and so the rules went on and on. Roxy looked really interested. You can see from the pictures what an impact this discussion had on her. But how could you deny her these things, just look at that face? Before long Roxy had *me* really well trained, she had me right in the pads of her paw. Nothing much has changed to be honest, I would do anything for my girl. I love her to bits.

It soon became apparent from Roxy's walks and just generally observing her, what had gone on in the 20 months of her life before we got her. It was very clear she had not been walked, hence her destructive nature. Everything she saw outside was a wonder to her, she just had no experience of anything. If I raised my hand too quickly to open a kitchen cupboard or something, or if there was a sudden loud noise she would cower away. She remains this way today. So I think someone bought her as a puppy, thinking "Oh, what a little cutie" because, looking at her now, she must have been. Then she got big, she wasn't walked, and with nowhere to channel her energy she became destructive. She is a powerful girl and capable of real damage for sure, then she was beaten for chewing the house up. I have no proof of this but that's my theory. Well, that was all to change.

Ben and Roxy became very close. They played a game that Ben dubbed "fighting and biting" a scary name for a scary game. Well... it looked scary. Ben would put his arm in Roxy's mouth and Roxy would soft mouth him while they rolled around wrestling. I had to discourage this eventually as I didn't want Roxy soft mouthing people, but I would never have imagined Ben playing with such a large dog in this way months ago. Roxy proved to be really good for him in many ways and it was truly heart-warming to see this relationship develop. It was almost as if she knew that Ben was a little different.

  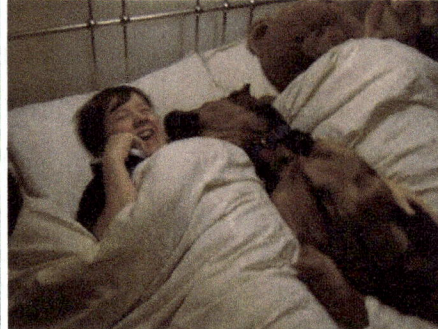

I took Roxy to have her spayed which was part of the agreement with the rescue. We had to use a specific vet for this operation as the rescue were paying for it. As Jo and I left her to be sedated you should have seen her reaction and the look in her eyes, it was a mix of sheer panic and utter helplessness, and she could not believe we were leaving her. Driving home I had a lump in my throat. However, with that episode out of the way, in the months to come, Roxy flourished. She learned to trust and so stopped trying to run away, she learned basic commands and became very obedient with an excellent recall. We could take her anywhere and do anything. Roxy came to work with us every day, the kids loved her and she enjoyed the attention, she was never alone. She started to put on weight and her exercise routine made her very strong. The walk plan was, and remains to this day, for me to walk a minimum of 100 miles every month, Roxy was off lead almost all of the time so God only knows what mileage she was doing. It would be at least three times the distance I covered. Come rain, snow, shine, or storm we would walk, every single day. Roxy has never been destructive in the house- she will skin the odd tennis ball now and again but that's it. Life was good, life was easy. Roxy was the perfect dog.

Christmas came and went. Our princess enjoyed a massive steak for her first Christmas dinner and got loads of presents. Roxy has more dog collars than Jo has shoes. Mind you, all those high heels have been swapped for walking shoes and wellies now. Jo and I were also experiencing a massive and very positive life change. Roxy became a very happy and contented dog, her life had made a U-turn for sure. Yet that fear and her timid nature was always there, just under the surface. The experiences she endured from a puppy would live with her forever, there was nothing we could do for her to change that. When she knew she was safe and secure, either in the car or on lead, she could project a real image of power and confidence, but off-lead and with nothing between her and another dog she was like a mouse. I recall on one occasion when out for a walk two miniature Jack Russell's approached her barking, and she was terrified- bless her. Her ears came back and that look in her eyes, her demeanour just didn't match her size and obvious power. Roxy has improved so much since then, being in a pack has been a huge help, but the fear, I think, will never leave her.

11 JANUARY 2011

Happy birthday sweetheart, our foxy Roxy is two today. We planned to do the thing Roxy loves more than anything else, we headed out to the Peaks for a whole day of walking. The weather was kind to us and we all had a great day, marred only slightly by the snotty attitude of the jobsworth waitress at the pub we stopped off at on the way home. Jo and I ordered food and I asked if I could have just a plate of sausages on their own for Roxy. The said waitress considered my request, while staring at the ceiling, and then simply replied with a blunt "Erm...no" without even looking at me and then walked off. No sorry, no explanation, nothing. It was one of those occasions when afterwards you think to yourself "I wish I had said that" as a clever and cutting reply comes to you five minutes too late. Never mind, I ate some of my food and Roxy had the rest. We had many lovely walks in the Peaks in the months to come. We used a long retractable lead quite a lot, as the risk of coming across sheep is always there. I really don't like retractable leads they are dangerous and if

8

you have more than one dog, they can be a risk to the dogs as well. For that reason, and because I like my dogs to be off lead, as our pack expanded over the years, we would not return to the Peaks.

MAY 2011

SO... WHAT'S THIS CAMPING THING ALL ABOUT THEN?

Resigning myself to the fact I will probably never set foot in an airport again, we bought ourselves a tent. Jo was still able to jet off now and again with her daughters but I wasn't going to put my princess behind bars ever again. That haunted look on her face while locked in that cage when we first met will never leave me. The tent we bought was a five man Vango, it was adequate for our needs and budget wise it was a good starting point for virgin campers. In my military career I have spent plenty of time under the stars on survival exercises all over the world, from Arctic to jungle, sometimes with a hunter force hot on my heels with the intention of capturing me and interrogating me for hours on end. What fun! But camping with a tent, a dog and a wife was new to me.

We found this lovely farm in the middle of Wales with a field for campers and a very clean toilet block. Our hosts were lovely, they did explain to us that a couple they had staying with them the week before had a dog that killed one of their lambs, so could we be careful with Roxy? After an incident like that, it was good of them to allow Roxy at all, but yes, we would be very careful. Roxy had shown an interest in sheep before, when we had her on a long lead she would attempt to chase but if the sheep stood its ground, Roxy's timid nature would kick in and she would shy away. That said, just chasing a sheep is enough to cause it injury and therefore gives a farmer licence to shoot your dog, so we would take no risks at all on this holiday.

Roxy really took well to camping, we had a fantastic time and went on some stunning walks. In the second picture I left Roxy with Jo while I walked on a little to get a very close look at a waterfall. Roxy was very

9

concerned she could not come with me, you can see that on her face. On another occasion we reached the summit of a high peak, and as we were coming down we crossed a ridge line and this amazing panoramic view just presented itself to us. Roxy stopped dead in her tracks and just stared in wonder, as if to say "Wow, this world is much bigger than I thought when I was with the other people I loved". I am sure she did love her first owners, despite the neglect, because that's what our beautiful dogs do.

On one of our walks things got a bit wet. Well, it was Wales! We stopped under a low tree to take shelter from the rain and we had a little snack. I pulled out a squashed sandwich wrapped in silver paper, it was a cold bacon sandwich I'd made that morning. I took a bite just as a huge drop of water rolled off a leaf and down my neck. I looked up, and in the sky flying overhead I saw an airliner, no doubt jetting off to somewhere hot. I turned to Roxy and said "See that thing up there, it's full of people that don't have dogs, going somewhere hot to sit by the pool and drink ice cold cocktails. That's what we used to do, but now we have a dog, YOU, and I am sat on the side of a fucking mountain in the middle of Wales getting piss-wet through eating a cold squashed sandwich". She didn't even bat an eyelid, she really didn't care... Shocking!

One day we took a drive to a beach. This was Roxy's first view of the sea. She darted straight into the water swimming like a fish, and took a massive drink. What she got was not what she expected, she had a face like a bulldog chewing a wasp. Had I not really felt for her it would have been hilarious, the look on her face. Our evenings were spent eating good takeaways and drinking supermarket brand wine while Roxy just relaxed with a bone, recharging her batteries for the next day's adventures. Perfect.

We stayed at the site for a wonderful week then it was time to pack up and go home. Roxy was incredibly well behaved and we had no incidents. Sadly we would not return, our future canine acquisitions would render this beautiful location inaccessible to us. It would be at best bedlam, and at worst dangerous, to dogs and livestock alike.

JUNE 2011

Jo enjoyed her time so much camping in the mountains of Wales soaking up the inclement weather (literally!), that only one month later she decided to sod off to Mexico with her daughter Leigh, and leave Roxy and me to our own devices. Well, I wasn't going to leave Roxy! As it happens we had a great time. "Right Roxy, we are going to do the Peak district, all of it!" This from the guy who only eight months ago hated walking. The things dogs do to you!

We had some amazing walks and it felt like a real bonding thing, just the two of us together. Until Roxy punched me in the face, that is. Giving a paw for a treat is always done with great enthusiasm and gusto. I offered Roxy a treat one evening and WHAM, as fast as lightning I got right hook square in the face! In fact, she really rang my bell. My nose was bleeding, my lip popped and did the same and then swelled up like a balloon. It felt like I had had a swipe from a bear. I did wonder at this point how Jo was getting on in Mexico.

When Jo got home, she had a lovely pink leather collar for Roxy, OK, Roxy is not a pink kind of girl, but it was a quality collar. I got a crap bottle of tequila with a dead worm in it.

AUGUST 2011

One very hot day in August we decided to go to a place called Illum for a day out. We had walked there before during the week, it was very picturesque and quiet. You could plan your walk to venture into the hills or to hug the river. As it was so hot, we planned to stick to the river. Roxy would have plenty of water to drink and she could take a dip if she got hot running around. The day we went was a Sunday and it was roasting hot, so as you may have guessed, the place was heaving with fair weather city types who venture into the wilds but rarely. Many of these people were just not equipped or dressed properly for this location.

We arrived at the car park and headed off along the path alongside the river. Roxy was very excited and was darting around in and out of the water. At one point, as she leapt into the river after some ducks which flew off, I saw looks of horror on some people's faces. I remember thinking then that this is going to be testing. We got to a crossing point in the river, it was quite wide but reasonably shallow with huge stepping stones. There was a one way system going on, a bunch of people from one bank would cross in one direction, then people from the other bank would wait, then cross the other way. You did not see people crossing in both directions at the same time. No problems, we got it.

As I started to cross, Roxy was behind me, she then pushed past me to get ahead. "Oops careful Roxy", It's a good job the stones are wide, then she bounded ahead past other people and I got a feeling of panic building amongst my fellow crossers. I didn't want to call to Roxy because then she would come back and push against the flow of people. I was now thinking "Maybe this is a bad idea". Roxy made dry land on the far bank and realised Dad was not with her. "Ohh no... where's my Dad? Ah there he is, in the middle of the river, I have to be with my Dad"- I saw this thought process going off in her head, I saw what was coming and thought to myself "Oh shit."

Roxy came bounding back to me, leaping from one stone to another like an antelope on speed. I could just see her bowling people over like skittles, people were shouting and screaming and waving arms around trying to maintain balance but thankfully nobody got wet. I grabbed Roxy and eventually we got across with no one falling in.

12

Once we were a quarter of a mile or so from the car park, there were no people so we could relax a bit. On our return to the car we found an ice cream van parked just off the path, surrounded by people, of course. Roxy took one last dip to cool down, and as she exited the water she shook off, right next to this substantial stern looking lady wearing her Sunday best and white trousers. OMG no! She held up her arms, her eyes went wide as she looked down at her not-so- white trousers and yelled "Oh, what a disgusting creature." I really had to bite my tongue. Perhaps I should have prevented Roxy from doing that but it happened so quickly, and we were in the outdoors after all. I remember thinking "Roxy is fit, she is strong, she is in great shape, and you call her disgusting!" On this day we also discovered Roxy really likes ice cream.

Roxy was very well behaved, bless her, she didn't put a paw wrong and she was just having fun in the water but Illum was another place that we struck off our list of walks, at least on weekends.

Later that month we saw the RSPCA were having a dog show at a local park. We thought to take our beauty along and enter lots of competitions, I was certain she would be festooned with rosettes and prizes. It was a lovely hot day, we had a look at the competition schedule and entered Roxy into best rescue, best cross breed and two other categories that I can't quite recall now. Competition one- we were not even in the top three. "NO WAY" I complained to Jo, feeling a little aggrieved. Competition number two... nope- again nothing. "NO IT CAN'T BE, there is something wrong here" I was actually getting a bit cross now. I am quite competitive but I can take it on the chin, however this was my beautiful girl. Competition three... strike three. "RIGHT WE ARE LEAVING, IT'S BLOODY FIXED" I ranted at Jo. I was hopping mad. We stormed off before competition four even started with me in a mood and Jo having a giggle at my expense. Roxy was none the wiser.

DECEMBER 2011

The months slipped by incident free and before we knew where we were, Christmas was rapidly approaching. My mum was getting on a bit and no longer travelled so we took Roxy up to County Durham to pay our

Christmas visit. All my family are dog lovers and both my sisters have dogs so Roxy always got a warm welcome. Being in that part of the world meant that we could take some lovely walks in Hamsterly Forest. The place is huge and is teeming with wildlife; we saw red kites and caught a glimpse of a large red deer as it melted away into the woodlands before Roxy could detect it. As always, Roxy was as good as gold.

We returned home after a few days to prepare for Christmas. My son Stuart and his partner Heather were coming to stay with us for a while, Heather is a fish eating vegetarian so we added a whole salmon to the traditional Christmas menu. In those days I did all the cooking in the house, Jo was not allowed since the time she set the kitchen on fire and the fire service had to attend to stop the house from burning down. She was allowed to use the kettle but that was it. So, dinner prepared, I had the salmon on the kitchen work-top with the foil off and I just popped into the living room, I don't remember why now, but whatever the reason I took too long and the price I paid was the whole salmon. Well, who could have done that, I wonder? I wasn't gone that long but the salmon was all gone. I yelled at Roxy to come, which she did. Then she did that thing she does to get out of trouble. She sat down, popped in her doleful eyes and put both of her paws in the air above her head, as if she is doing hands up. Then she slowly reared up on her hind legs and hooked her front paws over my arm, nuzzling her snout under my neck and snuggling into me, as if to say "Dad I am so, so sorry. I didn't mean to do it and I promise I will never do it again ever. Please forgive me, can't you see how much I love you". It works every time, Roxy is no longer in trouble and as soon as she realises that she wanders of as if nothing has happened, probably thinking "Ha, ha, what a sucker, I got him again."

11 JANUARY 2012

For Roxy's third birthday we booked into a dog friendly hotel-cum-pub for a long weekend. There was a nice big four poster bed which Roxy was not supposed to lie on, oops, and in the bar area there was a nice big open fire, which was perfect to sit by after a long snowy walk in the hills. The resident pub pooch barked at lot at Roxy but my princess just ignored the thing, good girl.

MARCH 2012

My birthday is in March, so as a treat, it was time to holiday again. Off we went to another location renowned for its characteristic weather, the Lake District. This time we stayed in a log cabin. The place was lovely and very cosy, certainly more so than our tent would have been at that time of year.

On day one we took a hike along a ridge line, just west of Lake Windermere. In the distance we could see a very large cairn. As we got closer Roxy, not having seen anything like this before, was unsure and so she started to stalk it. Much as she stalks the squirrels in the park. I think she'd been watching too much Nat Geo Wild on TV. It was fun watching Roxy discover new things. On day two we took a walk around Coniston Water and day three we planned Langdale Pikes. This walk was a quick six hours and it was truly stunning.

Since our hiking experiences in Wales, I was now the proud owner of a "Satmap" GPS mapping system. It's about the best you can get on the market and it is an amazing bit of kit for navigation. Accurate to within ten feet, it has excellent satellite acquisition and a four day battery life with the option of switching to AAA batteries if you are out in the wilds for weeks. I planned our route carefully using an Ordnance Survey map and dropped the waypoints into the GPS. The weather was stunning with clear blue skies. We parked the car in a pub car park so we could easily refresh at the end of the walk. The ascent went according to plan, it took some time and it was hard going but the views made it more than worthwhile. We eventually got to the top and stopped for a snack, Roxy had sausages.

We had planned a different route for the descent, and bellies full, off we went. Going down was not exactly easy-going either and about halfway down we were bang on course on the GPS, but the track just faded away into what looked like a bog. We had a choice, we could turn around and go back the way we came, adding three hours to the walk or we could press on and hope the track appeared again. I discussed the options with Jo and WE decided to press on. The path never re-appeared and the rest of the walk was heavy bog and very hard going. Roxy was fine, in fact she could probably have done the whole thing again but Jo wasn't fine, no, not at all, and it was all MY fault. The air was blue, and each half mile we slogged through brought Jo closer and closer to blind rage and meltdown. I had to choose my words carefully and tried to keep the conversation around how welcoming that pub would be when this was over. With the car park in sight we came across a ravine with deep fast-running water which we had to cross, although there was no obvious crossing point. After a search we did find a place but it looked challenging, certainly Roxy would need help as the rocks were very slippery, the ravine was steep, and the water was fast. Slowly and carefully as a team we made it across, albeit a team with one very angry member. We got to the pub, the thing that had been keeping us going for so long, and it was shut! We had a very quiet drive back to the cabin.

On day four and five we did short easy walks and avoided conversations about mountains, then it was time for home. The cabin was fantastic and we would return but we wouldn't be doing Langdale Pikes again.

While in the lakes, we toyed with the idea of getting Roxy a playmate. Roxy was so easy, the perfect dog, how hard would it be to have just one more? We had no idea what we were about to put ourselves through.

So... should we have a puppy or another rescue GSD? We postulated that given Roxy's timid nature and the fact she was only three, a puppy may be the best option. We were lucky with Roxy but another rescue dog may be a bit of an unknown quantity, and we didn't want to put Roxy into a stressful situation. One of the parents at our Martial Arts school, Amanda, was a GSD breeder, and her bitch was pregnant and due a litter soon, Amanda went to great lengths to ensure her puppies went to the right home, and she had no qualms about reclaiming them if things did not go to plan. Amanda always made a fuss of Roxy when we took her to work and she knew we loved her to bits. She often gave us advice with Roxy as she had considerable experience with the breed and she was the one that pointed us at the raw food diet. We asked if we could have one of her puppies and she agreed. FANTASTIC!!

When the litter of nine were produced, tragically seven of them died. Amanda and her family were devastated. She decided to keep one of the puppies and the other would go to her mother. Sadly, we had to think again about where to find a friend for Roxy.

For some time I had been looking at wolf hybrids and I found a kennel club approved breeder in North Devon that produced hybrids that were five generations removed from pure wolf. (This was a requirement to make it legal in this country.) They looked stunning and they were huge! We did some research on these animals and ended up shelving the idea as basically being too risky. Certainly our gentle Roxy may have struggled with a wolf.

In the meantime, Jo had spotted this wolf-looking Shepherd in another RSPCA shelter and drew my attention to him. This could be just the wolf I was looking for so a visit was arranged.

MAX

(Maximus – Gladiator)

APRIL 2012

On the day of the visit, my season ticket holding, football hooligan of a wife was at the match, so I went off to meet Max on my own.

I arrived at the shelter and one of the girls went to get him. I was quite surprised when she brought out this scrawny emaciated Shepherd. This didn't look anything like my wolf. I went up to Max and knelt down to stroke him and he gave me a big kiss. The young girl holding him looked very surprised, "Oh!" she exclaimed, "He doesn't normally do that". We were told Max had Exocrine Pancreatic Insufficiency or EPI, which is a condition that occurs when the pancreas fails to provide the necessary amount of digestive enzymes. Due to a lack of these enzymes, dogs with EPI cannot properly digest the nutrients in food. This means they can eat plenty of food but they will slowly die if not treated. The condition is not curable but if treated properly the dog can live a normal life with a normal life expectancy. It just meant Max would be on expensive medication every day for the rest of his life. At 24 kilos his ribs stuck out like piano keys and his hip bones protruded like bony lumps. We were told that when he came into rescue he was 22 kilos. His belly didn't have much fur, the insides of his ears were bald and he just generally looked a mess. Bless him, it looked like his body was giving up on him.

There were plenty of reasons for me to walk away from Max. He didn't look anything like what I was expecting, he was in poor shape and he had a permanent medical condition that would mean expensive medication for the rest of his life. People say that dogs choose you, and, in spite of these issues, I just knew Max would be ours. I asked all the important questions, is he good with children? "Yes" came the reply. Is he good with other dogs? "Yes" I was told, all the replies came back positive. Now I am not saying this young lady wasn't telling the truth, but when I think back now her body language and facial expression didn't match the words coming out of her mouth. Max was only one week younger than Roxy so that worked. I was sold anyway, I explained I would go home to chat with my wife then I would give them a call.

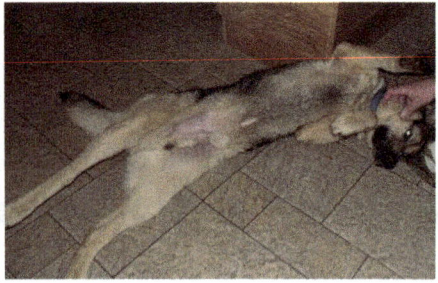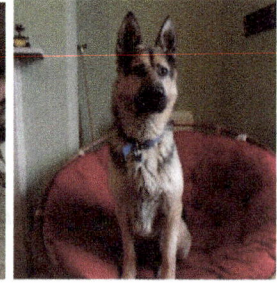

When I saw Jo that evening I explained I thought Max would fit in well with Roxy and the family. I explained the state he was but that didn't matter, we would soon sort him out. I paid one more visit to see Max and took Roxy, Jo's daughter Charlotte, and Ben with me, just to make sure everyone got on OK. We took the dogs for a short walk together in a small field, they had a little play fight together albeit Roxy seemed very unsure, but overall everything appeared OK. Later that day I called the rescue to say we would have Max, and as we already had a home check done by the RSPCA, we could just go and get him. Job done, we were all very excited. Well... maybe Roxy wasn't.

28 APRIL 2012

Jo, Leigh and her partner Emzy, and I took off to get Max. I was driving a Lexus RX400 at the time. It was a lovely vehicle, and we could easily fit 2 dogs in the boot compartment, but as a precaution we brought extra manpower in case the dogs fell out in the car on the way home.

We arrived at the shelter and I asked how we should re-introduce the dogs. The girl said that as they had already met we could just put them in the outdoor run together and let them get on with it. I wasn't so sure but I guessed she knew what she was talking about. Roxy, typically, paid no attention to Max. Max was quite lively and looking back and knowing what I know now, his body language said "I am primed and ready to go". Roxy jumped up at me to give me one of those "I am sorry Dad" hugs. Maybe she was worried we were going to leave her here or maybe she was saying we don't need another dog, who knows. This however, was the trigger for Max to go. As fast as lightning, things were happening. It wasn't a full-on dog fight, it was more a case of handbags with bricks in. Normally, my timid princess would shy away from such a thing but she had no choice, Max was all over her. For Roxy it was time to stand her ground and fight, because flight was not an option. Humans stepped in of course, but to watch this, everything seemed to be going in slow motion. In the short time it took for us to intervene Roxy gave a good account of herself, as indeed she should, she was heavier stronger and far more powerful than Max. However Max had that state of mind and the heart for it. Quickly they were separated, things calmed down and we regained control of the situation. Mmm, so much for being good with other dogs. The rescue girl said to me "Oh, he's not done that before". This would not be the last time I heard this line.

We packed everyone in the car, Roxy went in the boot compartment and Max sat on the back seat with the girls just to ensure there were no incidents in transit, and, loaded up with Max's meds we set off for home. To this day, I feel very bad that I exposed Roxy to that experience.

Pack gladiator - Maximus Decimus Meridius, commander of the Armies of the North, General of the Felix Legions, loyal servant to the true emperor, Marcus Aurelius, social hand grenade and general all round ticking time bomb had just joined the Robson pack.

Max would cause us many problems in the months to come, but at least as far as Roxy was concerned, when she was ready, they would become very solid friends indeed.

As soon as we got home, I took Roxy and Max out for a walk at Bestwood Country Park. It was obvious Max had received some training so when we got to a quiet secure spot I slipped him off the lead and tried several recalls and he came back just fine. There were no incidents between him and Roxy, in fact Roxy just completely ignored him. We met other dogs on our walk and Max didn't even bat an eyelid. Things were going to be fine.

29 APRIL 2012

A GLIMPSE OF WHAT WAS TO COME

In the morning, Jo and I took our pack out walking. We went back to Bestwood Park as Max had already been there. Bestwood is a great place to walk dogs, it has some lovely winding paths that cut through a variety of different trees and bushes, the place is pretty big and, if the mood takes you, there is a dog friendly hotel-cum-pub tucked away in there as well. As you can imagine, a place like this can get quite busy.

On this sunny Saturday morning the car park was full as we disembarked and prepared to walk. Jo wasn't sure about Max being off lead, but I assured her his recall was good and he had met other dogs and, like Roxy, he largely ignored them. Although Jo was unconvinced, we unclipped Max's lead at the start of the walk. Within 20 yards we came across a gentleman walking a very small, hairy thing which was off lead and like Max, was running around. Max ran up to the small, hairy thing to have a sniff, the little hairy thing ran underneath Max between his legs and in a flash it was in Max's jaws and Max was ragging it and shaking it, the way wild dogs do when then want to kill a small rodent before eating it.

Jo and I were horrified and I ran to rescue the little hairy thing. I got Max to let go and thankfully the little dog was alive and there was no blood. Understandably, the owner was very upset and Jo and I could not apologise enough. He explained that another dog had attacked and ragged his dog only recently. Fortunately he was prepared to leave things as they were and walked off with his dog in his arms. Max was on lead and we set off on our walk feeling a little dark and ominous about the future. Jo seemed to think the little dog nipped Max as he ran under him, I didn't see that, but no matter, we couldn't have Max doing things like that. I have no idea how that little dog survived this encounter with Max.

Over the months to come, Max was mostly on lead. We ventured into the Peak District a couple of times with both dogs on long leads, it was manageable but not easy going. Imagine two people standing right next to each other flying stunt kites in a strong wind. We were forever untangling them and taking care the lines didn't cut us or harm the dogs.

Back home, the only time Max was off lead was when I could see far enough ahead to be sure no one else was heading towards us, then when I approached a corner I would call him and put his lead on. I didn't want to risk him coming face to face with another dog on a blind corner when off lead. When he was off lead he seemed to really enjoy sneaking up to Roxy and grabbing her neck briefly in his jaws. Gentle Roxy didn't really know what to make of this at first, she seemed a little afraid. Eventually Max taught Roxy how to play, but dog walking now had become a tense and worrying affair. Nothing like when Roxy was our only child, oops, I mean dog! Max met many dogs while on lead, he often showed interest but most of the time all was well.

We still had incidents though. On one occasion, again in Bestwood Park, a young lady was walking a Staffie off lead. The Staffie made a beeline for Max who was on lead with me holding firmly. The owner seemed relaxed and was happy to let her dog run up to mine even though Max was clearly on lead. The Staffie seemed friendly so I thought I would just see how things go but I would be ready just in case. I failed to read the Staffie's body language. Max didn't. BOOM I pulled Max away but I was too late, Max had clamped onto the Staffie's nose and was not keen to let go. Eventually I prised him off, there was some blood and the lady was screaming at me because it was all my fault that she let her dog run up to mine when mine was on lead. She told me that Max should be put down. I told her she should be put down, and she may want to stop her dog from running up to other dogs when they were on lead. Things all get a bit heated. When her dog had approached Max, it's ears were pricked up on maximum alert, he made full on eye contact with Max and his tail was pointing straight in the air, Max didn't want to risk being attacked so he decided to get in there first. What a nightmare.

Behind all of this behaviour, Max was seriously ill and underweight, and he was afraid of everything. He had classic fear aggression. We can all be a bit grumpy when we are not feeling very well but I think Max had other things in his history to create this fear. These incidents were not restricted to other dogs, he also nipped people including one of my employees. On that occasion, he was trying to extract Max from my office as we were preparing for a meeting. Max didn't want to be separated from me so he gave a warning. The warning was not heeded, by any humans, me included, so Max bit and drew blood. If anyone got too close to Max in an enclosed space he would give of a low "Grrrrrr". He just didn't trust anyone, including me.

Within weeks of getting Max I leaned over him to give him a cuddle, much as I do with Roxy and Max let out one of his low "Grrrr" warnings. Being really stupid and ignorant of the ways of dogs, as I was in those days, I choose to ignore this warning and thought to myself "No you can't do that to me, I am your master", I pressed matters to force a point and Max, who didn't give a shit about any point I wanted to make, gave me a good nip. I was bloody furious, I yelled at him to get outside. Max looked terrified. I didn't know it at the time, but I was making matters worse. I grabbed Max's lead and took him into the garden- he was going to get a good hiding for that. Max reluctantly followed me, I turned to face him, I looked into his eyes and I saw fear. I took a deep breath and... I just couldn't do it. I have never beaten a dog and I never will. In utter frustration I threw his lead to the ground, I looked at him and just said "No Max you can't do that". Max looked back at me and something happened between us. I don't know what exactly but I distinctly felt it, from that point on things started to change.

Ben was witness to all this and in his innocence he wanted to know what was going on. I did my best to explain to him but I am not sure he really got it. Often when out walking with the dogs and Ben was with me, he would introduce Max to other dog walkers and add "My dad takes him into the garden and beats the crap out of him". Arrrgghh! No, no, no, no, no, Ben, I don't do that! Kids and dogs, you just have to love them all.

MAY 2012

Butter wouldn't melt in his mouth, would it? I found this post I made on Facebook. *"Mmmm, he is in the bad books at the moment. He tried to eat a Yorkshire terrier this morning."*

EPI AND DIET

Max had to have a compound on his food, to be taken with every meal. It is basically dried pancreas in powder form with a few chemicals chucked in to increase shelf life and boost profits. It would help him extract nutrients from his food. I am not a chemical fan and so did a bit of research to find that raw pig's pancreas would do the job far better than his meds, and cheaper. Well, the butcher provided me with this sticky gooey organ for free, and free is always good. The butcher minced it up for me and I would mix it in with his Kill-ble. Initially I thought, maybe the fat content was too high so I asked him not to mince it and just give it to me as it was. I bought my own hand mincer and would spend hours on end carefully trimming off all the fat and hand mincing the stuff into small containers and freezing it. I shouldn't have bothered! Dogs need more fat in their diet than humans do, 20% of their diet can be made up of fat, no problems. Today Max just gets chunks of it thrown in with the rest of his food, raw. Soon, on the raw pig's pancreas Max flourished, so we weaned him off his meds. His coat started to grow thick and glossy, his trust improved and he started to put on weight.

To help him with his fear and uncertainty, we bought him a thunder coat. This is a garment that wraps tightly around his body, supposedly making him feel more secure and relaxed in stressful situations. It's called a thunder coat because it's supposed to help dogs cope with noisy, scary storms. I don't think it made much difference to Max if I am honest.

Max looks so thin in these pictures, and he had already put weight on. In the second picture Roxy is sporting a fashionable country, outdoor girl, expensive branded mountaineering type coat. She ran into the woods one day and emerged without it, and we never saw it again. Remember all that useless crap we bought for Roxy and didn't need!

JUNE 2012

BRACE YOURSELF SCOTLAND, HERE COMES MAXIMUS

This was to be Max's first camping trip, we were off on holiday to Loch Lomond. We secured a great pitch right on the shore of the lake and away from other tents. It was stunning. For those of you who have been in Scotland that time of year, and especially near water, you will know the midges can drive you to suicide. We didn't really think about this and were not prepared at all.

The weather was warm when we arrived, I tethered Roxy and Max and started to pitch the tent. Soon I was sweating and the feast began. I was the main course for clouds of these little demons. Poor Max who still had bald patches was dessert. Roxy had a little more protection than Max and I could constantly hear her jaws snapping shut as she took on the impossible task of reducing the numbers of our assailants. Once the tent was up we took shelter inside, covered in little red bites. Jo's reaction to these bites was not good, she looked like she had measles. No matter, we would not allow this to spoil our holiday.

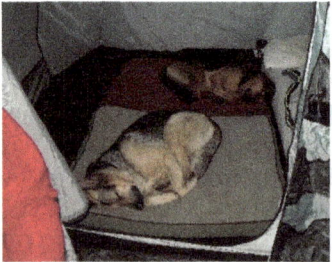

The walking in Scotland was fantastic and once away from the lake and in the hills the midges were not an issue. Unlike Wales, there were far less livestock to worry about and not many people around, so walking with Max was more relaxing. Paths were not so well defined but I had my trusty satnav with me so we would not get lost.

On day one we made a point of shopping for anti-midge stuff. We told the shop attendant about the location of our pitch and the problems we were having, he just smiled and said "Welcome to Scotland". He sold us a load of stuff to put on our skin and also some oil which when heated gave off a vapour that would deter insects. Loaded up with goodies we returned to the tent to do battle. The situation was manageable but basically the best strategy was to get in the tent as quickly as possible, batten down the hatches, then kill off anything that followed us inside.

Walks were a little difficult to find but when we did walk it was relaxing, quiet and blissfully uneventful with some stunning scenery. We didn't find any sheep but we did come across some fearsome looking cattle. Max, as you can see from the picture was not fazed by them at all. Here he is having a stare off with one probably wondering how many beef burgers it would make.

During the late afternoon and evening we could take shelter in the tent, but due to the fire risk, we couldn't cook inside. We had added a front awning to our tent and that's where the cooking took place. This of course, would leave me exposed to the killer midges, so it was time to try out the oil I purchased. I put a little oil in the bottom of a pan and gently heated it. The vapour it gave off was not unpleasant and it did noticeably reduce the number of flies. We were even able to enjoy sitting outside. The oil would burn down and I would top it up again. I discovered if I heated the oil up a little more it gave off more vapour, so I turned up the stove a notch. For a moment I was distracted, the oil sparked, I looked up and "HOLY SHIT THE TENT IS ON FIRE... EVERYONE OUT" Fortunately we were all sat outside under the awning. I got the dogs clear and quickly took care of the fire. The damage was limited to the front awning but that was a very scary moment. In the end the midges proved too much for us. They had won the war and we packed up the tent and returned home a day early.

Max was still a little unpredictable so Jo and I sought out a German Shepherd dog training class for us to attend. The classes were run by an ex-police dog trainer and were on a drop in and pay-as-you-go basis. Being in a group of dogs would help Max socialise, and with no smaller dogs involved I reasoned, would possibly limit any damage that Max may cause. On our first visit I explained to our large burly trainer the problems I was having with Max. He asked me to "Give 'im 'ere" I handed over Max's lead and the trainer took off towards a group of dogs with me in tow. Max snapped his head around to look behind at me, his eyes went wide and his draw dropped as if to say "What the hell are you doing, who's this guy and where am I going? Are you coming?" The expression on his face was priceless. Max was as good as gold at training, he had a couple of incidents but on the whole he did very well. After earning his first obedience certificate I stopped taking him. I am not really interested in teaching tricks and our trainer on a few occasions demonstrated methods I was not keen on.

AUGUST 2012

Having replaced the damaged awning on our tent, undeterred, we set off camping again, this time to Barnard Castle in County Durham. Ben would be coming with us this time and we would meet up with my son Mark and his partner Sophie- they would be bringing Tag (their rescue Staffie) with them. Mark is a pilot in the Royal Air Force and at the time Sophie was in the Navy, so they both travelled a lot and Tag would often stay with us. Max and Tag got on really well together, they would play fight for hours. Max would body check Tag, then Tag would try to grab Max's back legs. Eventually Max discovered if he grabbed Tag by the collar he could drag him all over the place and poor Tag didn't really have a solution for this. We deemed this unsportsmanlike and removed Tag's collar to deny Max this unfair advantage. If the game was on Max's terms then all was well, but if Tag wanted to initiate play, and play by his rules, which involved charging at Max full speed when he wasn't looking and torpedoing him in the ribs, then Max didn't want to play. Which was fair enough since Tag was a very solid little dog and that can't have been comfortable for Max.

During our week of camping the weather was mixed with some sunny days and a few days of very heavy rain. We did lots of walking as usual, the dogs were very well behaved and we managed not to upset anyone. It was great to be with Mark as I didn't get to see him that often. Also, as a massive bonus, we managed not to set the tent on fire this time. At the end of the holiday Mark drove Jo back to Nottingham, as she was planning a trip to Canada to see relatives, and Ben and I relocated the tent to a site called Allensford, near Consett, so I could visit my Mum and sisters. In the first picture is Tag enjoying the inflatable camping sofa, in the second picture you can see Max asleep without lying down. Max does this sometimes when he is afraid he may miss something. He really fights his fatigue and you can see his eyes slowly shut. Then his head starts nodding and he will wake with a start, forcing his eyes wide open and the whole thing repeats until he falls asleep with his head up. Finally a family shot outside the pub.

MARK TELLS OF TAG (ALONG)

"I'm not getting a Staffie"

The decision to get a dog with my wife, Sophie, may have been somewhat impulsive, yet I would like to think that despite this, the correct research and provisions were put in place prior to actually going through with it. Well, most of the correct research anyway. I will be the first to admit however, I had overlooked one key thing... My pre conceived prejudices on certain dog breeds I had no actual experience with. I mention this prior to going fully into the story of Tag, as I don't think I am the only person to have experienced this, and I see it on a regular basis (as I am sure many readers of this book will).

The day came for Sophie and I to visit the shelter where we were looking for a small dog, who was in need of human company and was relatively low maintenance. Other than this, our specifications were few and far between, but being a 5ft11 guy with pretty broad shoulders and a bald head, I didn't want a Staffie (as we all know, they are killers after all). After looking around the unfortunately underfunded and over populated dog shelter, we met a number of dogs and took one for a walk. This happened to be a three legged mongrel who sadly, other than providing a frankly comical display when weeing while doing a handstand on his front two legs, was definitely not the fit for us. Slightly disheartened we returned the dog and thought about other shelters which might have the perfect pooch for us. Just as we were set to leave, a lovely lady who worked at the shelter spoke to us and asked what we wanted. After listening, she said she had the perfect dog, but he was part Staffie... Although not a full one (stretching the truth a tad). Politely we said we would meet him and as she went off, I gave Sophie a look as if to suggest we will say hello, then get on the road. Clearly not being the boss in the relationship, I was told we would take him for a walk as he probably hadn't been out today. All I can say is we probably made it 30 meters down the lane before we knew; Tag (Ty as he was called then) was the dog for us.

We did not feel the name Ty suited him, nor was it far enough away from the common Staffie name, Tyson. We therefore went for the name Tag (or Tagalong when he is in trouble), an easy change to implement and a name which suits our boy perfectly. On our second visit to the shelter we learned about Tag's background. He had been in the shelter for approximately three years, before that no further history was known. The shelter had really stressed him out, his ears were completely bald and half his teeth were missing, presumably from biting on the bars. We needed to get him out. The staff at the shelter had recognized what a lovely dog he was and he had become one of their 'poster boys', helping them on meet and greets and advertising days. Prior to us taking him he had recently been adopted, yet the mother in the family which took him was unfortunately very allergic to him, which meant Tag was returned to the shelter. This did provide us with a glowing report however, to say what a good dog he was.

Overall I would say Tag's time with us has been largely plain sailing and we accept we have been very lucky, however we have had mishaps.

The first one occurred within a week of having our lad with us. We had just taken Tag to the groomers to get cleaned up. He smelt fresh and along with his pink ribbon, looked great. On our way home we stopped off at some woods to take him for a walk, but at this time his recall definitely left something to be desired. On the other side of the road happened to be a pig farm and this did not go unnoticed by Tag. With haste he ran to the pigs, through an electric fence (which based on the size of these monsters must have been incredibly strong), giving him one hell of a shock. Anyway he was in and ran to the pigs. They clearly realized before he did that the size difference was substantial and soon he was the one being chased. He was left with two options...get trampled by the pigs or take another huge shock. He showed a rare moment of intelligence and took the shock, returning to us filthy, stinking and in line for one hell of a telling off.

The next mishaps can be grouped. When left alone, he can be quite the cunning thief if food is left even in what should be considered safe places. Many times my wife or I have returned to the house, excited to finish the pizza we bought to aid the hangover from the weekend to find the box on the floor empty, even with the dip completely cleared out. Other occasions include (but not limited to) – 18 meatballs seared and ready to be cooked, doughnuts, toffee popcorn (licked to the point the bag was inside out), dark chocolate (an expensive bar when you include vets fees) and most recently a go at our wedding cake. We were obviously thrilled.

Surprisingly when we are in the house we can leave food around and he is good as gold. Most likely just plotting his next great steal.

We could not be happier with Tag. He is a loving dog, who wants nothing more than company. He loves sitting on the sofa with us and if my wife and I ever dare to actually sit next to each other, or God forbid, have an arm around each other, he is seconds away from climbing over us to wedge himself in between, for maximum attention. His favorite place (which fortunately is one of mine) is definitely the bar. We live on a military base and no matter which bar we are in, he is always a favorite of the staff and our friends. Two stools next to each other give him a perfect seat to join in with the conversations and get extra fuss (and the occasional pork scratching), along with plenty of other dog friends to play with.

I am very proud of the great ambassador he has been to the breed. It is heartwarming to see how many people's opinions he can change on the breed and how shocked people are to see how gentle and kind he is as a dog. While we moan about what a pest he is due to him always being under our feet, we would not be without him and bringing him home was most certainly one of our best decisions.

OCTOBER 2012

A LIGHTBULB MOMENT

Max was improving all the time. Certainly he was healthier, heavier and starting to look how he should. I still didn't trust him with other dogs though, so walking was still not relaxing because we had to be on full alert at all times. Max still spent a lot of time on lead, usually the long lead with which he was OK, but on the odd occasion we had to use a short lead he would pull like a train. I don't remember when this was exactly but I took Max for a walk on his own to Woodthorpe Park. This place has a dog walking area with loads of well socialised dogs off lead running around and interacting with each other. I used to take Roxy there all the time but with the arrival of Max, and having had an "incident" there with him not long after he arrived, I struck this place off my list of walk locations. So here I was with Max on a short lead with me trying to teach him not to pull and to walk to heel. I had absolutely no idea what I was doing.

I could see this man walking towards us with this little spaniel. He would throw a ball into some thick bushes then he would give his dog Holly directions. "Go left Holly" and Holly went left. "Go right Holly" and Holly would go right. "Holly away" and Holly moved away and found her ball. This was very impressive indeed. The man looked at me and said "Are you training him up" I explained I was doing some lead walking and also exposing Max to other dogs as he could be a little unpredictable around them. The man called to the spaniel "Holly come and say hello to Max" I quickly emphasised that Max could be aggressive and I didn't want Holly to get hurt. I took a very firm grip on Max's lead. The man calmly replied "Nah, Max will be fine" and beckoned his dog towards Max. He approached Max and knelt down in front of him and Holly came, tail wagging, up to Max. This man's aura of calm gentleness descended upon Max, wrapping him in a blanket of serenity, I even felt it myself. Max was perfect, I was truly amazed. The man gave Max a treat, after asking if he was allowed, then went on his way with Holly.

This meeting gave me something to ponder. From this point on I realised, when I was around dogs I would need to be more aware of my energy and manage it better. I had so much to learn.

NOVEMBER 2012

This was to be Max's first trip to the seaside, so we all took off to spend the day at Skegness. As cold as it was, Roxy, our water baby, ran straight into the sea. Max is no fan of the water, he briefly followed then exited the water barking at Roxy to get out. If ever Roxy spent too long in water of any kind, Max would tell her off when she got out.

As we were leaving the beach we noticed a group of young men had driven their car onto the sand and it had become bogged down. The car was way below the tide line and they were desperately trying to dig it out as the tide was coming in fast. This was a race they were clearly not going to win. We got back to our SUV which was parked some way from the beach. I raced back to the trapped car and quickly spun around in front of it. A tow rope was hooked up and the car was dragged free of the beach. A really awesome moment.

DECEMBER 2012

While Max had no problems at all chewing other dogs of all sizes, he did seem to have problems chewing things he was allowed, like food and treats. He would just pick them up and hold them in his mouth, as if to say "I know this is valuable because you gave it to me but I don't know what to do with it". On Christmas Day, Roxy and Max got a massive juicy steak each, the steak was cooked because that's what I did in those days. Roxy did a vanishing act on hers, but Max just didn't have a clue. I had to cut his steak into bite size chunks for him to manage it. That Christmas was quiet and uneventful. Tag came to stay with us as Mark was away somewhere. We just ate, drank and relaxed. Roxy got a ridiculous pink sparkling collar which just didn't look right on her. We were still prone to buying silly crap for our fur babies.

JANUARY/FEBRUARY 2013

We had some heavy snow in January, and this opened up lots of possibilities for new doggie games, like knocking the snowman's head off, and snow ploughing through drifts with noses, leaving little snow pyramids on the end of the snout.

As a joint birthday treat for the gang, we booked back into the hotel we had taken Roxy the year before. I was a bit concerned about Max with the resident dogs but although they barked just as much as last time, Max was as good as gold. This place advertised itself as a walkers' pub, a haven and a shelter for the outdoor types venturing into the wilds come what may, regardless of the weather and muddy paws welcome. After one long walk in the hills we cleaned off the dogs outside and stamped off our feet then made our way upstairs to our room. After a short while we heard a heavy knocking on the door, then without invitation the door burst open and the owner stuck his head in and gave us a right telling off for leaving a muddy footprint on his stair-carpet. I was speechless. So much for all the outdoor bullshit and whatever happened to "Let's look after the paying customer that brings repeat trade"?! Well, no more repeat trade here I am afraid. If he was that upset about a bit of mud on his stairs it's a good job he didn't see the dogs as in picture three, because that was NOT ALLOWED.

A DECISION IS MADE

In our pre-dog years, Jo and I would holiday abroad, with Cyprus being one of our favourite locations. We are not the types to sit on a sun bed all week so we would hire the biggest motorbike we could find and head off with no real plan in mind, drifting as the mood took us. It was tremendous fun and this is how Jo got into motorbikes. At home we had a monster V Twin cruiser, a Honda VTX1800 and it was a beast. I loved this bike. However once Roxy arrived, we were just not using it, and certainly when Max came along, it seemed even less likely that we would ride. When the weather was nice, perfect for riding a monster heavy cruiser, our preference was to walk the dogs and make a day of it somewhere. The bike was just not getting the attention it needed, we were no longer able to fulfil its needs, and it really wasn't fair on this lovely bike to not get the exercise it should be getting. So with a heavy heart we decided to re-home the Honda.

On Facebook I posted

That's it... it's done... arrangements have been made... it will be gone on Monday. My baby. My monster V-Twin. I will be a biker without a mount, a biker no more indeed... Just another driver, not a rider. No longer a member of that band of brothers, the bond will be broken- no, not broken, more like torn out of me. A chapter closes. Something else dear to me fades away into the background. Monday will be a sad day, it is quite possible I will cry.

MARCH 2013

When Jo asked me what I would like for my birthday, I told her I wanted another rescue Shepherd. Clearly by now I was smitten, and so was Jo, because she agreed. We would often see Amanda our GSD advisor in our workplace and she suggested we look at a breed specific rescue. We looked at the website and joined the Facebook page and found a whole host of dogs available, some with very sad stories attached. I really wanted to help a dog that needed it most, and although Max was still a bit of a handful, I thought I could cope.

We found a lovely old girl called Kiera. She was in a pretty bad state, and had been used on a puppy farm to produce a conveyer belt load of puppies. When no longer able to produce, she was booted out. This was a dog that needed help for sure, and it would not be an easy task but we had made progress with Max, so that gave us confidence to cope. We applied to go and meet Kiera but the family that were fostering her fell in love with her and decided to adopt. Good for Kiera, but for us the search was back on.

In the meantime, whilst Max had improved no end, he was still prone to the odd gladiatorial bout given half the chance. He was far healthier for sure, the EPI was fully under control, his coat was full soft and silky, but I still couldn't fully trust him. I just couldn't get him to that place I needed him to be, so it was time to enlist help, I needed training. It's called dog training but it's not really, it's people training.

For a chunk of cash up front we enlisted the help of a National Dog Training Organisation. The deal was the local representative would come to your home and do an assessment then get to work with you. It was private assistance and for this fee you would get life time support until you got the result you wanted. It was not cheap but I thought it worthwhile if we could get Max to be as trustworthy as Roxy.

Our trainer arrived and took a good look at Max. He listened to me describe a list of his little misdemeanours and I explained where I wanted to be with him. He drew up an action plan for me that would span months, then showed me exactly what to focus on for the next couple of weeks and how to do it. He would then return, check I had done what he told me to do, and then give me more stuff to work on. It struck me that I just didn't really have the time to do this as the schedule he created for me was quite demanding. I would just have to find a way, but there was no doubt about it this was going to be hard graft and take up a lot of my time.

Our trainer explained that he couldn't fix Max, all he could do was teach me how to fix him. Fixing Max was my job, not his. He explained that many people used his company and threw money at them expecting the magical dog training fairy to wave a wand and instantly transform naughty dogs into saints, while the owners sat on the sofa watching TV. I think this was my dog trainer's way of telling me he would expect no excuses from me, this is what he wanted me to do, now I had better damn well get on and do it. Fair enough!

We would start with passive leadership in the house, this would mean massive changes in rules that would affect Roxy as well. Poor girl, she was as good as gold but now restrictions would be placed on her because of Maximus. In the months to come, Max and I would spend hours, and hours, and hours together in fields, parks, and streets just ploughing through our action plan.

When I wasn't trying to make Max bend to my will, we continued to look for our next pack member. Coincidentally we found another Kiera that needed a home. She was living with her family which included children, in a pub. The family had to move out into rented accommodation and dogs were not allowed. Time was of an essence here. Kiera needed a new home quickly. We thought this may just be the girl for us and so we arranged to drive to Boston to see her, and if all went well, take her home.

KIERA

(Our Beautiful Lady)

24 MARCH 2013

With the pub location set in the satnav, we all set off, humans and dogs alike, to drive to Boston to meet Kiera. Naturally I missed the pub, driving right past it, but in so doing caught a quick look at her. She was sitting in the pub car park with her owner and the rescue volunteer. I mentioned to Jo how big and beautiful she looked. We got out the car to meet her, leaving the dogs inside, at least at first. She was a beauty for sure, she looked a little strange though because her coat had been sheared all over so her fur was a lot shorter than it should have been. It made her look a little like a puppy. No matter, it would grow back. We decided to take the dogs for a walk on lead then we would let them mix in the pub garden and if all was well, we would remove the leads. I was worried about Max but he barely paid Kiera any attention. Max was a funny one, I just couldn't predict which dogs he would take a dislike to.

The walk went fine, but in the garden Kiera was a bit bossy towards Roxy, whose ears went back a bit, but no problems really. We were told Kiera did not travel well in the car, this would need to be sorted as I drove out to the woods every day. We were also informed she had been socialised with other dogs by taking her to car boot sales. I thought this an unusual way to socialise a dog. Jo and I had a quick chat and we decided to adopt Kiera. With the paperwork done we prepared to leave. I did notice Kiera seemed a little shaky on her back end and her hocks, or ankle joints, were very close to the floor. Roxy and Max leapt into the back of the Lexus but Kiera couldn't manage, she had to be lifted in. Emotions were running high as Kiera's Mum got a little upset as we got Kiera in the car. It brought a lump to my throat I admit.

What on earth must Kiera be thinking bless her, she had been with this family for eight years, and had no idea what was happening. All she knew was that she was being bundled into this strange car with no familiar smells, with strange people and dogs, and her owner was upset. Then we took her away from her family that she had been with for eight years. Dogs do have emotions and feelings - that is beyond dispute. I know sometimes re-homing can't be avoided but how often are dogs' feelings considered? Whenever I transport, foster or adopt a dog I always try to tap into how they are coping emotionally. It really is difficult sometimes to look at their confusion and fear.

On the drive home, we discovered Kiera was very noisy in the car, barking a lot. I thought maybe this was in part to her being taken from her home, but no, this would continue… forever. If we were driving at a constant speed she was fine, but if I slowed or put on the indicators or worse still, stopped, she was off. Barking at the top of her voice and she had a very piercing bark. The other thing I noticed on the way home was that my Lexus was not big enough to put three dogs in the back. I really am not a car man but I did really like my Lexus. Maybe it would have to go.

Kiera came to us with her Kennel Club (KC) pedigree certificate. A KC pedigree certificate is a dog's version of a family tree. In Kiera's case, we could trace her pedigree back to her great, great, great grandparents. The names on the certificate are shown in red if that dog had been a show champion. There were thirteen names in red in Kiera's family tree. Dogs registered with the KC often have very flamboyant names. This is to ensure if they are shown in competitions, there will be no duplication of names and there are some strict rules when registering your dog's name. The name must be more than one word and it may include the name of the kennel. If it does, then the kennel name must be the first name of the dog, and so the rules go on. At home you may choose to call your dog Fido, but the kennel club name may be, as in the case of Kiera's father or sire "Iolanda Lancio by Albesa". Her mother, or dam, was called "Albesa Night Runner".

So on this day Kiera, or "Albesa Midway Lady" as she was known to the KC, a beautiful eight year old, joined our pack.

When we got Kiera home, the dynamic between her and Roxy changed somewhat. I remember being in my study and hearing a commotion behind me, I turn around to find Roxy lying on the floor on her back with Kiera standing over her. Roxy looked terrified. I don't tolerate falling out in the pack so Kiera got yelled at. I really felt for my Roxy, this was not what I wanted at all. She was my first dog so she should be the boss. That's not how it works though. Pack order cannot be engineered, the pack will figure it out and it will be what they decide. That evening, things got worse. Roxy couldn't be in the same room as Kiera, she was very afraid. It got to the point where Roxy went upstairs to our bedroom, which is where she slept, and wouldn't come down. I felt so bad for her, first her introduction to Max did not go well and now this. I did wonder if Kiera should stay. I don't give up on things, but I had to put Roxy's needs first, I could not have her becoming an unhappy dog.

The next day when I woke, Roxy was on her bed, and jumped up full of the joys of spring, as always. Then she heard Kiera downstairs. Her facial expression visibly changed, it was like she instantly became depressed at the thought of Kiera in her home. I couldn't have this so I called the rescue to explain what was happening. They told me it was very early days and I should persevere, and eventually matters would sort themselves out. I was not so sure but I took the advice I was given. Kiera would stay.

Roxy was given lots of love, I tried to re-enforce her position as alpha female but all I was doing was putting her under more stress. I learned from Max's trainer just to let them be and arrange the pack order themselves. Although I was reluctant to accept that my sweet gently Roxy would be subservient to a newcomer, that's the way things went. Kiera was a very strong character and Roxy, given the experiences she had as a puppy probably, was in no position to compete.

In the months to come the girls got on better. Roxy would always give way to Kiera and let her be first in the car in the morning. Kiera would give Roxy room but she would not tolerate Roxy playing with Max. This was a great shame as Roxy was only just learning to play. The girls managed to be with each other but they would never be friends. In the long term I think this experience has been good for Roxy, maybe even made her more confident and stronger. As far as Max was concerned... well he was a warrior, not a politician, he wasn't really bothered and he just let the girls get on with it.

25 MARCH 2013

On our first walk with Kiera, we had some heavy snow, the drifts were up to my knees. Roxy and Max loved it, Kiera needed lots of rests, I don't think she was used to this level of exercise. Back home we discovered Kiera did not really have any boundaries in place. Jo was sitting eating a pizza one evening, Kiera just sauntered up to her and helped herself off Jo's plate, paying no heed to our objections. Responses to commands were virtually non-existent, she just got on and did what she wanted. Kiera did have obedience certificates she was awarded when a lot younger, but I don't think anything had been re-enforced with her for a while. It appeared that maybe she had just been left a lot to her own devices. Some work was needed here for sure.

14 APRIL 2013

I'd already re-homed the Honda, and I knew her new owner clearly cared for her, spraying her matt black. Now it was time to think about the Lexus. With the addition of Kiera to the pack, the Lexus, as much as I loved her, was just not up to the task. We constantly had to have the back seats lowered, as in the first picture, and mud would get all over the leather interior. This also meant that in essence, it became a two seat vehicle. Sadly, it was time to re-home the Lexus as well. We looked at options to replace her and decided to go for the Mitsubishi Barbarian. This was the version of the L200 with the largest rear cabin. It was a bit higher off the ground than the Lexus so I made a ramp to make it easier for the dogs to get in and out, and a false floor to stow the ramp when not in use. Aside from the poor mileage on the automatic version it was fit for purpose, and the dogs seemed to like it.

By the end of April, Kiera had learned some basic commands. She had learned recall and so was now off lead and running around with Roxy and Max. Tensions had eased considerably between her and Roxy and although they were not the best of friends, Roxy at least was more chilled out and comfortable. Regular exercise had made Kiera stronger, she was developing a little muscle on her back end and her coat was growing back and becoming soft and silky. If Roxy was a water baby, then Kiera was a fish, she adored the water. She did this curious thing, she would stand in a pond and put her head completely underwater, then she would toss her head in the air and shake the water off. Just as those pretty, long-haired girls do in shampoo adverts. After the walk it was time for dinner, (just look at the focus in picture two), then a snooze on the sofa, leaving plenty of room for the humans on the floor.

20 APRIL 2013

This was our first outing in the dogmobile, the L200 in the previous pictures was a demo model. The gang fitted nicely in the back, and from left to right we have Tag, come to stay with us again, Roxy, Max, and then Kiera. We took off to the old colliery at Watchwood for a nice long walk, then a swim. I noticed that Staffie's don't really swim that well. Tag gave it a good shot but his little compact body was just a bit too solid. He went in the pond after the others, then started to sink a bit, so he employed a very frantic swimming technique that involved a lot of splashing to get back to shore. I did wonder at one point whether I might have had to go in after him. We ended the walk at the butcher's for doggie goodies. Aside from Tag almost drowning, we had a fantastic day. You can see Kiera feasting on a large load bearing knuckle bone. I don't feed those any more as they can damage teeth, smaller rib bones are much better.

MAY 2013

Kiera's first camping trip was at a site near the Malverns. The fire damaged Vango was gone and in it's place we acquired an Outwell Wolf Lake 7. This tent was in a league of its own, and a massive step up from the Vango. This was obviously the first time Kiera had been in one of these weird cloth houses, and bless her, she was totally confused. As we zipped down and settled in on our first evening you could just see the cogs whirring in her brain "Oh no... where's the door? Can I poo in here?

Where do I wee? Where do I sleep? Following the lead of our seasoned campers Roxy and Max she soon settled down.

The weather was uncharacteristically hot for a bank holiday. It was very busy walking across the Malverns, there were people, kids, dogs, and bikes everywhere. Thankfully our crew were very well behaved, even Max.

15 MAY 2013

Our lovely lady Kiera had her first birthday with us, she was eight. On this special day, she enjoyed pate on toast for breakfast, then we all took off for a long walk. As was customary, whenever she could find a nice big patch of mud she would stick her head in it. This skin care routine kept her looking young and beautiful. Being an older girl she didn't range far when out walking, she would pretty much remain by my side. When out and about she loved to grab the lead off me and play tug-o-war. She was settling in very well and was clearly a happy dog. For birthday dinner she chose from the a-la-carte menu and went for raw heart and liver mixed up with a few biccies. Then time to relax on the sofa.

Diet wise, I was getting there but it was still not quite right, and soon the dry complete would be gone. Certainly, I wouldn't mix raw with dry commercial. There is a train of thought that suggests as the two types of food are digested at different rates, it can cause an excess of gas, which in turn could lead to bloat. A condition not uncommon in large breeds of dogs that causes the stomach to rotate or twist. It traps blood in the stomach and blocks it from returning to the heart and other areas of the body, often causing organ damage. Bloat is often fatal. I asked my vet on his opinion of the cause of bloat and the party line was that there is no single cause that can be pinned down. He was not convinced on the mix of food but I would take no chances.

With the birthday celebrations out of the way, it was time to prepare for our next camping trip.

5 JUNE 2013

Fully loaded and ready to roll, we were off to the New Forest to upset a whole new bunch of people. Roxy, Max, and Kiera go on tour. We flea treated the gang just before we left as this place is well known for ticks. With three dogs, it was getting harder and harder to find camp sites that would have us, as many sites have a maximum limit of two dogs per tent. As a rule though, camping and caravan club sites don't limit you but they may ask you not to visit at busy times of the year. We were at such a place and our pitch was in a corner out of the way. We still managed to upset one fellow camper though who told his young son "Those are nasty dogs". What an education that young fellow was getting!

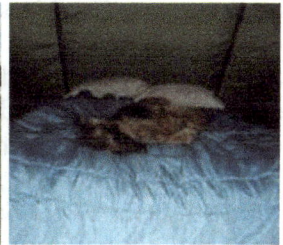

Our walks were largely uneventful. Roxy got lost for about 20 minutes in the woods, that was very scary and on another occasion Max wandered into a children's playground. He was walking ahead of us and we didn't see it. Someone went nuts at us for having our dogs off lead. Max had done nothing wrong, he was just curious but we still managed to upset some one. As you can see in the third picture Kiera's fur had grown back nicely, she was looking truly beautiful.

LEAD WALKING AND RECALL

The subject of lead walking and recall can be a tricky one. The law states that you are not allowed to let your dog be "dangerously out of control". "Dangerously out of control" includes "Making someone worried that your dog might injure them" Now that is a MASSIVE grey area. Only yesterday, I was taking my dogs out of the house to load them into the car. Saxon as always had stuff to say. A lady was about to walk past my house and she stopped and froze in fear. I saw this and closed the gate so the dogs couldn't get out and she walked by in terror. She was obviously worried that "My dogs may injure her" so had I broken the law? Technically I suppose so. I do know people that never allow their dogs off lead, just to play safe.

Opinions differ and people have criticised me for what I do but I want to allow my dogs freedom to run around and just be dogs. When I take on a new dog the first step is to make sure it's socialised and safe. Max was not always predictable so he would be on lead if there were people or dogs around. If we met dogs or people on a blind corner and Max happened to be off lead, he would usually be OK. When you meet people on a blind corner they don't have time to panic and worry, which means negative fear vibes are not passed to the dog, and consequently the whole situation is more relaxed. That said, as we approached corners I would still usually put Max on lead. The next step is to establish good recall, and it's not enough to tick that box if your dog returns to you when it's got nothing better to do. It's very important that they obey, if possible even establishing good recall when the dog is in a state of distraction or excitement. This is very difficult and will never be certain. Finally I like to be confident that if my dog approaches an aggressive dog that is on lead, they will retire on their own and not react badly. Once I am sure of these things, my dogs go off lead.

I choose to walk my dogs in quiet places away from people and other dogs, not because I am worried about my dogs, but because people often make wrong assumptions when they see a pack of five or six Shepherds walking towards them, and then situations can develop. If I see another dog owner coming towards me and they keep their dogs off lead then I do the same. If they lead up then I follow suit, usually then we get lead reaction and the dogs go a bit nuts, in some people re-enforcing the idea that "Yes, I thought they were nasty". Had I kept them off lead they would have been fine but then the other dog owner may get upset.

If my dog runs towards another dog, where possible I call ahead and ask permission if they can say hello. If I can't do this or if I can't hear the reply (because I am as deaf as a post,) then I recall. If the recall fails, which happens sometimes, then I don't yell or recall in an angry voice at my dog. I just let it go. I don't want the other dog owner to think I am panicking because I am afraid my dog will rip their dog's throat out. In effect, I am trying to manage human emotions. If the recall failed, then it's failed- me yelling, screaming and hopping about will not improve matters. I just remain calm and apologise that my recall failed. If people get upset at me, which happens, then fine.

I love to meet professional dog walkers when out and about. Their dogs are usually off lead and they are so calm and relaxed. Dogs meet and mingle and do what social pack animals are supposed do.

I have had incidents, (ask Max) but I do my best to strike that fine balance between freedom for my dogs and keeping people's faces straight.

JULY 2013

Max and I were progressing very well on the schedule the dog/human trainer created for us. I did everything that was asked of me, to the letter. I was determined not to fail Max. Our trainer was happy how things were progressing and so, as a kind of graduation, I suppose, we arranged to meet him at Woodthorpe Park. Max and I got there a little early and did some revision as I wasn't sure what was going to be asked of us. All work at this point had been done on lead. Our trainer arrived and announced we were going to walk Max off lead through the park, from one end to the other then back again, and we would stick to the main path which was the busiest place to be in the park. "Holy shit". I had visions of Max leaving the park looking quite smug with himself, with dog body parts strewn all over the place behind him. Almost as if he knew what was going through my head our trainer interrupted this very negative train of thought and asked me a very direct question. He said "Are YOU ready to do this" I remembered the man that introduced his spaniel to Max, I recalled his demeanour and energy and I calmly replied to our trainer "Yes, I am ready".

Our trainer took verbal control of Max for the first half of the walk, Max walked to heel off lead and if he showed the slightest sign of losing concentration or taking an interest in another dog, he was verbally checked immediately. We got to one end of the park then it was my turn to do the return leg. I projected a mental image of calm assertiveness and an image of what I expected of Max. The lad had done well on the first leg so I was feeling confident. Half way back a little dog came charging up to Max barking. Max showed interest, of course, but I checked him and Max was spot on. Training session over and Max had done very well. Our trainer told me to keep up the work and he warned we may have the odd regression here and there but as long as I didn't forget the training, things should be pretty much sorted. He was absolutely correct. Over the years we have had a couple of incidents but Max is a very trustworthy dog now.

Max went from seriously ill and full-on fear aggressive, to fit, healthy, calm, relaxed, and trustworthy, in 16 months. The essence of our training was that I had to become a stronger pack leader and Max had to trust me. In doing so, the pressure of being pack protector was lifted from his shoulders and he could relax. I think because what we have been through together, the frustrations and fear we have faced and the success we have shared, Max and I have a very special bond. More so than any dog we have had before, Max is keenly tuned into my emotional state. If I am feeling the slightest bit out of kilter, Max knows and he comes to comfort me. Certainly when we first got Max he could not tolerate what you see in the following pictures.

Walking once again became a relatively relaxed affair. I say relatively because we were adding to the pack all the time. It's fair to say the more dogs you have the greater the probability of incidents.

TRAINING MAX

Again I want to stress that I am no dog training expert, but the following exercises I did for Max and with time and effort it worked. Max realised I was the pack leader and he started to relax, then he started to trust, and I think, combined with his improving health, his aggressive tendencies started to fade. The following steps I took to help me give Max what he needed.

Step 1 – Review the training check list provided by your trainer.

My trainer gave me advice on use of tone of voice. Dogs can only memorise so many words but they will understand your tone and energy. The praise voice is soft happy and higher pitched, and you need a warm fuzzy feeling. The command voice is clear and in a normal speaking tone, feel calm yet assertive. The correction voice is loud and guttural. Almost like a growl, don't use the dog's name, instead a one syllable sound that comes across as gruff, maybe "BAH". With correction, you need to stand tall and feel assertive and in command. As an aside with five or six dogs I find I have to use the dog's name on correction sometimes just so they know who I am yelling at. My training checklist was quite long and offered some good tips. Above all you must relax and stay calm, always be in control and remain confident and focused.

Step 2 – who's the boss?

While you may think you are the boss, just ask yourself a few questions. Does your dog tell you what time to get up, when it's feed time, or when it's time for a treat? Does your dog drop a toy in your lap and then stare at it waiting for you to play? Does your dog tell you when it's time to fuss him by nudging you or rolling on their back? Does your dog dictate to you who may or may not visit your house, who walks past your property, etc.? If the answer is yes to a number of these questions you may well find that your dog has YOU quite well trained.

Step 3 – Passive leadership - I am the boss.

Quite simply we need to ignore certain attention seeking behaviour. If your dog pokes you and looks at you with those "melt my heart eyes" then ignore the dog. The dog gets cuddles and tummy rubs when you decide. If your dog stands at the door waiting to go out, just give it a few seconds and when the dog turns away from the door, then open it. The door is opened when you decide, not when the dog tells you. That said, if the dog looks desperate for the toilet you may want to just open the door. Moving around the house, passing through doors, the dog is ALWAYS behind you. You are the first one to enter a new space, the dog follows. No sitting on the sofa, not allowed upstairs, it's hard I know but until we have established very clearly who the boss is, this is how it has to be. All the decisions are yours, never concede to the dog's attention seeking. This must be done without compromise for a good month or so. Then you may need to revisit it occasionally. Remember dogs are a pack animal and they may challenge you from time to time. Signs that your dog may be submitting to your leadership are head down, ears back, licking lips, rolling over and a low wagging tail.

Step 4 – Back lead training

This is a walking technique done with a 6ft lead. Allow your dog to walk ahead of you and as it does so start to walk backwards, as the lead goes taut give it a firm check and call "BAH" then direct the dog back to your side. When the dog returns, give huge praise. Repeat this exercise, hundreds of times if needs be, until the dog knows to walk by your side.

Step 5 - Attentiveness training

This step follows back lead training and is a great way to re-enforce your position as pack leader, and teach your dog to pay attention to you. It's best to start this with a 6ft lead which can be lengthened as your dog improves. Also, it's best to start this in an area where there are few distractions. Start with the lead loose in the hand and head off in random directions or change direction as soon as the dog tries to get in front of you, at first you may need a little pull or check on the lead to grab attention. Direction changes should be random and never dictated by the dog. As the dog improves you can lengthen the lead, or even as I did with Max, dispense with it completely. Before this exercise is done off lead you must establish sound distance control and recall. This exercise had to be done for 15 minutes a day, every day for a month.

Step 6 – distance control and recall.

This can be done alongside step 5. Make sure you establish good eye contact with the dog and teach him or her to sit. You may need some gentle pressure on the dog's rump while applying a little upwards movement on the collar just to help the dog understand what you mean by sit. As with any success the dog achieves, it needs massive and instant praise. Once sat down, move away from the dog using a stay command. If the dog motions towards you then a very assertive "BAH". Once a short distance away circle the dog, as you pass behind the dog he or she will be tempted to move, they must remain seated until you give the command to come. As the dog improves you can increase the distance you do this exercise, even walking behind a corner out of sight, always the dog must remain sat until you call.

Step 7 – understanding dog aggression

This was more about me understanding that dogs are not born aggressive, to make them so, something has usually happened. If a dog is confident and trusts, with a strong pack leader, then aggression is rarely a problem. With Max I had to watch his body language carefully when approaching or passing other dogs. Signs I had to look for were: ears forward, hackles up, stiffening of the body, low growling or tail up. Any of these would require immediate correction.

For Max though this period of training had transformed his pet human into a pack leader. Max could now relax as this responsibility was no longer his. I demonstrated my leadership and he believed in me and trusted me. The aggression started to melt away. Max still has his moments from time to time, and around other dogs he is certainly not submissive, but Max had become a very different dog.

For the money we spent on training Max, and for how quickly we achieved results, our trainer asked if we would like help with one of our other dogs for free. Straight away I thought of how irritating Kiera's barking was when in the car. I thanked him for his very kind offer and I explained about Kiera.

AUGUST 2013

Our dog trainer made arrangements to come to our home to have a look at Kiera. We bundled her into the car and went off for a drive. Kiera did not let me down, each time I slowed down or used the indicators she would be off, "WOOF, WOOF, WOOF" at the top of her voice. She was at her worst when I stopped the car to get out to enter a shop or fill up with petrol. Over the weeks to come, various strategies were suggested and tried but all to no avail. Then our trainer suggested water bombs! The idea was that when she was barking in the car, assuming I was stationary, I get out of the car and throw a water bomb at the vehicle. The resulting explosive splash would distract her from barking and stun her into silence.

So with a washing up bowl on the back seat full of watery munitions I was good to go. I beckoned the dogs into the car for our morning walk, I closed the rear hatch on the truck and Kiera started barking at the top of her voice. BOOM! The first water bomb landed and Kiera was as quiet as a mouse... amazing. In fact there was a look of stunned silence on all three faces. Roxy's ears were back and Max's eyes were wide open as if to say "What the hell was that?" It looked like we had a solution. I did notice however, when parking at public places, as soon as I started bombing my car I did get a few strange looks. It must have been akin to that famous scene in Fawlty Towers when Basil beats the crap out of his car with a branch. Kiera remained quiet though, I am not sure if it was because of the water bombs or because she was embarrassed for me. Maybe in her silence she could pretend she was not there and this crazy human was nothing to do with her.

What I didn't realise however, was while this assault on my car silenced Kiera, it was terrifying my gentle Roxy. After only a few days Roxy refused to get in the car, she jumped up at me and hooked her paws over my forearm and gave me one of those irresistible manipulative cuddles. That was it, I couldn't have my Roxy frightened. Just look at the uncertainty on her face. I dispensed with my arsenal and decided to tolerate the barking. Our trainer had been very kind to offer to help with Kiera and he had done so much, so I didn't bother him again. The barking was here to stay.

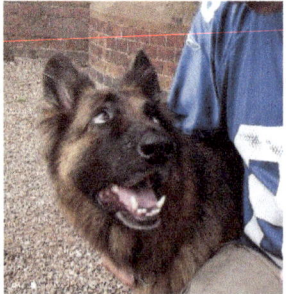

As August rolled into September, Kiera was flourishing, she was clearly a very happy dog. The relationship between the two girls continued to improve. It was almost as if a mutual understanding and feeling of respect was developing. They were still not best friends, that was for sure, but they could be content in each other's company. Max didn't really care who was first in the car, that cheeky boy was more interested in getting up to mischief.

Towards the end of the month we heard of a dog show that was being held in Lincoln where the rescue were going to have a stall on display. We decided to take the gang and have a look. Kiera's previous owner had kept in touch with us and when she knew we were going she asked us if she could meet Kiera again. Jo and I discussed if this was a good idea as we didn't want this meeting to affect Kiera in a negative way; after weighing things up we agreed. Our pack were very well behaved at the show, Kiera met her old family, and since she had been with them for a good eight years she did recognise them. She went up to the children who fussed her, then soon after she came back to us and stood behind us. The meeting went so well, Kiera was fine and she knew where her place now was. It was very reassuring to see this.

We had a chat with the volunteers at the rescue stall and asked how we could become volunteers ourselves as we were keen to do more to help. We filled in paperwork and were told someone would be in touch with us. Our volunteer work would include doing home checks for potential new families, assessing dogs that were being re-homed, helping transport dogs and fostering, if we could. Our application was accepted and life turned a corner. We didn't enter any competitions at this dog show.

SEPTEMBER 2013

Jo became addicted to the GSD rescue Facebook site and was forever pointing out the plight of this dog and the next. I always did, and still do, avoid this as it makes me feel bad to see how some of these lovely creatures are treated. It would probably lead to me having more dogs than I could handle. However on one particular occasion when breaking this rule of mine, I came across a desperate case. This lovely boy Luther had been handed into a pound as a stray. He had not been claimed, his time was up and he was scheduled for destruction. The rescue site was alive with activity trying to come to the aid of Luther. It didn't take long for Jo and I to agree that we should foster him until a home could be found.

A QUICK WORD ON STRAYS

To date I have fostered or adopted a number of stray dogs, one in particular was heavily overweight and another (Luther) was in very good condition. Clearly they were not strays at all. Someone had got bored with them, or maybe they had suddenly become an inconvenience and so it was time to get rid of that faithful companion that loved its owner with its whole essence. So the collar is removed and the dog is handed into a compound (pound) as a stray. Many of these places have a kill policy if the dog is not reclaimed, which it won't be of course since it was the owner that handed it in and lied about it being found roaming the streets. This often means that within seven to ten days, this beautiful dog, which is no doubt missing its unworthy owner, will be killed. If the pound is at capacity when a new dog is handed in then that may accelerate the killing of another dog to make room for it. Often people use the abbreviation PTS, meaning "put to sleep", a gentle way of avoiding the nastiness of the situation. In cases like this I don't care to hide behind the screen of an abbreviation, they are being killed. That's it.

If they escape this fate and are re-homed, there is a possibility they will end up in the wrong hands. Puppy farmers are always on the prowl for cheap breeding stock, and unlike most rescue organisations, dog pounds don't usually take measures to ensure dogs go to good homes. An entire dog can be acquired cheaply or even for free, then spend it's life as a breeding machine, abused, starved, and locked in a dirty cage for as long as it is of any use. Once it has outlived its usefulness, what happens to the poor dog then? You can imagine. Recent puppy farm raids have found dogs that used to be family pets.

This is not the worst fate though. Dog fighting is illegal in this country but it still happens. The foul people that engage in this activity are always on the lookout for bait animals. Bait animals could be rabbits, cats or even that faithful, loving ex-family pet that got in the way of that exciting holiday. These fighting dog "trainers" will ruthlessly acquire animals to use as live bait, their methods include posing as a "good family" to acquire animals from council pounds, or scouring newspaper advertisements for "free to a good home". Or just plain theft. The bait dogs are often torn apart to feed the blood lust and savagery of the fighting dogs. Again many dead dogs have been traced back via microchip and have been identified as being family pets.

Then I hear people claim "but the dog had issues". Then put some effort in, I say, and help the poor dog. If I could "fix" Max, then many, if not most dogs that have had issues could have been "fixed", and like Max become a loyal, loving, faithful friend. Then you have to consider why the dog needs fixing in the first place, how did it get broken? Who wants to take responsibility for that?

At least handing the dog into a pound and telling a load of lies may be better than just kicking it out by the roadside. I don't know who to give credit for this picture I found on Facebook but it says it all.

Luther was supposedly a stray, but at least he would be saved, he would not suffer any of the dreadful fates I spoke of earlier. It was arranged with the rescue that he would be ferried from the Bristol area to a service station on the M42 near Birmingham, where Jo and I could pick him up. The two volunteers that gave their time to transport Luther were Linda and John.

LOUIE

(Sweet and Gentle)

15 September 2013

This was the day we had to pick up Luther. It had to be this day, as on the following day he was due to be terminated. I was feeling really ill, I had an upset stomach and I was throwing up. I took Jo with me in case I ended up being unable to drive but delaying the pickup was just not an option. We arrived at the service station to find John walking Luther calmly on lead while I dashed to the loo. Luther looked like a lovely boy. John couldn't tell us much about him as he was a stray but he did say he travelled well and seemed to be a delightful, calm dog. On meeting Jo, Luther gave her a great big snog. Clearly a friendly chap as well! Following another trip to the loo we set off home with Luther in the back of the truck as happy as you could imagine and as quiet as a mouse.

We got him home and he just wandered around the house like he had lived there forever. The rest of the gang accepted him with no problems. Max seemed especially happy to have him around and went straight into play mode. A nice change for Max after having to put up with the tensions that had existed between the girls in the past. Luther was the name given to him by the staff at the pound. He didn't respond to his name and it didn't really suit him so we decided to re-name him Louie

Linda, who collected Louie from the kennels contacted us to say she noticed he had a worry spot on his back leg. A worry spot is when a dog, usually through stress or boredom, starts to nibble at himself, causing an open wound which often becomes infected. Then, because of the infection, the dog continues to lick at it, preventing the healing process. If this continues for a while, even with proper attention the dog can get into the habit of gnawing at that particular body part. Much as a baby finds comfort in a dummy and then can't do without it and it can be very difficult to stop a dog from doing this.

In Louie's case the worry spot was quite large, some of it looked like it had healed some time ago leaving a large, bald, scarred area, but there was still another large area that was just raw flesh. The pound told Linda when she picked up Louie that a vet had looked at it and said it was OK. Well, it didn't look OK to me, I would have my vet look at it.

I had switched vets to one of my black belt students who had his own practice. It was some distance from my house but Uncle Jon, as he came to be known, was a very good vet and I knew he wouldn't sting me. As the pack was growing, vet bills were a serious consideration. Also, Uncle Jon would often treat the dogs at the dojo when he came training, which meant the dogs didn't stress out visiting his practice.

17 SEPTEMBER 2013

I was still feeling crap, so I went off to see the doctor. It turned out I had gastroenteritis. I was passing my days in the smallest room of the house, usually with Max for company. The pack, sensing all was not well with me, decided to administer some canine comfort. Max is clinging onto the front of the sofa to be as close to me as possible, whilst Roxy, and little Tag, are sitting dangerously close to the action end. Tag should probably have worn a gas mask.

After six days of having Louie we failed as fosterers. The rescue posted this on the social media page:

"We have another happy ending!!! Louie has settled in so well into foster care, he has been adopted!! Go Louie!! Enjoy yourself little chap! Congratulations and thank you to Ken Robson and family."

I responded with the following:

"Louie- a wonderful natured and very loving dog was picked up as a stray in the Bristol area, sent to the dog pound and after 10 days he remained unclaimed. So his time was up. Time for the long sleep. But here he is now in my house as our new pack member, he fits in perfectly and the gang have all accepted him, awesome. Plan A was to foster Louie (the handsome chap on the left). Plan A didn't really pan out at all. WELCOME to the pack Louie, why he was ever a stray totally escapes me, he is a lovely natured boy, and he is very loving with impeccable manners. My pack love him, so Max (he's the guy at the back, in the first picture) had a word with me and now Louie stays. I am so happy to have him. A happy ending."

Our pack was now four.

Louie was just not used to exercise. In the early days he would need to stop and lie down to rest. When I say lie down, I mean flat out on his side. His worry spot was not getting better and after every walk I would clean it and apply a new dressing. If I caught him nibbling I would yell at him and the look he gave me was as if his universe had just imploded. He was very sensitive to correction.

He was coming out of his shell though. He was starting to bark and make little yipping sounds when he was excited. We delighted in buying him all the usual stuff, bed, toys, collar lead, etc. Louie decided to sleep on the first floor landing while the other three were in the attic bedroom with Jo and me. He would sleep there every single night without fail. With the rest of us upstairs I think he took it upon himself to be the protector of the den entrance. He was the early warning system while everyone else slept. Dogs need a job in life and if we don't direct them to one they will find one for themselves. If we leave a position vacant, like pack leader, then they will take that job as well. Then a dog owner might lose control, and label the dog as having issues and decide to dispose of it. In reality the dog owner was weak and the dog just tried to help out by taking the job it knew they couldn't handle.

Louie strangely enough would never sleep on his bed, he would always sleep next to it. In the morning he would dash into the attic yipping and yapping, so full of joy and excited about the adventures that lay ahead that day. He would barge around the bedroom to greet everyone, knocking dogs and furniture flying, then he would give me a good morning kiss that involved an uncomfortable amount of nibbling with his teeth. If I got up he would sit on his hind legs and hook his paws around my forearm so I couldn't brush him away, then he would look right into my eyes and yip away. He was clearly so happy. If I were to put a human slant on this, it's almost as if he knew what was going to happen to him in the pound, that at the last minute his life changed and as a result he was so grateful for every single day he was alive. It's easy to think of this notion as a fantasy, but trust me, our dogs are far more in tune with things and far sharper than we give them credit for. Truly, they know things that humans don't.

Greetings done, he would boot one of the other three off their beds to have a quick power nap. His barging antics soon earned him the nickname "The Bomb" or "Loo Bomb". His lack of ability to wait orderly in a queue for his dinner earned him a Shrek blanket for his bed, which he never laid on, but did look cute with. I soon found this spot on the left side of his neck which, when rubbed, would cause him to stretch his neck out, crank his ears at a funny angle and then his back foot would thump on the floor like a machine gun. Louie had the most amazing eyes I have ever seen on a dog. To think only weeks earlier someone wanted rid of this beautifully natured dog and he was going to be killed, probably just because he had become inconvenient. I wish I could dispose of all the inconvenient humans I have come across.

18 OCTOBER 2013

I posted a piece on Facebook introducing my pack to my fellow rescue volunteers. I include it here because it was written at the time and it does highlight the different characters our dogs have; they are as diverse in nature as humans. Also reading it now I can see I made a few errors in my character assessment.

"Don't you just love the individual characters of our dogs? Roxy centre stage (picture one) is the alpha female and pack hunter. She is also the fun police- if pack fun is happening and she has not authorised it then she has something to say. She is a powerful girl that could run all day, given the chance, and is also a great swimmer. After feeding time she does the dishes for me. Given her history she is sometimes a little under-confident as pack leader (after me of course) but she gives it her best shot and stands her ground when she has to.

Max at the back is the court jester, with bells on. He is in charge of the play fight schedule (when Roxy allows), and when out walking he keeps the pack on its toes by quickly sneaking up on the others and slipping their heads in his mouth. He then runs off and looks to me for approval. NEVER a dull moment with Max around. This fella has had a very hard time, dumped at the R.S.P.C.A at only 22Kgs with EPI (the disorder with his pancreas). He was a skeleton with fur on, very afraid and, because of that, aggressive and would have a go at anyone or anything. This cheeky boy is as good as gold now, great around other dogs and people and weighs in at a healthy 36kg thanks to raw pig's pancreas.

Kiera is the pack protector, especially when Roxy is out of sight hunting. She is always first in to meet other dogs to make sure they are not a threat to the pack. She is never aggressive but her approach to this role often scares the life out of other dog owners. I am working on this. She starts by stalking them from a distance then she will bolt at them full on. It's not uncommon when people see me coming to gather up their dogs and scuttle of in a different direction. Kiera is also the mouth of the pack and will sometimes challenge Roxy if she senses her lack of confidence in certain situations. It's the pack way, I guess, you can't have a weak pack leader.

Finally we have Louie, Mr Laid Back, he is the master of chilling out. Only been with us a few weeks so is still finding his place and role in the pack. He is such a lovely boy and apart from eating a cushion on one occasion, is proving to be unnervingly perfect.

I am so lucky to have them"

My first error was that Roxy was not the alpha female, not by a long way. She did take on the role of pack hunter though. I know now that Max was and remains the herder, he likes to keep the pack together. My next error was with Kiera. The pack protector's job is mine, I should have been a good deal firmer with her. Also, I should have put more work into her high distraction recall, as she did bolt at other dog walkers. She was never aggressive but I should not have allowed that. Roxy never challenged Kiera. Kiera was a very strong character and after me she was the boss.

22 OCTOBER 2013

When we first got Kiera I noticed she had a lump on her back foot, so we contacted her original owner who confirmed it had been there for a while. I was of the opinion that it was getting bigger, so it was time to have a chat with Uncle Jon. Whenever discussing dog ailments with Jon, he always takes time to explain all possible treatments and all the possible outcomes of each. He gives as much information as possible so I could make an informed decision. My decision was usually to ask him what he would do if it were his dog, and I would go with that. With this being a lump, of course, Jon mention the cancer word. He reassured me it was unlikely as the lump seemed very localised but we couldn't be certain. Although I am a "glass half full" kind of guy, that did worry me quite a bit. He suggested removing it as soon as possible because if it got any bigger he would have trouble stitching up the wound since there wouldn't be enough skin on her foot to stretch over the area where the lump had been.

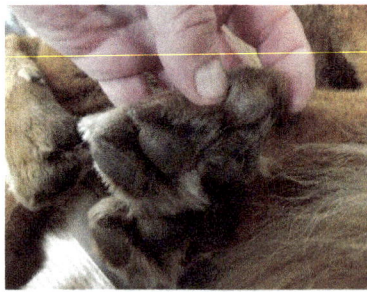

Kiera was booked in for surgery the following day. The operation went well and Jon confirmed everything seemed localised and cancer was unlikely. However the lump would be sent off to the lab for analysis just to make sure. It was a very long eight days before we had confirmation that all was well. It was just a lump of fatty tissue. On receiving this news, I felt as if a weight had been lifted from my shoulders.

After her operation, Kiera spent the next thirteen days stuck in the house. I hated going walking without her, and she hated being left behind. Jo took pictures of her while I was out with the others and she looked really fed up. Often she would just sit and stare at the window until I returned. When she did make it out for her first walk, although we didn't go far, she did get tired. Back from our walk she seemed to go missing in the house, we just couldn't find her. It transpired she had taken herself off to our bed for a little lie down- the madam!

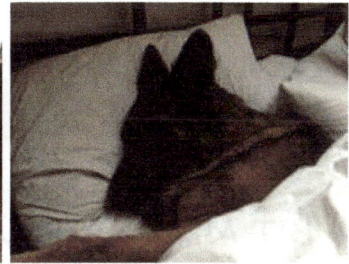

16 NOVEMBER 2013

This was to be Louie's first holiday. We wanted to go back to the log cabin we hired last year in the Lake District. Unfortunately there was a two dog maximum policy in place, and we now had four. I was certain that the dogs would not cause damage to the cabin and in the unlikely event they did, I would pay for it. Although Kiera would probably bark a bit, outside of that I couldn't really see us upsetting anyone. So rightly or wrongly, we decided that on this occasion, if needs be we would seek forgiveness rather than permission. We made the booking, no questions were asked and we took off on holiday.

With four dogs we would be keeping well clear of the hills and sheep. All of our walking was in Grizedale Forest. The place was big enough to spend a week walking the many tracks and trails and we were guaranteed to find no sheep or livestock. It was quiet at this time of year, the scenery was amazing and the dogs could be off lead the whole time. The pack were very well behaved and Louie had great time. He did get frightened on one occasion when crossing a very narrow bridge over a stream. The bridge was about twelve inches wide with a six foot drop into the stream. Nothing too dramatic but half way across it just got too much for Louie who lay down flat in fear and just wouldn't move. Louie was not a light dog, it took a lot of effort to man handle him over, poor lad. The week sailed by and we only upset one person, and I caused that. I reversed my truck into a gentleman's car... twice.

I just LOVE picture three. The pack on patrol, Roxy has point with Louie on right flank and Max and Kiera on the left. It gives a really good feel for the walking in Grizedale.

DECEMBER 2013

Christmas is a great excuse to spoil the dogs even more than normal, especially with dinner.

A BIT MORE ABOUT DIET

By now the kibble was gone and I was using the "bones and raw food" diet, or BARF. Raw chicken wings, offal and muscle meat formed the bulk of the diet. I also included vegetables, cooked and pulped, and carbohydrates in the form of mashed potatoes or rice. To make the carbs more appealing, I would include cooked and skinned sausages, all chopped up. I spent hours and hours preparing dog food for the week.

The BARF diet includes fruit and vegetables which I know now can't really be processed properly by dogs. However some people include them because they believe that, in the wild, carnivores eat vegetable matter from the stomach of their prey. The world's leading wolf biologist, David Mech, is very clear on the fact that wolves have no interest in stomach contents. The stomach lining and intestine may be consumed but the contents are just left scattered around the kill site.

David's book "Wolves: Behaviour, Ecology, and Conservation" is a compilation of decades of studies, observations and experiments. I quote from this work:

"*The wolf's diet consists mostly of muscle meat and fatty tissue from various animals. Heart, lung, liver and other internal organs are eaten. Bones are crushed to get at the marrow, and bone fragments are eaten as well. Even hair and skin are sometimes consumed. The only part consistently ignored is the stomach and its contents.*"

Only this morning, when out with my pack, Roxy caught a small rabbit. Max asked her if he could carry it for her, and suckered her into letting him have it. He carried it for about two miles or so before he could resist no longer. He ate the whole thing, skin fur and all. I have never fed my dogs anything with fur on but Max just knew what to do with this kill.

You may argue that you don't have a wolf, you have a domesticated dog. Well, in fact you have "Canis Lupus Familiaris" who is genetically identical to the grey wolf to within 0.2%. Even that little Chihuahua.

My Saxon especially, will often eat the odd leaf when out walking, it's always the same kind of leaf and he probably does this because he simply likes it. The vegetable most often eaten by dogs is grass. There are quite a few theories as to why dogs eat grass but, in truth, the reasons remain largely unknown. I do know however that when a lot of grass is eaten, often by my Roxy, the undigested grass frequently causes things to get a bit stuck when it's time to go to the toilet. I then have to slip my hand into a poo bag and pull the grassy poop out of her bum. The things we do for our dogs.

The BARF diet was a massive leap in the right direction for my pack, but from what I now know, it still wasn't right

JANUARY/FEBRUARY 2014

Roxy and Max had turned five. Canine birthdays are always fun, probably more so for Jo and me than the dogs, but they didn't seem to mind wearing silly hats and they certainly enjoyed the special dinners, treats and of course the birthday cake. Pork pies were a quick and easy birthday cake substitute but going forward I found the most popular cake by far was liver cake.

I have yet to find a dog that will turn it's nose up to this delight. It's a simple mix of liver, eggs and flour. A quick whizz in the food processor and bang it in the oven for about 40 minutes. When done, chop it into little squares and you have the perfect dog treat. For dog birthdays, my special kind of madness usually compels me to write the dog's name on the cake in sausage meat. Light the candles and take a load of pictures to post on Facebook, just to prove to the world that we are totally bonkers in this house.

In the third picture Max seems a little confused as to why I have set his pork pie on fire.

16 MARCH 2014

Kiera had been with us for a year on this date, that's 365 days of barking in the car. As we lived pretty close to the city centre I would drive a minimum of five miles every day to take the pack somewhere interesting and pleasant for them to walk. We would mostly head out north to one of the many forestry commission locations. Every single day, rain or shine we would go, and every single day Kiera would bark all the way there and usually all the way back.

We had started meeting up with other GSD owners to do social walks. We would meet at a pre-arranged location and walk with ten to twenty dogs or so. The busiest walk we attended was in Sherwood Pines, we had forty eight Shepherds, all off lead with no incidents. There was the occasional disagreement between dogs but it was usually a case of handbags at ten paces. You could guarantee, though, if there was any kind of spat going on, Max would be in or around it somewhere. Max was well behaved on the whole and his aggressive tendencies were long gone, but he remained full of mischief. He loved to whip a group of dogs into a frenzy, then retire to watch the fireworks. GSD social walks were a great way for people with difficult dogs to meet and socialise with likeminded people who understood the breed and can relax around them. On the first rescue social walk we attended we met Chris and Vicky and their two white GSDs, Wolf and Krystal. Chris and Vicky are dedicated to their dogs and very active in the rescue. Whilst walking Chris told me about Krystal, her story of cruelty and abuse is not uncommon, often we have no idea what our rescue dogs have endured and suffered but Chris knew about Krystal, and kindly contributed the following: (Including a piece about Krystal's pack "The Mad Whites")

KRYSTAL'S STORY

In October 2013 we took our usual weekly trip to the supermarket in Doncaster, our route passing the local dog pound. For whatever reason this time we stopped to have a look. We met a lovely looking black and tan GSD and so made enquiries to bring him into rescue. We were asked if we had seen the "black" GSD, which we hadn't, and so we were taken to "his" kennel.

To our horror we found the dirtiest "white" bitch cowering at the back of her prison cell completely giving up on life. I fought back the tears and immediately phoned the rescue to bring her in. Arrangements were made to take her to the rescue kennels, as I already had a new foster due into my care.

This little girl's new life had now begun and she had been given a new name. She was to be called "Krystal", with a kicking K, as she would become Krystal clean once more.

Following Krystal's move to kennels we received news that our intended foster dog had gone straight to a new home- we didn't need any excuses, we set off to the kennels to collect my Krystal.

Kennel staff had already begun operation "Deep Clean" finding all sorts of nasty metal shards and springs in Krystal's fur as well as gallons of diesel, tar and grime. It was clear that this lady had been a scrap yard or garage dog who had outlived her usefulness. We discovered Krystal to be partially deaf, which is hardly surprising given the amount of compacted dirt that was becoming detached from within her ears.

Clean and loved, in her new home the sparkle soon returned to Krystal's eyes. She would very quickly bond with Wolf, her adoptive brother, and they would become as thick as thieves. These two would soon become firm favourites at fundraising events both in local pet stores and at galas.

However, over time, Krystal's past life would take its toll and her health would deteriorate. Over a period of months we would have to deal with asthma, bronchitis, diabetes, and myasthenia, which is a degeneration of the throat muscles. This proud lady was a fighter, though, and she refused to give up on life. Although her exercise routine was now to become limited she would discover hydrotherapy and love it. Through her swimming we discovered further hip problems.

Age and health have further impacted this grand old girl to the point where she is no longer able to enjoy swimming or walking, but where there's a will there's a way. Krystal became the proud owner of a chariot. It's a custom made pushchair specifically for dogs. Wherever possible Krystal would enjoy being pushed around by her human slaves with her very own pack, Bonnie, Summer, and Wolf.

She still maintains discipline amongst the younger dogs and still chases balls, (albeit at a very sedate pace) and can still manage to get upstairs to bed. At the beginning of April 2016 the vet gave Krystal only a couple of weeks to continue on this earth. As of, 1st September 2016, she is still fighting.

ABOUT THE MAD WHITES

In 2010 we founded the Mad Whites, with the adoption of Simba from Barnsley and Royston Animal Rescue. At the beginning of 2013 Simba was eight years old and we thought some stimulation would be beneficial in the form of a young friend. We were not certain as to how Simba would respond to another dog in the house so we approached a German Shepherd rescue and applied for a foster/adoption home check, and to become fund raisers. The idea being we would foster, and if all was well, then adopt.

With the home check passed in February 2013 Wolf became our first foster. Simba and Wolf got on like a house on fire and became inseparable. So we had no choice but to adopt Wolf. Both dogs enjoyed numerous camping trips and fun times in the great outdoors. Unfortunately Simba became ill with Anal Furunculosis which eventually led to his passing over the bridge in late 2013. At the time we said "no more dogs" but Wolf had other ideas, he pined for two weeks following Simba's death. So... we took in two urgent foster dogs, both black Belgian Shepherds, which gave Wolf a new role in life.

Shortly after our foster dogs found their new home we discovered Krystal, (see Krystal's story). Now we had two dogs we thought that would be enough. Until that is, in April 2014, we saw that a six month old bitch needed urgent placement, so we fostered Summer. She had been with us for less than an hour before we made a phone call to turn our foster dog into a permanent new addition, (we were not doing well at fostering).

The final member of the Mad White pack came in the form of Bonnie in late December 2015. She had been discarded by an unscrupulous breeder who had no further use for her.

From left to right below we have Summer, Simba (superimposed), Wolf and Bonnie with Krystal in the foreground.

APRIL 2016

My Mum's health was slowly deteriorating as she aged. My sisters were real angels and dedicated their lives to taking care of her as things worsened. Eventually though, she needed more care than they could give, and she was moved into a lovely home. My sisters chose this place carefully, it was a new building and the staff were very good. When my sisters explained to the manager that I lived two hours away, and it was difficult for me to visit regularly, they also mentioned I had four dogs. The lady manager was delighted and said that Jo and I could come and stay at the home in one of the empty rooms so I could spend more time with my mum, AND we could bring all four dogs to stay with us. Now that's dog friendly!!

On our first visit we arrived with the pack and after saying hello to my Mum we were given a tour and shown to the suite where we were staying. Kiera who was keen to leave a good impression squatted down and did a massive runny puddle of shit in the hallway, all over the brand new carpet. She had never done that before- Jo and I were mortified! Without batting an eyelid the manager said in her Geordie accent "Oh no worries pet, the old folks do that all the time. We have some really good carpet cleaners, and we'll get it sorted". Sure enough the carpet was cleaned and there was not a mark on it. It was lovely to be able to visit my mum and take the dogs to see her. Apart from that one incident, they were all well behaved.

MAY 2014

It was our turn to arrange the next rescue social walk for the Midlands. I thought Ransom Woods would be a good location so we took off on a reconnaissance mission. Ransom is located about twelve miles north of Nottingham, and has a business park in the woods that would provide a safe parking area to get the dogs in and out of cars. We went on a bank holiday Monday to have a look around and found it to be very quiet. The walk was through woodlands and open heath, with two clean lakes to provide swimming opportunities for the dogs. With no livestock around, dogs could be off lead; we would just need to keep an eye out for the wild deer that roam there. This was an ideal location and the social was arranged for the following month. We ended up with twenty Shepherds and little Tag, my son's Staffordshire bull terrier, on the walk.

14 MAY 2014

The beautiful Kiera was nine on this day, she was spoiled with all the usual things, nice food, gifts and a special walk. For a GSD, age nine would put her at an equivalent human age of around the late fifties. So it was no surprise to us that she started to slow down a bit. On Sunday 15th June she literally slowed to a stop. It was a lovely day and we were exploring a new walk location at Haywood Oaks. Every now and again Kiera would need to have a little sit down, but with about a mile to go she just lay down, and looking into her eyes Jo and I knew something was wrong. Slowly and gently we coaxed her back to the car, we would take as long as she needed. Being Sunday, Jon's practice (Dove Vets) was closed, but I called on his private mobile anyway. He told us to monitor her closely and bring her in to see him first thing in the morning. If we were concerned, we could always opt for the PDSA practice as they would be open. At home she seemed quite lethargic and was content just to sleep, not wanting to disturb her we thought it best to let her be and take her to see Jon the next day.

First thing in the morning we arrived at the vets, Jon took a good look and explained that he felt fluid on the stomach, which could be water or blood. Either one could point to something very serious.

The rescue community on Facebook has always been very supportive of those needing help, there is a wealth of experience there and often good advice. Whatever you need help with, someone will have been there before and will be able to advise.

The following are Facebook posts I made regarding Kiera. I include them here as they accurately capture how I felt at the time.

16 JUNE 2014

"Of Kiera

Thank you all for comments, I love her so much, I am literally feeling sick with worry. I should have more information by three o'clock tomorrow. I will post again tomorrow with updates. Thank you all again so much.

Our Kiera has fluid on her stomach. Initial blood tests did not show anything worrying but the fluid is building. She is scheduled for an X-ray tomorrow.

If the fluid is blood, then the Vet is throwing around the possibility of a bleeding spleen, possibly due to a tumour of some kind. If the fluid is clear then there is a possibility of chronic heart disease. She was exhausted after a short walk yesterday, and so a heart condition would explain her fatigue. We had very little in the way of good news from the vet other than her bloods are good and she is pretty fit for age nine. I am worried sick at the moment. Has anyone had experience of fluid on the stomach?"

We had a massive response in terms of support, it was quite heart-warming. Lots of people were asking after her and were keen to know what was happening. Over the next few days I made a series of posts as news came in from the hospital. As much as anything else, writing about it seemed to help me process and deal with what was going on.

17 JUNE 2014

"Kiera update.

The X-rays are not conclusive however her heart looks OK. The fluid is blood so we are looking at a bleed on the spleen from a mass or growth probably. The X-ray shows some separate problems with the lower intestine. She has been referred to a specialist consultant hospital. I am sat there now with her waiting to be seen. We are expecting more scans and surgery at some point."

Note: Jon had referred Kiera to Pride Park Veterinary practice. It was a new state of the art facility with the equipment to deal with anything that unfolded. I made the first post from my phone, I was worried sick and trying to busy myself.

"More X-rays show nothing conclusive other than her heart is the correct size and shape. The fluid on her stomach hid much on the X-ray. To compound matters, though, an anomaly was discovered on her lower intestine, with pockets of gas and the possibility that the intestine may be stuck together. Fluid was drawn from her stomach and it was confirmed to be blood so the most likely cause is a bleed on the spleen. This could be a haematoma or a benign mass in which case the spleen will be removed. In the long term this would not impact her greatly. If the mass is malignant then anything could happen and none of it is good. She has been referred to the Pride Veterinary Centre which is a specialist hospital with consultant surgeons, so she is in the best place she can be. I had to leave her there an hour ago for a CT scan followed probably by surgery tomorrow. Walking away from her was very, very hard, she knew I was leaving and didn't want me to go. I have had worse days in my life but not many."

Note: In the big scheme of life in general, it may be considered a little extreme to say that a seriously ill dog worried me so much. However, in instances like this, the pain you feel is the price you pay for the love you have, and I love my dogs with all my heart.

"I hope to hear the results of the scan maybe tonight or possibly tomorrow morning. All being well she could be back home on Thursday or maybe Friday.

Thank you all so much for your comments and positive thoughts, my girl needs all she can get now. I hope to have more positive news soon

The hospital just called Kiera is going in for emergency surgery now to have her spleen removed as it does contain a mass. We won't know what kind of mass it is until after analysis. They are not worried about the intestine but they may have found another mass on the heart. I hope to God not. I will hopefully have more news in two hours or so after the operation.

The surgery is over and it went well, the spleen has been removed. The surgeon found four litres of blood in her abdomen, some of this would have been old blood, but it seems she has had an acute bleed sometime today before surgery. Thank God we acted fast or she could have been lost. Looking around inside her there seems to be no spread and the liver appears clear. This is all good. We are now just waiting for the image specialist to report on the possibility of a mass on the base of her heart. We will get that news in the morning, then we will have a wait of three to five days for the analysis results on the mass she has had removed. The scales I feel are slipping in our favour bur we are not out of the woods yet by any stretch. Thank you all for so many thoughtful comments. I will show Kiera the thread when she comes home on Thursday."

18 JUNE 2014

"Kiera update.

Kiera had a good night, her heart remained stable and she even had food last night, the surgeon is very happy with her so that's another hurdle crossed. The results of the scan came back and did not show anything on the heart, which is great news, however they did show some nodules in the abdomen. It was explained to me that these could be inflated lymph glands or possibly a spread of a malignant growth on her spleen. It was stressed to me that we won't know for sure until the biopsy of her growth. That will now take five to seven days. The surgeon did start to talk about the possibility of chemotherapy (this was not a good conversation). The fact remains we have removed the possibility of a life taker in the form of a heart tumour and replaced it with the possibility of something still nasty but hopefully less so. We are going to visit her today and are taking a tray of liver cake. I can't wait to see her."

 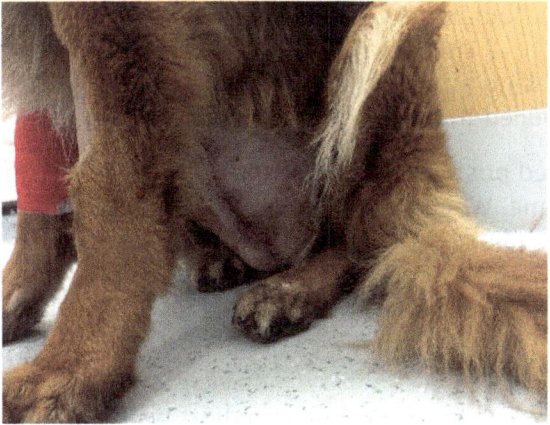

We were able to stay with Kiera for about an hour, we fed her some liver cake and left the rest for her to eat after we had gone. Turning away from her to leave was very difficult, the look in her eyes was heart breaking. From her perspective she had no idea what was happening. She was in a strange place and feeling very sore no doubt. Her pack were not with her and for all she knew, that's how things were going to stay.

19 JUNE 2014

I went to pick up Kiera from Pride Park, Jo stayed to look after the others. I would also get to speak to the surgeon, which I was feeling very nervous about. After what seemed like an age Kiera was brought to me, as she was handed over she slipped her collar and ran for the exit. Poor girl, she hated it there and desperately wanted to get out. I was able to catch and calm her and we went back to speak to the surgeon.

We had a long chat and in her opinion she said she would be surprised if the biopsy came back benign. She suspected a type of cancer that cannot be cured. I asked her how long Kiera would have left in the worst case scenario. Her reply seemed to take an age, and when it came it was as if she was speaking in slow motion. She started "The best we can hope for is one (As I am listening to this slow motion reply my brain is racing and processing the "one" and I am expecting her to maybe say year...) to three MONTHS". As this sank in I felt numb, I remember thinking "No you are wrong, you don't understand, this is Kiera, she is strong, this can't be right".

It was explained to me that we could subject her to chemotherapy and possibly add one to two hundred days to her life. The chemo would be administered gently to extend her life and if she reacted badly to it, then treatment would cease. I wondered though about the quality of her life, since I couldn't exactly explain to her what was happening. Possibly, if it came to it, there may be a way I could extend her life naturally. My mind was racing and I had no idea which way I would go. I felt like someone had pulled my heart out of my chest.

I stayed positive for her. I didn't want Kiera picking up on any bad energy from me. When she got home she got a nice greeting from the rest of the pack and she devoured two packs of cooked chicken and some sausages. Kiera was about to get very spoiled indeed. Her progress on Facebook had over two hundred people commenting and offering support.

20 JUNE 2014

Kiera was allowed to go for a short walk and she absolutely LOVED it, she was clearly very happy to be home. She had to stay on the lead but she still insisted in trying to play with Roxy and she did pull a lot trying to join in with squirrel hunts. She was so alert and bright, it was a joy to see, it was like she had a new lease of life. Back home, she had a hearty breakfast of lightly stir-fried steak chunks and chicken on a bed of rice mixed with kale spinach and sprouts, after that she had a nice fat chicken wing. It was amazing to have her home and see her so happy. I was hoping against all odds that the test results came back clear. Below we have Louie, Kiera, Roxy then Max

21 JUNE 2014

It's fun time!

Jo left to go on holiday to Turkey with her daughter Charlotte. This was not a good time to go as Kiera's test results would come through while she was away, but the holiday had been booked for a while, so it had to be done. I took ten days off work to be with the pack. Kiera was going to have the best ten days of her life. We would do all the things she enjoyed most, fun walks, lots of time outdoors, great food and when her stitches were out we would do plenty of swimming. Tag would be joining us as my son Mark was away again. It would be just the six of us, it would be awesome. Kiera seemed really bright and chirpy.

Over the next few days I relaxed the rules a bit with Kiera and she started taking a few liberties, "Oh well... clever girl" I thought. I would spend our walks mulling over the issue of, if it came to it, whether we would opt for chemotherapy or not. I was starting to lean against the idea. Preferring instead as much exercise as she was comfortable with, I would cut out the sugars in her diet, so no more rice. I would add lots of turmeric and powdered green tea on her food. I was going to see if I could give her a little more time naturally. Advice from Uncle Jon was to go for quality of life not quantity. I just couldn't leave her alone, I was always fussing her. She seemed so full of life and energy, almost like she was a puppy again. At times I felt very positive about her future.

24 JUNE 2014

I posted to Kiera's followers on Facebook

"I have just had her test results back and the worst is confirmed, we are going to lose our beautiful girl. My heart is broken. I feel physically sick".

25 JUNE 2014

I was determined that the time Kiera had left would be the best time of her life. I changed my work schedule to a three day week to spend more time with her. She would eat the best food and have lots of short walks. I would try to extend her life naturally by adjusting her diet, using herbs, and as much exercise as she was comfortable with. I had prepared a comprehensive anti-cancer protocol for her. Obviously it would not cure but it should delay things and keep her comfortable. To look at her she seemed the picture of health, her eyes were bright, she was active, and clearly a very happy dog. Sometimes I allowed myself the thought that against all odds she would pull through. Eating bones in the house (picture two) was not allowed but Kiera could do no wrong at this time.

30 JUNE 2014

The situation was getting worse with my Mum, and over the last couple of months it became apparent that things were coming to an end for her. My sisters would call me if they thought I needed to dash North to visit. I was spending a fair bit of time on the road. Sometimes I would pop up just to say hello, sometimes I thought I may be saying goodbye. On this morning

I got another call from my sisters, they thought that I should get up to see Mum as soon as I could. I was out in the woods with the dogs on our morning walk so I would need to get back to the car and get the dogs home before I did anything. Late morning I set off for the two hour drive to the home where my Mum was staying. On the road I was in frequent contact with my sisters, they urged me to drive carefully but hurry. This must have been the most frustrating drive I have ever done. The motorway stretch was clear but then, on the last leg to the home, it was torture. Anything and everything that could have slowed me down did. I was getting quite anxious as the last call I received indicated things were very close for my Mum. When my Dad died I was there by his side with my sisters and my Mum. I desperately wanted to be there for my Mum.

I raced the car into the car park and just abandoned it outside the front door of the home and dashed inside. In the foyer, my sisters were waiting for me, they should have been with Mum. "NO" was all I could manage. My Mum died 20 minutes before I arrived. The three of us went to her room and sat with her.

10 JULY 2014

Time to go camping again. This time it was at a site next to Lake Windermere in the Lake District. The site would only allow two dogs per pitch but we were going with friends that didn't have any dogs so that worked.

Kiera was now three weeks post operation and she was looking fantastic, so when our friends saw her they couldn't believe she was ill. This was what I wanted for her rather than chemotherapy. However, every morning I woke I would wonder if she would start to deteriorate, or indeed if that day would be her last. It would be the first thought that entered my head every single day. My elder sister Val had dogs for many years and she had lost quite a few, she told me that when it was time, Kiera would let me know. So every day I looked for signs, and when she seemed sprightly I would relax. Certainly at this time she was like a dog reborn.

This would be sweet Louie's first camping trip. As always, he took everything in his stride and was as good as gold, apart from one occasion, more of that later. He still nibbled at the worry spot on his leg, I tried all sorts to stop that but all to no avail. After every walk I would clean and re-dress his foot. If I caught him having a nibble I would yell at him, and his ears would go flat, his head down and he would look up at me with those amazing eyes of his. He hated being yelled at, so I would give him a cuddle to reassure him and all was rosy again. Loo-bomb was the most outwardly happy dog I have ever come across.

We arrived at the site and on checking in we had a few issues as they weren't aware that the four dogs we were bringing were deadly vicious, child-eating German Shepherds. My friend, seeing how furious I was, dealt with the site owners. They gave us a pitch in a fenced field separate from everyone else, which as it turned out was perfect. In addition, only fifty yards from our tent was the lake. The weather was scorching hot so by the time the tent was up I was soaked with sweat so it was into the lake, clothes and all with the dogs for a good old romp and splash around. Max is no water baby so he quickly retired to the shore to guard the towels. Our fellow campers on the other side of the fence seemed quite amused. In the last picture Louie has his plastic camping plate which he commandeered, I think he thought it was a Frisbee.

Our friends enjoyed fishing, so in the mornings we would take off to Grizedale Forest walking while they would attempt to catch lunch. We would re-group mid to late afternoon to swap stories, drink wine and cook.

THE INCIDENT

Each morning we would go for a quick walk along the shore of the lake There was a well-marked path only yards from the water and the fields to the side, which contained sheep, and which was securely fenced off. Other campers would take early morning walks here with their dogs, often off lead. The first time we used this path we kept the dogs on lead as we were not familiar with the place, but once we were happy it was safe, the dogs were free to run and swim. It was a handy early morning and bedtime walk for them.

One morning as Jo and I took the pack along the lake side walk, suddenly without warning all four dogs took off and disappeared from sight around a corner. They behaved just as they do when they chased a squirrel or rabbit. I hurried around the corner just to make sure all was well. Horror... I saw two sheep which had somehow escaped the field and were on the path with the dogs almost upon them. The sheep had nowhere to escape. I started screaming at the dogs to come back, but at this point they were deaf to my calls. The two girls Roxy and Kiera backed off, Louie chased one sheep while Max without hesitation grabbed another by the throat. I sprinted to Max and managed to prise his jaws free, and in doing so the sheep ran off back towards our site. In the chaos of Jo and I trying to grab all four dogs, Max managed to get free of my grip and he and Louie were in pursuit again. In an attempt to escape, the sheep took to the lake and started to swim away. Max not liking the water, gave up the chase but Louie was a good swimmer and a very strong dog. Louie soon made ground on the trailing sheep, he swam alongside it then rested his head on its shoulders and pushed the sheep underwater. He was trying to drown it! On reflection I thought that quite clever of him but at this point I had to act. I was in the lake fully clothed again, this time with my new walking shoes on, and wading out to the sheep as fast as I could. Jo was screaming at him at the top of her voice. When I got to the sheep I was chest deep in water and it was sinking, its eyes open and vacant, it had given up. I briefly thought to let the evidence of this crime sink to the lake hidden out of sight, but no… I couldn't do that. I reached down and grabbed the sheep which was on the bottom by now and lifted it above water. This was not a small sheep and it was very woolly and wet. It was damn heavy.

To make my task a little more challenging, Louie, who thought Dad was helping bring the kill home, started trying to chew on it as I waded for the shore. Meanwhile Jo kept screaming at him, she had Roxy and Kiera on lead now but Max was still free. I was now in waist deep water trying to carry a really heavy sheep with one hand while fending off Louie with the other. As the water got shallower the sheep got heavier, the water was no longer supporting its weight. Now Max rushed in to "help" me land the kill. It was bedlam, energy levels were through the roof and with all the shouting going on, the dogs probably thought Jo and I were excited about chucking a sheep on the BBQ that evening, so they were encouraged rather than deterred.

Eventually I got the sheep on dry land and all four dogs on lead. I collapse absolutely exhausted and just stared at the sheep lying there lifeless, who by now was joined by the second sheep. Jo and I were contemplating our next move when with a start, the "dead" sheep suddenly spluttered, jumped to its feet and the pair of them ran off as if nothing had happened. Wow, that was a lucky escape and we would not be off lead on that path again.

We abandoned the walk and returned to the tent, with Jo sitting nervously, scanning the horizon for a farmer with a shotgun. Our friends return from their fishing trip "Did you catch anything?" I asked. "Nope" was the answer. "We did" I replied.

Thankfully, although this all took place close to the camp site, there were no witnesses and no repercussions. We had always gone to great lengths to ensure our dogs didn't come into contact with livestock. However on this occasion, as good as our dogs were at recall, and as well behaved as they were, by the letter of the law they were not under control, so it was not only the sheep that had a lucky escape. On a more positive note the people who owned the camp site, who were nervous of having four Shepherds, commented on how well behaved they all were. That incident aside, I hope we changed their opinion of the breed.

On our final day, our friends came out walking with us. We took ourselves off to the sheep free zone of Grizedale again. The weather was glorious and the dogs had a great time. Towards the end of the walk Louie and Roxy got out of sight for a while, I recall and Roxy came running. Louie appeared soon after about 100 yards away on the trail behind us and started running towards me. His back legs suddenly just gave way from under him and he fell. I looked on in horror "That's not right, there's something wrong" I thought. Louie picked himself up and came limping towards us, he'd clearly hurt himself a little in his fall but why did he fall in the first place? He was running in a straight line; he should not have fallen. I had a really bad feeling about this.....

15 JULY 2014

Arriving home after our holiday I had a lot of messages from people on the rescue social page asking about Kiera. I posted the following update:

"*Kiera post op +1 month*

She has just got back off her holidays, camping by the shore of Lake Windermere with her pack. She still has not had any bad days yet in fact she is full of beans and having a great time, her coat is silky and glossy. Our friends camping with us could not believe she was ill. The lake was just fifty yards from the front of our tent. Louie managed to hurt his leg on the last day charging around like a mad thing so we are off to see Uncle Jon for a once-over this afternoon. Lots of people commented how well behaved the dogs were, I am so proud of them all.

Keep going Kiera my beauty"

17 JULY 2014

We arrived at Watchwood at around 9am for our morning walk. Less than half a mile in Louie collapsed and started breathing heavily. I could not coax him to stand let alone move. I picked him up and carried him back to the car, Louie weighed in at 39 kilos so the best I could do was about 100 yards at a time. On the way home, I was on the phone to Jon the vet who said he would pop around the house to have a look. When I got Louie home, he could get up and potter around a bit but he was very weak and he was deteriorating. He wouldn't eat but he was drinking loads of water but then would just vomit everything up again. He was constantly vomiting. Jon arrived to have a look and suggested emergency treatment. The fastest way we could do this would be to take him to the local PDSA hospital.

The PDSA kept him in for tests as they were not sure what was happening but recognised Louie was really poorly. We were worried sick. They say things happen in threes, I hoped not. First my Mum, then Kiera, now maybe Louie. It was so hard turning around and leaving him with strangers. He made eye contact with me with those eyes of his and I could see his helplessness and fear.

Louie had all manner of tests and scans throughout the day and the picture that was emerging was not good. At around 10pm that night we received a call and were told he would not make it through the night. If we wanted to see him again, we should go to the PDSA now. The drive was indescribable, I wasn't expecting this. Jo and I arrived and were ushered in to see him. Bless him, he recognised us straight away and tried to stand to greet us. He was in this horrible strange place and laid out on a metal trolley, he just wanted to go home with us. He didn't manage to stand and collapsed back onto the trolley. I rushed over to him and gave him a cuddle and did my best to soothe and reassure him. Louie was riddled with cancer, the same killer type that Kiera had, it had got to his heart and he was slowly suffocating. We were advised to end his suffering as the poor lad was in pain. We immediately agreed and then they started to take us through the whole paperwork rigmarole, when all I was thinking was "For God's sake, just end his suffering now". When the end did come for him he was in my arms, I held him and kissed him, and told him how much we loved him. He knew I was there and I think that gave him comfort. My sweet, gentle Louie took his last breath in my arms at 10:25pm.

I felt numb, I couldn't believe it. Here we were waiting for Kiera to die and then from right under our noses Louie was taken from us. Only that morning he came yipping and yapping into our bedroom and gave me one of his characteristic kisses nipping my lips with his teeth, full of joy and ready for the days adventures. Just over twelve hours later he was dead. I walked out of the theatre with his collar in my hand and a thousand yard stare.

The next morning Jo told me I was calling his name in my sleep. Days later, shortly after going to bed, I was just dropping off to sleep and I felt Louie give me a kiss. I was not asleep, I knew this for sure, this was no dream, but neither was I awake. Similar things have happened to me before but this time it was very different. That special kiss Louie gave me every morning was as real as could be. I knew it in my heart, without any doubt whatsoever. That last kiss will live with me forever.

On hearing of Louie's story everyone in the rescue group was very supportive. I decided to write a little tribute to him and post it for the group to read. Every time I lose a dog I now write a tribute to them. Of Louie, I posted the following:

"**21 JULY 2014**

A Tribute to Louie

His story

Louie was a wonderful boy, gentle in spirit and very good natured, he had the most amazing eyes I have ever seen in a dog, wide and bright yet full of vulnerability. He was very dearly loved and is sorely missed. I feel honoured that such an amazing animal spent time in my life. It escapes me how anyone could give up such an incredible dog, but whoever you are, I am pleased you did, in fact I wish you had done it sooner so he could have had a better life for longer.

On 13th September 2013 we saw this lovely dog called Luther on a website who desperately needed foster care, he was in a pound in Western-super-Mare and scheduled to be put to sleep. He was handed in as a stray and no one claimed him. Jo and I quickly decided we needed to foster this lovely boy until a full time home could be found. We needed to save him. As he was not our first rescue, arrangements were quickly made through the rescue for us to foster. Luther was collected and ferried from the pound to Birmingham area by Linda and John. I am so grateful that they helped Luther/Louie be part of our lives. John mentioned to me when he handed him over what a lovely good boy he was. He was not wrong. The first thing Luther did when he met Jo was give her a great big kiss. Before we got him home we decided this boy was staying with us. The name Luther didn't work for him we thought, but Louie definitely did.

He integrated with our other three seamlessly and was a joy to have around. Some things I noticed about him was that every time I entered the room his head would go down, he would look up at me with his big sorrowful eyes and his ears would go flat on his head. I think this handsome boy had seen some bad times. Well that was going to change, every time this happened he got lots of love and cuddles. He had a worry spot on his back leg, if ever I left that uncovered then he would have a chew. So every day I would remove a wrap from his foot for his walk, then cover it again for the ride home and give him a clean wrap when we got home. He never got out of that habit. On his first walk with the pack he had to have a little lie down after a mile, he had clearly not been properly exercised, this would also change. Louie was off lead in no time enjoying his long daily walks in the woods. He was a water baby for sure, he loved to jump in lakes and ponds, the first time he did this we couldn't get him out, when he did get out 100 yards down the trail he turned around and ran back in again. We just had to wait for him to finish his play. Soon the mention of walk got him so excited he would yip and yap and charge around the house bowling the others out the way and head butting me as I bent down to fasten my shoelaces. He soon earned the nick-name "The bomb" or "Loo Bomb" this behaviour earned him a Shrek blanket for his bed.

His sleeping habits were strange. At first he was afraid of stairs and would not attempt them but after a while he got over this. The rest of the pack sleep in our bedroom but Louie liked the top of the landing so we put his bed there, he would never sleep on it at night but he would sleep right next to it. He would never sleep in our bedroom with the rest, yet first thing in the morning you would hear him padding upstairs and he would barge past any of the others in his way to give me a bit wet kiss which involved tongue's and teeth, then he would share a bed with a random pack member until they got fed up and abandoned their bed to him. As soon as I got out of bed he would get so excited and come yipping and yapping at me. He would sit at my feet and give paw after paw, sometimes two at a time. Almost like he was so happy to be alive and had another fantastic day ahead of him. When he gave a paw he hooked it around your hand so you couldn't let go. He loved attention, if ever I was fussing one of the others he would barge between us just to remind me he was there, as if I could ever forget. His favourite fuss spot was just to the side of his throat; he would lift his chin, stretch out his neck, lean into you and his back leg would be thumping like a rabbit.

Louie loved his toys and loved to take tennis balls out for walks but not many came back. He really grew to love his walks, he was the meeter and greeter of the pack. Always gentle and cautious with other dogs, if they snapped or were vocal he would turn around and run for his dad.

His first holiday was in a log cabin in the lakes in November. He had such a great time. On one occasion we had cause to cross a narrow bridge with a 6 foot drop into a stream. Louie got half-way across and decided he was a bit scared so he lay down in the middle of the bridge and wouldn't move. He could be such a timid soul at times, bless him. His second holiday was his last, camping in the lakes, just a few days ago. We had no idea he was ill, no inkling of what was about to happen. He took to camping like he was a pro.

We had him a short ten months before he left us. In that time he found his way into every corner and crevice of our hearts and souls. When he died in our arms at 22:25 on Thursday 17th July, a bit of both of us went with him. You are welcome to it Louie my boy, you earned it, keep that part of me safe until we meet again. Mum and Dad love you, and you will live on in our hearts forever.

Louie died of cancer, he had a large mass on his spleen from where it had spread throughout his body including his heart. This gave poor Louie no hope of survival at all. The tumour on his heart was slowly suffocating him. The onset of this was literally hours. As soon as we realised what was happening we had to end his discomfort. Left to its own devices Louie would have had a drawn out painful death. Cancer is not natural in dogs but it has become very normal. We have to ask why, I have my own ideas and am doing something about it. But for my dear Louie it was too late."

18 JULY 2014

Louie would be collected and taken to be cremated. I didn't want a group cremation with other dogs, I wanted his ashes and his ashes alone. I did wonder about the process though, how could I be sure I had my Louie? After Louie was taken from the PDSA, I visited the crematorium to ask a few questions. It's not uncommon for people to make enquiries like mine, so the staff were forgiving of my suspicions. I was given a tour and shown the whole process. We got to the furnace and I was warned that Louie, who was to be cremated that afternoon was inside, I was invited to take a look if I wanted to be certain it was just him. I so wish I hadn't. There was my sweet Louie, laid in this furnace with his body all contorted, which was too much for me, I just broke down in tears. I asked why they had to lie him out that way and they explained to me that with larger animals their dense bones, like the skull and hips, had to be placed next to the burners to ensure the job was done properly.

The next day Jo and I went to bring our dear Louie home. He had a lovely cask with a brass plaque on top, the inscription reads "LOUIE sweet and gentle". He now resides in my study with his collar and name tag draped over his cask. Around his collar I have tied his last bandage I wrapped around his foot that morning. There is also a small box with a lock of his hair. Behind his cask I have made a backdrop from a photograph from his first holiday. Louie would run pain free and wait for me at Rainbow Bridge. The people at the crematorium gave us a nice card offering their condolences and some forget-me-not seeds to plant. I bought a plant pot for the patio and inscribed his name on the side and we planted the seeds. We would not need flowers though, to remember our sweet Louie.

THE STORY OF RAINBOW BRIDGE

The story tells of a green meadow located "this side of Heaven" (i.e., before one enters into it). Rainbow Bridge is the name of both the meadow and the adjoining bridge connecting it to heaven.

According to the story, when a pet dies, it goes to the meadow, having been restored to perfect health and free of any injuries. The pet runs and plays all day with the other pets, there is always fresh food and water, and the sun is always shining. However, it is said that while the pet is at peace and happy, they miss their owner who had to be left behind on Earth.

When the owner dies, they come across Rainbow Bridge. It is at that moment that their pet stops what they are doing and sniffs at the air and looks into the distance where they see their beloved owner. Excited, they run as fast as they can until they are in their owners arms, licking their face in joy while their owner looks into the eyes of their pet who was absent on Earth, but never absent in their heart. Then side by side, they cross the Rainbow Bridge together into Heaven, never again to be separated.

29 JULY 2014

Kiera was now six weeks post op, so she was half way towards her maximum life expectancy and two weeks past her minimum. Her illness was starting to weigh heavily on me, every day I knew it was more and more likely that I would start to see signs. So far, so good, though, she was still doing very well, bless her. I was so pleased I did not opt for chemotherapy. Every day since her operation had been a good day for her. Maybe all the natural supplements I was giving her were helping.

LATE JULY 2014

It has been said that the best way to honour the memory of a lost and loved rescue dog is to rescue another. I know many people can't bring themselves to do this- their loss has just been too painful. They feel that a period of grieving must happen- getting another dog too soon could seem callous in the sense that they found it so easy to replace their lost friend.

I felt intense pain when I lost Louie, it physically hurt me, and he was constantly in my mind. But my take on this is that while I am repairing my emotions and healing my pain, somewhere, a dog is suffering, maybe starving, maybe being abused and beaten. So I need to step up to the plate, put my pain to one side and take action. That doesn't mean Louie is forgotten, he's certainly not replaced, nor does it mean I loved him less. It means I need to help another.

SAXON

(The Big Guy)

So here I was again, engaging in the forbidden activity of perusing the rescue Facebook pages and website looking for lost or injured souls. My preference would always be to look for urgent cases or for dogs that no one else wanted, usually the oldies. The soul I found was not necessarily injured or lost, but he was a soul in very urgent need of change. I found Saxon.

Life deals you a bum hand every now and again, that's just the way it is. Saxon's owner, Lisa, was on the receiving end of a particularly bad deal. Life had changed for her and things were not good. Saxon was being impacted by these unwanted life changes and was suffering. Lisa recognised this and made the brave decision to surrender Saxon to the rescue where she hoped a good home would be found for him.

Before a dog can be re-homed, it needs to have an assessment done. After that, it would usually stay with the owner until an adoption with the right family can be arranged. If the dog can't stay with the owner then the options are foster care, or, if there is space, a rescue kennel. There are rarely any spaces in kennels. Things were happening fast for Lisa, Saxon urgently had to be moved. With no time for an assessment, an adoption could not be arranged, (unless the adoption was with an experienced volunteer) so the call went out for an urgent foster place. I spoke to Jo and we quickly decided that we would step in.

Saxon was in Scotland and travel arrangements were rapidly made. Saxon's owner would do the first leg and hand him over to Linz, then Linz would ferry him to Manchester where I would pick him up. We would foster him for as long as it took to find the right home.

6 AUGUST 2014

I arrived at the service station near Manchester and, within minutes of parking, a small car pulled up beside me where a massive black bear of a dog sat on the front seat as happy as could be. I took one look at this dark prince and I called Jo. We would no longer foster, we were going to keep this handsome boy. This was given the green light by the rescue and we logged the fastest foster failure ever. Saxon had a great time on his little road trip with Linz enjoying treats and custard creams. I made a fuss of him and he seemed delighted to see me. Later we would find he was very nervous of men he didn't know, so he and I must have hit it off at first sight.

Linz and I chatted for a while and the conversation soon moved to canine diet, Linz told me what she thought of vegetables and carbohydrates for dogs. This conversation was a turning point for me, setting me on the path of full raw prey model diet.

On getting Saxon home, he did brilliantly. He had lived with another dog before so there were no issues between him and my gang. In fact Kiera started showing off and displayed behaviour I had not seen her do before. I got the distinct feeling that she fancied Saxon. Given all she had been through I thought this would be very good for her. I was also saddened by the thought that she had found this handsome prince to connect with, yet she had so little time left to enjoy his company.

Saxon destroyed his first raw dinner of beef skirt, then we had a little after dinner sing song. The information we received about him told us he loved Amazing Grace on the bagpipes. We put this to the test and sure enough the big guy started to howl and sing along, with Max and Roxy joining in. It was a treat to watch!

7 AUGUST 2014

Off we went for our first walk with the big lad. We quickly discovered Saxon liked to bark in the car. Kiera primarily barked when the car was stationary and Saxon mostly barked when the car was moving. So between them they had the whole noise thing covered.

Saxon was fine on his walk, his recall was OK, and he met other dogs, horses and people all without incident. It appeared he had definitely won Kiera's heart and she spent most of the walk by his side, as in the first picture. The previous day I was getting a little worried about her, I thought things were maybe catching up with her but on this day she really was on form, maybe it was for Saxon, who knows. I remember on this walk how much I missed my Loo-Bomb. Later that day Saxon came to work with us all, he barked a bit but everything was strange to him, I was sure he would settle down in time.

11 AUGUST 2014

This day marked the wettest I have ever been with my clothes on. We took the pack off for a GSD social walk to a local reservoir and woodlands. I was worried about the distance we were doing for Kiera but she did fine. Someone managed to lose a dog so we split off from the main group to search for him. He was found within half an hour or so but that was a very worrying half hour for the owners. We got split from the main group and got lost but eventually met up with the main body towards the end. We had walked further than I wanted to with Kiera. This was Saxon's first social walk and he was a real gent; it was Kiera's last.

12 AUGUST 2014

We were now two thirds of the way towards Kiera's maximum life expectancy and I feared my beauty was slowing down. She would often sit on her walks and sometimes she wouldn't move until she knew we were returning to the car. We had a couple of days like this but on the social walk she was fine, and so I was hoping she was just a bit tired since the walk was quite long. Or maybe I was just kidding myself. Living under this shadow was awful, having seen how quickly Louie was taken from us and each day was filled with painful anticipation. "Will this day be her last"? It was made worse by the fact she didn't really know what was going on and it wasn't as if you could sit down and talk with her and explain. She couldn't tell you how she felt, you just had to carefully watch, all the time, constantly looking for signs. This meant the shadow never abated.

In all other aspects she was good, alert, bright eyed, and as bossy as ever with a good appetite. We planned a short camping holiday for the following day because she enjoyed that, and if she was too tired to walk far then that would be OK, we would all hang around the tent with her. Right next to the site there was a large field and a river to play in, that would be fine for Kiera. She loved the water so a trip to the seaside in Northumberland was on the cards. In the picture you can see princess Kiera relaxing in her pool and being hand-fed morsels of steak. The last shot is a picture of her asleep on her last camping trip.

13 AUGUST 2014

This was Saxon's first camping holiday and he did brilliantly, a bit vocal at times but at least that ensured no one pitched near us. We went back North with Ben to see my sisters, and we planned to meet up with Mark, Sophie, and Tag. Kiera, bless her, did really well but we let her call the shots and walked only as far as she wanted. On a couple of occasions she declined to come walking at all and just stayed at the tent with Jo for grooming and treats. She LOVED her beach trip though, as they all did. Roxy found a partially submerged rock with sea weed swirling around it. Cautiously, she stalked it thinking it some sort of weird sea creature. We took a quick trip to Go Outdoors where Saxon caught a glimpse of himself in the mirror and gave himself a good barking at. He just couldn't believe the cheek and the arrogance of this big black GSD that barked back at him. It was an awesome holiday- why would anyone trade this for a trip abroad? We booked Kiera an appointment at the groomer's on the following week as she wanted to look her best at all times. We were also planning a Reiki session which would happen at home just to help her out a little. The shot taken with the gang in the car are from right to left Mad Max, The Mighty Saxon, Foxy Roxy, the Beautiful Kiera and Tearaway Tag. In picture two you can see Kiera has hijacked all the blankets and the third picture gives you an idea of how stressful Saxon found camping

19 AUGUST 2014

Kiera was nine weeks post op, so the best we were told we could hope for was another three weeks. In reality it could come any day now.

We were getting a bit worried on our final day of camping and over the last few days. It seemed things were beginning to tell on her, she could not manage walks well at all and would often sit and not move, so I just packed everyone up and went home. Jon had a look at her and it seemed her hips, which had never been good, were getting worse and becoming quite painful for her. This may explain why she struggled on her walks; it may not have been her illness. He did think however that there was some muscle wastage on her back legs. I also thought this was the case, something to be expected if the cancer was taking its toll. So I had her weighed and in the last two weeks she had put on a kilo. "Good girl" I thought, however this turned out not to be a good sign. Now she was on pain control for her hips and things improved significantly, she was much brighter.

My princess had a busy day. First thing, she was off to the beauty parlour (she still had that horrible hospital smell about her) then home for dinner of mince, liver, heart, and mackerel. Then she had a gentle Reiki session at home with a local Reiki master. Late in the afternoon she went off to the dojo to supervise the junior black belt tests and to socialise with the parents and students. Then we had some private Dad time to go to the vet's for a weigh in. We ended the day's activities with a short walk just to stop her hips from getting stiff, another yummy dinner then some chilling time. Maybe it was a mix of pain control, the grooming and the Reiki but she was bouncing around like a puppy, bless her. I told her "Long may it last girl, keep it up my sweet". In one picture she is with her new boyfriend Saxon and in the last picture she has just finished her Reiki session.

2 SEPTEMBER 2014

Kiera was now eleven weeks into a twelve week maximum life expectancy. Some weeks ago I was hoping beyond hope that there was a mistake in diagnosis, or that against all odds she was winning this fight. She looked too healthy to be ill. But the last two weeks had taken its toll on my beautiful lady. She had been finding it harder and harder to cope with even short walks. One on occasion I loaded up the truck with the pack and drove five miles to one of their favourite parks. We arrived and disembarked, Kiera just looked at me, and with her eyes she said" Sorry Dad I can't do this today". "That's OK sweetheart" I replied "let's go home to Mum". I drove home to leave Kiera with Jo to be made a fuss of and I went back out with the rest for our morning walk. I was sure she was not in pain but I think she was starting to feel uncomfortable at times.

The previous night she could only make it up the first flight of stairs to the spare bedroom so I slept there with her, I didn't want her to be alone. I had been torn apart by not being there for my Mum, I was going to be there for Kiera in the event anything happened during the night. On some days she looked quite chipper and bright, she would maybe manage 300 yards or so on her walk then we would all sit with her for a while before returning to the car to go home. From the pictures you can see how good she looked.

Her belly, though, had started to fill with fluid again. It was unlikely to be blood since she no longer had a spleen. This could have meant the cancer had spread to her liver, however she was not displaying symptoms of a large tumour there, so it was more likely just to be bodily fluids accumulating as the cancer grew in her stomach. That is why she would tire easily. She had put on over three kilos in three weeks, now I was sure this was due to fluid accumulation. She still enjoyed food and cuddles, she interacted with her pack and still watched TV. She remained alert and bright so it was not her time yet, but it soon would be.

As the days passed by we only ventured as far as the local dog park two miles away. We would take a slow walk to a tree stump Kiera liked and we would all sit and have a feast of a picnic in the sunshine. On the menu were cocktail sausages, chicken, raw burgers and mackerel, all of Kiera's favourite things to eat. We would just sit and watch the world go by, sometimes for an hour or more, on one occasion I wasn't sure how long we sat by the tree stump. I would look at Kiera and think how happy and contented she looked. It was interesting to note that the rest of the pack would sit quietly with us, even after the food was gone, even with other dogs passing nearby they were content just to sit with Kiera. They knew it would be soon, of that I was certain.

I had found the last eleven weeks to have been both very warming, as I had spent so much more quality time together with her, and also incredibly heart rending. Kiera was a fighter and I didn't think she would slip away in her sleep. We would have to make that hard decision at some point, I didn't want her to lose her dignity, but I didn't want to lose my baby either. When the time was right, Jo and I would do what was best for her. She would have no pain, but mine I knew would continue and grow. How do these beautiful creatures so completely get into your heart?

KAY – THE ANIMAL COMMUNICATOR

Kay was a member of the rescue Facebook social page, she had been following the many stories of my pack and she was following Kiera's progress. She contacted me and explained she would be happy to communicate for me, to maybe help me and help my dogs.

It is said that animal communication is an intuitive language between humans and animals, where we listen with the heart instead of our minds. It is also known as interspecies communication or animal telepathy. It is also said that it is possible to connect with our pets after they have crossed over. There is a tremendous amount of scepticism about this kind of thing, but experiences I have had in my life cause me to keep an open mind about such matters. If you have ever wondered about life after death, and you are willing to open your mind, it's worth looking at a book called "Proof of Heaven" by Eben Alexander.

Kay asked me to send her pictures of my dogs and a date would be arranged for a consultation by phone. During this consultation Kay told me things she couldn't have known. I would ask myself "Has this information come from one of my posts?" Some information could have but some most definitely not. Kay told me that Louie was all around us, including Kiera, and he was reassuring her. She knew her time was short but she was not afraid, she was very accepting. This appeared to be reflected in her demeanour. Louie was with her and he would help her when her time came. It is said that "feathers appear when angels are near". Go back and look at the second picture in the last but one set, just by Kiera's left elbow was a solitary white feather

9 SEPTEMBER 2014

I posted to Kiera's followers on Facebook.

"Twelve weeks post op today, the surgeon suggested her max life expectancy would be twelve weeks.

This last week has seen a decline, her tummy is swelling, and she is very tired. She can't make it upstairs any more so I have been sleeping on the sofa to be with her for the last four nights, or maybe it was five, I don't know. My vet is on two weeks' leave so I took her to his house yesterday and he agreed time is close if not now upon us. Yet she fights on, she will still have a little play in her pool, she will still tell the others off for playing too rough. But the spark has gone. Last night at 2.10am she threw up everywhere. Yet a few hours later she is barking at the bin men. She is eating very little and the weight is dropping off her. She is a

89

strong, determined girl, but her dignity is slipping and most of the time she is not looking happy. My worst fear is something will happen during the night, maybe she develops an acute bleed like she did with her spleen, and she will have hours of suffering before she passes. I don't want her to leave us too soon but if I leave it too late I will never forgive myself.

I had a long chat with the vet today on the phone, and it looks like, unless we see a dramatic change, tomorrow may be the day.

I feel a physical pain in my chest, it's like I am the one on death row waiting for tomorrow. I had to explain to my autistic son Ben who, is with his mum this evening, that Kiera may be going to Rainbow Bridge very soon, he asked his mum to drive him to mine to say goodbye, he lay in the garden and cuddled her and kissed her, he spoke to her softly about meeting Louie. Jo had to walk away. I felt torn apart.

I will be with Kiera again tonight, but I am not expecting much sleep.

Louie my boy, be there for her and take care of her.

Kiera has only been with us for eighteen months, but we love her with everything we have.

That night we all slept downstairs with Kiera. We wanted to be close to her. She slept on her bed next to the sofa I was sleeping on. Often in the night I was aware of my hand touching her. She was loved so much.

10 SEPTEMBER 2014

That morning Kiera looked me in the eyes and I knew, beyond all doubt. My sister had told me that dogs let us know when the time has come, and Kiera did. She spoke to me with her eyes and she said "It's time for me to go Dad, please help me". I called Jon who then made his way to the house. This was where things would end for her- in her own home, on her bed with her family. I asked Jon what she would feel, he explained to me that the injection was basically just a large overdose of the same drug that is used as a general anaesthetic. Having had a few of those, I know it's quite a comfortable feeling as you slip off to sleep. Kiera was laid on her bed in the living room and I held her in my arms, Jo was by her side, I whispered in her ear how much I loved her as Jon administered the needle, she was calm and relaxed and she knew she was loved as she slipped from this world. I continued to hold her in my arms and just cried and cried.

Jon left her with us to be taken to be cremated later that day. We sat with her for a while and stroked her, then we introduced the dogs back into the room one at a time so they could sniff her and know that she had gone. When the time came to move her I made a dog stretcher out of one of our camp beds and we gently lifted her on it to carry her to the car. I cut a lock of fur from her to keep next to her cask. As we left the house to take her to the car the pack howled, a haunting howl. At the crematorium, she was carefully laid out while things were prepared. Jo said to me "She looks so peaceful now, take a picture of her" Her fight against cancer was over, she was at peace and running free at Rainbow Bridge. I did take her picture but I can rarely bring myself to look at it. In the first picture we are waiting for Jon to arrive, in the second she is at peace, and in the third she is with her pack brother Louie. The plate on her cask reads "Kiera, our beautiful lady"

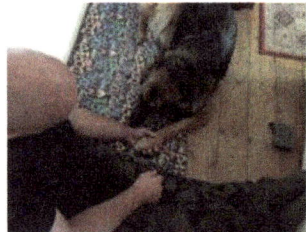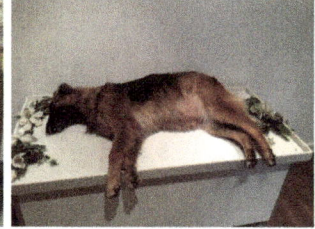

I posted to Kiera's followers on Facebook

"Our baby has gone, our vet came to the house and at midday, she slipped away peacefully in our arms. This is all I can write now. I still can't believe it. Just want to say a big thank you to everyone following her updates, and offering support and help. It meant a lot to Jo and me. We are heartbroken"

The lady who was a volunteer with the rescue at the time and did the handover when we picked up Kiera, sent me this message and picture.

"Ken, Joanne, and family, I am so sorry for the loss of the beautiful and loving Kiera. As you know I held a torch in my heart for this beautiful girl, I have loved watching her blossom in your care and following her many

adventures she has been on with you. I met her when I assessed her and it was love at first sight. I feel your pain, having lost ones so dear in the past, she is now at peace, and like Louie will live on in your hearts forever. Treasure those memories you have made, they are what helps ease the pain. Kiera had such an amazing 18 months with you and I am so glad she had the chance to live with you and experience so many things. Ken you are one in a million and Kiera would thank you from the bottom of her heart for the wonderful life you gave her".

13 SEPTEMBER 2014

As with Louie, I posted a tribute to Kiera. I found that doing this helped me with closure.

"A Tribute to Kiera

Her story

Kiera was truly a most beautiful girl, and a real lady. She liked things done her way and liked nothing more than telling everyone else what to do. She was so cute and loveable, and had a look that would melt your heart. In the morning she really enjoyed jumping into bed with you for a cuddle. Her passing has left a hole in my heart and our family, the house is quiet and empty without her huge presence and character. Watching such a strong girl fade and decline over the last 4 weeks has been torture for me. True to her nature though she fought hard to the very end and never surrendered her dignity.

In March 2013 Jo and I saw Kiera needed a home, she had been with a family for around eight years and the family were moving house into rented accommodation where dogs were not allowed. As we drove past her house we caught a glimpse of her sitting waiting for us and I said to Jo, "WOW look at her". Roxy and Max came with us to meet her. Introductions done, it was time to take her home, this was an emotional experience as she was leaving her family of eight years. She struggled to get in the car and needed some help. On the way home she barked all the way. Bless her, she didn't know who we were, where she was going or what was happening.

We got home after a very noisy journey. Roxy was not happy having Kiera in the house. The girls didn't really hit it off at first and I was worried about the effect this would have on my Roxy. Roxy wasn't coping and I was worried things may not work out. However things did improve.

Clever Kiera, though, played her part. Kiera was the boss right from the start. Looking back now that was clear although at the time I didn't want to accept that. Roxy was here first so she should be the boss (I have learned so much since then). I think Kiera understood the nature of Roxy and she gave her a lot of leeway, Roxy began to relax and relations between the girls improved. All along, of course, Kiera was the boss and she knew the score even if I didn't. Max didn't care really, he's not into politics and is only interested in getting up to mischief.

Soon we had Kiera on a raw diet and her coat, which had been clipped, grew back, soft long, and glossy, she was beautiful. She didn't give a paw at first but she soon learned and she did this in the most elegant ladylike way you could imagine. Regular exercise made her strong and getting in and out of the car was no longer a problem. In the morning as soon as she knew we were going for a walk she would get so excited and she would start bossing me around telling me to hurry up. I was never able to stop her from doing this. I give my dogs a lot of freedom, they are hardly ever on lead and they come to work with me, but for all this to happen they have to do as they are told. With Kiera it took some work on my part to teach her to comply but she only ever did so up to a point. Almost like she knew she had to behave, and so she would only do just enough to satisfy me- beyond that she had to have a measure of control. So eventually the two of us came to a compromise and things worked. She always had to be first out the door after me and first in the car. Roxy and Kiera would race to the car and Kiera would be first in. Roxy is very strong and very fit, she could easily have won every time but often she would let Kiera win. I think Kiera knew this and a mutual respect started to blossom between my girls. If I stopped the car for any reason on the way to the walk, boy did she have something to say.

On our walks she was the meet and greeter. Her greeting was not always welcome amongst other dog owners as Kiera would charge the potential intruder, quickly come to a halt in front of the other dog then rest her head on its shoulders. I can imagine her saying "Look, see this pack here, well it's mine and I need you to know I am the boss- OK?" I could never break her of this habit. Kiera LOVED the water although I never saw her swim. She would just stand there then put her head right under water then toss her head in the air, much like models do on shampoo adverts. She also liked to rub her face in mud, looking like she was giving herself a mud pack.

Kiera enjoyed some great holidays with us and had many adventures. On our first camping trip, though, she didn't really know what to make of this weird cloth house. It had no doors she recognised, how do I get out? Where do I wee? She soon got the hang of things though.

In early July of this year Kiera seemed to get unusually tired on her walks, and on one particular day it became apparent something was wrong. Our vet is a family friend and is always on hand and he thought she had an accumulation of blood in her stomach. One thing lead to another and Kiera was quickly in the hospital having an urgent operation. Her spleen had a tumour and was leaking blood into her stomach. It must have been close to rupture because the surgeon said he emptied about four litres of blood out of her gut. He was amazed she survived, well... he didn't know my Kiera, did he? The tumour was found to be malignant and a CT scan revealed multiple nodules in her stomach. I asked what the possible outcomes were and I was told she had maybe four weeks certainly no more than twelve weeks to live. We were totally devastated. I thought "no... this isn't happening to my girl, you don't understand this is Kiera, this can't happen". But it was happening.

Kiera did not like being in hospital, when I went to pick her up she slipped her collar and ran to the exit. I took my baby home and was determined to give her the best three months I could. She dined on steak and liver cake, we took her on holiday and lots of visits to ponds and lakes. I cut my schedule to a three day working week so we could do more things together. The next two months were amazing, she was like a puppy again, and she had a new lease of life. Sadly during this time we lost our boy Louie, with no notice, to the same type of cancer. With Kiera though I began to think that maybe the surgeon got it wrong. She looked so *healthy and happy, but he was right, well up to a point. During her last few weeks she couldn't really manage her walks, but I would not leave her behind. We would all head out to the park and only walk as far as she could manage, even if it was only 100 yards, then I would sit with her and wait, when she was ready we would all go home. I would drop Kiera off with Jo then I would take the others off for their walk. When the end did come typically Kiera did things her way, she lasted her maximum of twelve weeks plus one day.*

On that day, bless her, she was ready, the stairs had become difficult for her so I had been sleeping on the sofa for four or five nights so she would not be alone. On her last night we all slept downstairs in the same room. The vet arrived at our house on 10th September and Kiera passed away in our arms at 11:55am, she didn't stress at all and she was comfortable, for that I am grateful.

We miss her so much, my girl, my beautiful Kiera. Nothing will ever fill the void she has left. Where ever you are my girl, I love you, and long to meet you and Louie again."

14 SEPTEMBER 2014

Kiera was not gone. The previous night I had a dream, a very vivid dream indeed, a dream like no other I have ever had. In fact, I am certain it was no dream at all. I was just standing around, I don't know where I was, and someone said to me in a cheerful, matter of fact voice "Look here she is, she has been to the pub to see her first family and now she is back." Kiera came running up to me healthy and happy, she was there with me, I could feel her fur it was soft and real. I could feel her very essence... Kiera was with me. Many times on walks I have glanced down and seen her by my side. I don't see her in a way we see things with our eyes, it's not like that, but I see her nonetheless and I have felt her. Sometimes she is with me when I am sitting at my computer in my study, usually sitting on my left. Often I felt compelled to put my hand out to stroke her as I usually did. I am sure people could argue that this was my imagination but it felt so different to me imagining something as I usually did.

Lately as the years have passed by I have felt her less, but when I wrote this piece, she was with me again.

15 SEPTEMBER 2014

This would have been Louie's "Happy Gotcha Day", we would have had him a year on this date. We didn't know his date of birth so we were also going to make this his birthday. At a guess he would have been seven or eight years old. It felt very strange walking with just three dogs, often I would find myself looking around or into the woods for the fourth as a habit, then my thoughts would turn to Louie and Kiera. I miss them to this day.

Saxon's first Mum, Lisa contacted us to check on Saxon, I didn't mind this at all, she clearly loved and missed him, and I can't imagine what it would be like to have to give him up, but it was nice that Jo and I could reassure her that the big guy was doing well and loving life. Some years later Lisa would find out for herself.

17 SEPTEMBER 2014

On our walk today we would trial the new ramp I fitted to my truck. With the tailgate lowered it was quite a jump for the dogs to get in and out, certainly on one occasion Max hurt his leg on exit. To stow the ramp, I made a false floor out of chipboard, the ramp would slide in and out as required. I used a jigsaw to shape the false floor around the wheel arches in the back cabin. The ramp itself was made from lengths of decking, the ribbing effect on the decking would give the dogs some traction. The decking was secured with screws to two lengths of angle steel. As I have a tow bar fitted I had to clad the rear bumper to stop the tailgate impacting the tow bar when fully lowered. About £150 and three hours later- job done. It didn't take long for the dogs to get used to it. This proved to be an essential modification for older dogs.

Our walk found us at Harlow Woods. It had been a week since we lost Kiera and her presence felt really strong around me.

1 OCTOBER 2014

IS THERE SUCH A THING AS A DOG AMBULANCE?

We headed out to Watchwood, one of our favourite haunts, just me and my three pack. It's a nice easy walk of under four miles and the weather was lovely. Saxon loves to chase and bark at stones, and every now and again he likes to carry a stick. I found a nice, smooth, two foot long stick for him. I take care to avoid pointy or sharp sticks - if they lodge into the ground when thrown, the dog can run onto it and get injured. This stick was perfect. I picked it up and tossed it to the ground about six feet in front of me, Saxon got all excited and ran for it, then with a massive YELP he fell to the floor and started crying like a baby.

I rushed to his side to check him out and he just lay on his back, legs in the air, with his head on my lap and cried. I checked his pads and found no obvious problem, and after about ten minutes I tried to coax him to stand without success. Our route on this walk had us about as far from the car as we could get, it would be just under two miles back and Saxon couldn't stand let alone walk. Here I was stuck in the middle of nowhere with a forty plus kilo dog that couldn't stand and another two dogs to look after. What do you do?

First off, I called Uncle Jon who talked me through an examination but nothing was revealed. I called a friend at the rescue to see if anyone knew of such a thing as an animal ambulance, but again no solutions. Then I called Jo to see if she could bring my dog stretcher from home and park near a firebreak in the woods that has a locked gate leading to the main road. This would mean we, meaning Jo and I, would only have to stretcher Saxon about half a mile or so. Then using my phone I found the Forestry Commission phone number and called them to explain my predicament. I asked them if they could send someone out to unlock the gate to allow Jo access to the fire break where she could drive closer to me, they very kindly agreed and arranged to dispatch someone. So we all sat around waiting as the cogs of this rescue machine started to turn.

A walker passed me and stopped to ask if all was well, I explained about Saxon and our rescue mission and his reply was "Pfft, you spoil that dog". Well, maybe so, but that was my choice. Thirty minutes passed by and Jo was getting close. THEN Saxon jumped to his feet and trotted off like nothing is wrong, GAHHHH... I stood down all rescue forces and walked Sax the half mile to the firebreak gate where Jo was waiting. He hopped in the car for a ride home with Mum while the rest of us trekked back to my

97

car. I would be late for work that day, but at least the big guy was OK. Here he is looking sorry for himself in this picture taken at the dojo just after our little drama. Uncle Jon checked his foot and leg and could find nothing.

8 October 2014

These pictures with Max would have been impossible two years ago. Even with me, this close, his eyes would go wide and he would look slightly away from you and growl. If you didn't take heed he would get his fangs out. The transformation took eighteen months and was worth every second of effort and every penny spent. Now Max was trusting, relaxed and very loving, here we are me and my cuddle monster watching TV together.

HOW MUCH DOES DOG FOOD COST?

The pack had been on the prey model diet for some time and were looking good for it. "But how much does it cost" I was once asked. First of all you need to figure out how much stuff you need. My three dogs weighed in at 118 Kilos and I feed them 3% of their body weight a day over two meals. My local butcher supplied me with a weeks' worth of heart, beef skirt, chicken wings and carcasses, liver, kidneys, lungs (including the trachea and assorted squidgy bits) all for around £50 to £60. Then I add whole tripe - two weeks' worth for £5. Finally sprats or sardines at about £15 per month. The pig's pancreas used to control

Max's EPI was free. So we were looking at a total of about £65 per week. Not all food items were used at once, this was just the list of things I would choose from. This was much cheaper than the commercial dry complete I was using and it was far less hassle than the BARF diet. It took a while to source and prepare everything but the dogs loved and thrived on it.

MONTY

(My Old Soldier)

16 OCTOBER 2014

With the passing of Kiera, Jo and I started searching for another soul in need. I saw an appeal on the rescue Facebook page *"Seven year old Monty needs a forever home please. A lovely friendly boy, in foster care in Cumbria"*.

Monty had been picked up as a stray, he was very overweight and had not been exercised. He had been taken from the pound and put into foster care with a rescue volunteer, but he now needed a forever home. I was working from home when I spotted him and Jo was at work. I sent her a text about Monty, coincidentally she had been looking at him as well. I called her and we quickly agreed to adopt.

19 OCTOBER 2014

Arrangements were made for Monty to be ferried to the Midlands where I would collect him. As I left home, Max somehow managed to get past me and stood at the front gate waiting for me. It looked like Max was coming. I thought that would work, Monty could meet Max on a one to one basis before being introduced to the pack at home. As can be seen in the first picture below, Max made himself very comfortable on the back seat of the truck. A rescue volunteer kindly drove hundreds of miles to collect Monty and get him to me. The meeting place was at a hotel with a secure field right next to it where we could walk and introduce the dogs.

Sure enough Monty proved to be a lovely boy. Max was awesome with him- Monty was very unsure at first but Max soon enticed him to play. In a very short space of time they were both trotting around the field together. Later I told Max that I was very proud of him and he was being promoted to Pack Ambassador. Max asked me if this meant he now had diplomatic immunity. "No chance" was my reply.

With the introductions and handover paperwork complete, it was time to go home. Poor old Monty was very afraid of the ramp on the truck and no amount of liver cake could entice him in. In the end I had to lift him in which was no easy task as he still had some weight to lose. He was as quiet as a mouse all the way home. As I left the motorway to drive into Nottingham a big rainbow appeared overhead, the picture does not do it justice, and the colours were very vivid, mmm..., I fancied, Kiera and Louie giving their approval maybe?

Monty was introduced to the pack and things went like a dream, it looked like he had been with them forever. From what I was told, I understood that this old feller has not had a great life, his foster mum had done a good job to restore some confidence, trim him down and start exercising him but there was still a long way to go. Uncle Jon would visit him the next day to give him a once over. Monty's days of existing were over, now he was going to LIVE.

Later that day the rescue posted:

"Well, our Lord Monty of Montague Hall has totally hit the jackpot today! He is now a fully-fledged member of the Robson family! Couldn't be happier for this lovely lad!"

21 OCTOBER 2014

Monty was very inquisitive when I got him home, he stuck his nose into everything but eventually he settled down and relaxed. Within a day he had mastered getting in and out of the truck using the ramp. He watched the others first, then just copied them. Max stuck pretty close to him on our first walk, he was taking his job as ambassador very seriously. I thought it best to wean Monty off commercial food and onto raw gradually, but old Mont had other ideas, he knew what was good for him and he went straight for the raw food wolfing down a chicken wing and a chunk of beef heart. Jon came to visit him and thought him to be a bit heavy but otherwise in good shape. He explained his droopy ear would have been caused by an untreated ear infection or it could have been due to impact trauma, in the same way a boxer can get a cauliflower ear. Monty wasn't head shy so I suspected it was probably due to infection.

After just a couple of days, it was like Monty had been here forever, he had settled in really well. He chose to sleep on the first floor landing as he struggled a bit with the steep stairs into our attic bedroom. Monty followed me everywhere, even more so than Max. He had been to the dojo and proved popular with everyone, he really enjoyed the fuss and attention. Slowly I was increasing his exercise levels. His foster mum told me when she first had him he could manage no more than 100 yards before he needed to sit and rest. His recall was poor to non-existent so I would have to work on that if he was going to be off lead like the others. I made sure on our walks he got to meet other dogs and he behaved perfectly. He was on a steep learning curve but with the others to lead him he was improving fast. In no time he was giving a paw for his dinner, which he LOVED. Within a week he could jump into the back of the truck without using the ramp.

25 OCTOBER 2014

IF DOGS COULD TALK....

Occasionally I would have to leave the house without the dogs, and on those rare occasions that I did, they would let the whole street know about it. Typically Max would start howling like a wolf and then the rest would join in. Sometimes dogs can get separation anxiety and this was a worry I had about them, so I set up a camera to video them when I went out.

Happily I learned that they quickly settled but initially things were a bit frantic. If dogs could talk then the dialogue may go something like this:

MONTY (Running to the front door as he realises I am leaving) "Guys, he's gone out... I just saw him go out the front door, he's walking down the path... I can see him"

ROXY (Jumping up on the window sill to look out) "Yeah... I can see him too... he's going to the car without us... this is outrageous... he's going for a walk WITHOUT US... that's it, we need to be re-homed, Max get me the phone"

MAX (Next to Roxy looking out the window) "Maybe he just doesn't realise he has left us behind, you know how stupid these humans can be, let's call to him... this is so serious, I am going to howl... Roxy howl with me"

SAXON (Wanders into the living room not realising I have left) "What's up? What's going on? Oh... everyone is howling, great I think I will join in"

MONTY (Running from the front door to the back door) "Hang on... maybe he has gone around the back ... ah no... This is terrible, he's goooooooooonne."

While they may settle after a while, I don't. I have to admit I suffer from separation anxiety and I can't do a thing about it.

28 OCTOBER 2014

IF DOGS COULD WRITE...

After getting a new addition to the pack I always post on the rescue site to let people who have an interest know how things are going. On this occasion I let Monty do it.

"Hi, my name is Monty

Dad said I could make a post to tell you all how I am getting on after my first week at my forever home. That's me in the first picture, one of my ears is a bit wonky but Dad said it makes me look cute so that's OK. It's really nice at my new home and the best bit is that I am part of a pack now and people love me.

Max. That's him in the next picture, he's my best friend EVER. He came to meet me with Dad and I was a bit scared of him so I pretended to be tough. But Max is really clever and he knew I was just pretending so he told me to stop being silly and relax, so I did. Max was really kind to me and the first thing he did was show me how to play. I want to be like Max one day.

Then there is Saxon... he is MAHOOSIVE and he barks A LOT, he has always been nice to me but I still get a bit scared when he barks and I sometimes have to leave the room. Saxon likes to lie down in smelly puddles, I don't know why yet.

Then there is Roxy, she is the boss after Dad. I have never seen anyone like her, she is so strong and fast. We don't see her much on our walks as she always goes off hunting, she must be very good at it because we always have nice things to eat.

I have learned a lot of things in just a week and Dad says I am a very clever boy. I give paw for my dinner (which I love) and I can sit and stay and recall now. This means I go off lead on my walks just like Max and the rest. I can also get in and out of the car properly using the ramp, I was very scared of that at first. I have met lots of other dogs on our walks and everyone is so nice to each other. I can now sleep in the pack bedroom, I couldn't do that at first because the stairs were too steep and scary but Max showed me how to do it so I can sleep with everyone else now.

Dad says we are going on a holiday next month to Cornwall, I don't know what or where that is but I don't care because I have a pack now, and at last I am loved. Lots of people have helped me get to my forever pack so I just want to say a big thank you to you all. I have got to go now as Dad has got us all a bone.

WOOOF"

31 OCTOBER 2014

My main focus was to get Monty's weight under control and start building up muscle mass on his rear legs and hips and improve his fitness levels. Aside from an ear infection that was quickly treated, he was fit and well. His coat started to take on that silky glossy look that results from raw feeding. Within four weeks he could easily manage a three mile walk, and looking at him from above, his waistline was beginning to appear. Since we were doing lots of short walks a day, to save money on petrol, I would drive out to our closest haunt at Bestwood Quarry. In the first picture you can see Monty far left looking a bit on the chunky side, and in the last picture there he is looking slim and trim.

29 NOVEMBER 2014

Monty's first holiday was at a place called the Bed and Basket in Cornwall. It consisted of a number of converted barns and farm outbuildings, each with an adjoining heated outdoor kennel, should you ever want to go out and leave your dog (why would you do that?) and two shared secure fields to use as dog runs. There was no limit on the number of dogs you could take and no charge for them either. Dogs were allowed in the accommodation and towels and throws were made available so they could relax on the Chesterfield sofas. On arrival, a basket of goodies was presented, containing tennis balls, towels, toys and dog tags with the Bed and Basket address on should a dog get lost. In the first picture Monty is looking quite pleased about the complementary dog goodies, in the second Roxy and Monty are watching me unpack the car and in the third picture Max trying to get comfortable.

There were lots of lovely woodland walks to choose from. Dog friendly beaches were all around us, but our preference was woodlands. On beach walks, although the dogs loved it, they would often drink sea water resulting in them ejecting unpleasant fluids from both ends. We would take them to the beach but we would leave that for the end of our holiday.

Towards the end of our stay, we planned a walk at Goss Moor, a nature reserve with lots of footpaths and trails. I planned a route of three miles, because that would be enough for Monty, and programmed my hand held GPS. The paths were supposed to be easy going but it had been quite wet and the mud made things a little more difficult than anticipated. The walk went well until we were about half a mile from the car. My route planned to take us across a railway level crossing for the last leg to the car. After about three miles we arrived at the place where the crossing was supposed to be and found... nothing. The railway was fenced off and there was no way to cross. Our choices were to retrace our steps back to the car, thereby completing a six mile walk, or try to make it back to the car using the shortest route possible, but that would be off the path. I didn't want to force a six mile walk onto Monty so we went for option two.

Option two was a massive mistake. Each time we made some headway we would find our way forward blocked with bog or mud and we would have to turn around. Walking off path was hard going, very muddy and wet. I was very concerned about how Monty was coping. After getting lost a few times and doubling back and weaving around all over the place we eventually got back to the car, having covered six miles, and much of it was hard going. This was way more than I wanted to do. We should have doubled back at the railway track. Give Monty his due though his character started to shine through. Monty proved to be a real trooper, this was a trait he would continue to demonstrate. He was single minded and determined. On getting back to the barn we were all a bit tired but Monty didn't display any ill effects for his experience. A trip to the local butcher's provided treats and rewards for all. It is possible though, given the events that were about to unfold, that Monty would pay a price for this long hard walk.

The next day, to give ourselves a rest, we planned a short walk along the beach. The dogs had a great time splashing around in the water. What we were not aware of, until over a year later, was that tankers were dumping raw palm oil into the sea just off the coast of Cornwall. The oil was being washed up on Cornish beaches and there had been reports of dogs becoming very ill as a result.

4 DECEMBER 2014

ILLNESS

Not long after getting home, the whole pack started throwing up, and they all had the runs. Our vet thought one dog had maybe picked up a bug and then passed it onto the others. Like us, Jon was not aware of the palm oil, which may or may not have been related; we will never know. Of all the dogs, I was worried about Monty the most, it seemed to hit him much harder than the others. It's possible that fatigue from the long walk made him more susceptible and less able to cope with whatever was happening to him. I didn't know if it was related but he was having trouble standing, his back end seemed very weak. He was also a little dehydrated. I thought maybe that was because it was uncomfortable for him to stand and get to his bowl. I made sure his water bowl stayed next to where he lay and he did drink a little water. If he wanted to go to the toilet I would have to help him stand up, he couldn't manage that unaided. Jon, our vet, had another look at him and thought he could feel that his spleen was enlarged, much as Kiera's was. I thought to myself "PLEASE GOD DON'T TAKE ANOTHER FROM US SO SOON". I was told to monitor him very closely and if needs be I would take him to the 24 hour animal hospital.

5 DECEMBER 2014

Monty and the gang had been sent dozens of prayers and best wishes from the rescue community. Monty had been settled through the night and in the morning he was more hydrated and more willing to move. I took him to see Jon first thing in the morning and he was less concerned about a possible lump in his abdomen. He was given a course of antibiotics and I would continue to watch him like a hawk. Monty did seem considerably brighter and he was keen to eat his dinner. The rest of the gang seemed to have fully recovered from whatever it was that made them ill, and they were back on form.

7 DECEMBER 2014

Monty was very slowly improving, he was a real fighter for sure. He had a good life and he was determined to keep it. This picture showed him in a much improved state. He was still not well, as you can see, but things were heading in the right direction. He managed two very short walks but I remained very concerned over the effort it took him to stand. Jon suggested full blood tests and wanted to see him again in a few days.

9 DECEMBER 2014

I felt a weight had been lifted. Monty had a massive improvement on this day. Jon didn't feel the need to take bloods. His abdomen felt normal and his mobility was getting back to normal. He had started following me around everywhere again, and as usual he was first in line for dinner. Jon did think, following all Monty's recent examinations, that he may have an arthritic condition in his hips and front left elbow. Also, we found a lump on his back foot, similar to the one Kiera had removed. We would have that taken care of when he was feeling better, and we would get some X-rays done at the same time to determine if arthritis was an issue. I felt both relieved and emotionally drained at Monty's improvement. It had been a very tough year and I really didn't want things to get worse. As always, the rescue community were a huge comfort in the support they offered.

ROMAN & TROY

(The Brothers)

18 DECEMBER 2014

Just before Christmas, and with Monty not yet fully recovered, for some reason that escapes all logic, I started scanning the rescue Facebook pages. I saw this post.

"*************URGENT************
All of these dogs and more need to come into rescue urgently.
Three year old white Honey.
Nine year old brothers Mottu and Sheru.
Four year old Luna.
Four year old Titan.
IF YOU CAN HELP PLEASE, PLEASE DO."

They say dogs pick you rather than the other way around. This must be true because fostering the brothers Mottu and Sheru made absolutely no sense at this point in time. It was just before Christmas and Monty still needed a lot of attention. The rescue confirmed the brothers were good with other dogs so that was it. The boys were in Northampton, which is not far from me. I would just go get them and bring them home with me. The brothers were outdoor dogs, apparently they had never been indoors at all and they were left to roam in acres of grounds that formed part of an old people's home. The home was being sold on soon and the brothers had to go. If they were not brought into rescue they would go anyway. I am not sure where they would go, maybe they would become strays, or offered "free to a good home". These boys needed urgent help as no other option would be good for them. It was arranged that I would pick them up in three days.

I wondered how I would transition them from outdoor dogs to indoor dogs. Maybe I would need to buy some kennels, or possibly I could convert my garden shed for them to use. Jo and I really had no idea what to expect. We were back on to fostering... here we go again, once more into the unknown.

21 DECEMBER 2014

Jo and I arrived at the grounds of the retirement home in the late afternoon. It was dark and the owner hadn't bothered to turn up. Instead we were met by his cousin and the grounds man. I caught my first glimpse of the boys, they were shadowing the grounds man in the distance, but all I could make out was two silhouettes. They seemed a decent size, but they paid us no heed and were very quiet. The owner's cousin introduced himself and told us what little he knew of the dogs. We were told they were devoted to each other, which they were- all they had in life was each other. So much so, he went on to say, that they shared and ate out of the same food bowl. I took that to mean they had a trough into which kibble was thrown from time to time. I asked lots of questions but got few answers and the answers I did get sounded a bit suspect. I asked what shelter they had, and I was assured that they had a blanket to lie on. That was not what I meant by shelter. I was reassured though, that when the weather was extreme they were allowed in the foyer of the retirement home. When I asked about them travelling in vehicles, and vet visits, he looked confused. I was told they were very friendly and the resident old folks would stroke them and make a fuss of them when they could. It was suggested that they had an idyllic existence with acres of land to roam in and they were free. I was not convinced about the idyllic bit. Mottu and Sheru were from the same litter and were nine years old. On asking the meaning of the names I was told Mottu meant chunky or large or well built, while Sheru meant tiger.

The cousin called to the grounds man to bring the brothers over to us and it was time to get them in the car. The lighting around the car was very poor and it was pitch black, so I still couldn't get a good look at them. I lowered the ramp for them to get in but nope... no chance, they were terrified. The grounds man tried to man-handle them in, without much luck, so I gave a hand. Their coats were filthy, at my first touch they felt grimy and as I disturbed their fur it gave off a horrible smell. I tried to grab the first one by the collar, I am not sure which one it was but I couldn't get my fingers inside, their collars were so tight it had to be restricting, if not choking them. Even in the poor light I could see one of them was carrying his head wrongly, and when I helped him in the car my hand brushed the side of his face and it felt sticky. My hand was covered in some black goo. I really couldn't imagine the residents stroking these dogs without having to have a full biological decontamination afterwards. Eventually both boys were in the back of the truck, they just sat, both in the same corner, huddled in close to each other as far away from me as they could. We would just have to give them a good once over when we got home and make a plan from there.

On the way home the boys were a quiet as mice. Arriving home I couldn't get them out the back of the truck, they just sat next to each other in the same corner and wouldn't move. I had to climb in and give some heavy assistance. We took them into the back garden first and introduced them to the pack, my lot had a good sniff, and given the effectiveness of a dogs' sense of smell I am surprised they didn't pass out. Introductions done, we ushered the boys through the back door, into the kitchen and into the light, both literally and metaphorically.

These boys were handsome and looked like two distinguished old gents turned tramps. Aside from dirt, grime, and smell, and being a little underweight, Sheru looked in decent shape. Mottu, on the other hand, clearly had problems. His face and eye were drooping, the way a human face does after having a stroke. The drooping side of his face was black and sticky. It transpired that his ear was rotting, he had an ear infection that had gone untreated and now his ear was literally in decay. His stroke-like features were due to the pain he was in, poor boy. The first thing to do was to cut the collars off, I couldn't unbuckle them as they were too tight and the buckles were jammed with dirt and rust. I needed to arrange for Uncle Jon to take a look at them as soon as possible as the ear infection would need urgent treatment. Also a trip to the groomers would be in order as soon as we could arrange it. Until then, I would do my best to clean all the gunk off Mottu's face. I had to cut some of his fur away since no amount of soaking and cleaning would dislodge the hardened discharge. He had clearly been in pain for a long time. No wonder the cousin I talked too seemed confused when I mentioned vet visits, he clearly didn't know what a vet was. This type of neglect is just another form of animal cruelty. The stench they left in my truck after the drive home seeped into the front cabin and took days to go away.

The brothers didn't respond to their names, maybe I was pronouncing them wrong, but either way I thought I would rename them. OK, so Mottu could mean chunky, but from my own research Sheru, as well as meaning

tiger, could also be translated as glans, as in penis. I didn't fancy trying to teach recall in the local dog park yelling "CHUNKY PENIS... COME"
I live in a very multi-cultural place and someone was bound to be able to translate. I thought I would find names like Saxons, in keeping with the race/warrior theme. I did ask for suggestions on the rescue page, and while good ideas were forthcoming, so were the bad ones. Tom and Jerry... no. Reggie and Ronny... no. This would need some thought.

Here they are in the kitchen having a little dinner with the rest of the crew. Sheru did not know what to do with raw food. Sausages seemed a new experience but the guys quickly decided that sausages were good.

WHAT NAMES?

We thought of calling them Roman and Spartan. Roman was fine but neither of these guys could carry off the Spartan name (my Max could), particularly since there was a lot of modern popular imagery and ideas surrounding the Spartan name following the release of two movies featuring Spartans. Roman worked well and was in the theme of Saxon's name, so Roman was one and that would go to Mottu. The other name we thought of was Trojan, but then someone pointed out to me that Trojan was a brand of condom. However, in my mind the word Trojan conjured up images of the warriors defending the city of Troy. Trojan was a bit long winded but Troy would work. So that was it Mottu would now be known as Roman and Sheru would become Troy.

24 DECEMBER 2014

Day three with the big brothers in the house. Roman and Troy settled in nicely and were responding to their new names already. They had a solid night's sleep which meant Jo and I enjoyed the same. For two dogs that had never been indoors the sentiment seemed to be "Done that to death and we are not going out again" They really did like being in the house. Troy enjoyed sitting on the sofa and was fascinated by the TV.

These gents knew little of the outside world. They didn't know how to react on a lead, they pulled like mad and bounced around in all directions. They would get in the truck but were too scared to get out.

Troy was the more adventurous of the two, if I could coax him out the truck then Roman would follow. Although they were outdoor dogs, walks seemed to be a wonder to them, in a good way, it was like "My goodness, planet Earth is much bigger than we thought". The boys needed a little work with house training but since they had never been indoors, that was not surprising. They were very close and went everywhere together. I took Roman off to see Uncle Jon to get his ear sorted, at this stage I thought it best not to separate them so Troy came along for the ride. When ear infections are an issue, Jon's opening move is to have a good sniff, but on this occasion he nearly passed out. Poor old Roman was given a course of battleship sized antibiotics and Jon would see him again in a few days. He was surprised at how underweight they both were and suggested they both needed to add about ten kilos.

On our walk, by the end of the day I felt so proud of them. They were both off lead running with the pack, and we had established a decent low distraction recall. The smell was still pretty bad though. Given the time of year, our groomers was closed, so we planned a trip to the self-service drive through groomers. In the picture we have first Roman then Troy, both sporting nice new CLEAN collars, and the third picture the brothers are off lead with the pack. Roxy is missing from the picture, as always she would have been off hunting somewhere.

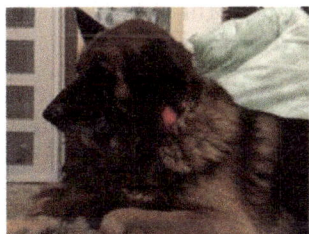  

Since Monty had been ill he had lost a lot of strength in his back end and struggled with stairs, so he now slept downstairs in the study. This is where Roman and Troy chose to sleep, as stairs were an unknown to them and a bit scary. I thought it nice for Monty to have a little company in the night. With daily doses of supplements and golden paste, marvellous Monty's strength was slowly returning.

RECIPE

Golden paste is a turmeric-based mixture that is taken orally on a daily basis and provides health benefits to humans as well as animals. Turmeric, known for its anti-inflammatory properties, has been used medicinally for thousands of years. It is reputedly great for arthritis, skin health, boosting the immune system, and can even help with cancer. I

114

included this as part of Kiera's treatment. Recent studies have revealed it may be as effective as many prescription drugs but without the side effects. It was developed by Doug English, a veterinarian who has utilised the ancient healing spice in all manner of animals. His research can be found on his website TurmericLife.com.au.

You will need:

½ cup of turmeric powder

1 cup of water

1 ½ tsp of ground black pepper

70 ml of olive oil or coconut oil

The pepper and oil dramatically improve the body's ability to absorb curcumin, which is the active ingredient in turmeric.

Directions

Add turmeric to the water in a pan, heat gently and stir until you get a thick paste. You can adjust the thickness of the paste by adding more water or turmeric. Once the paste is of the desired consistency, then stir in the pepper and add the oil. The oil will cause some marbling, you just stir vigorously until everything is nice and smooth. Allow the mix to cool then refrigerate in a jar with a sealed lid. It can be stored for up to two weeks.

For a GSD size dog just put a teaspoons' worth on their food each day. My lot don't seem to notice it. Roxy seems to really like it.

25 DECEMBER 2014

This would be the brothers' first indoor Christmas. We had a hectic Christmas morning going for two walks, everyone got presents and we had to prepare a very special Christmas dinner for the gang. "Surf and Turf" was the main course, cooked salmon and raw beef skirt medallions. Bless him, poor old Troy didn't quite know what to do with it, I think he was hoping for biscuits. My crew on the other hand knew exactly what to do. Roman's ear had stopped discharging and he had stopped shaking his head every five minutes. All we needed to do now was fatten the boys up a bit. You can see in the first picture how hard Troy was finding it adjusting to indoor life. The third picture is Christmas dinner- for the dogs, not Jo and me!

28 DECEMBER 2014

The brothers had been with us for ten days now and I was really getting to understand their characters, so it was time to do a little write up on them to send to the rescue. The report would be used on the website and Facebook page to try to attract an adoption.

The report read:

"NINE YEAR OLD BROTHERS, UPDATE FROM FOSTER DAD Ken Robson; Were Mottu & Sheru- renamed Roman & Troy.

A TALE OF DEVOTION AND BROTHERLY LOVE - and a few pictures from this morning's walk.

Roman and Trojan (Troy) have lived together as brothers for nine years and have never been indoors. They have never been separated, in fact they were puppy number seven and eight in the litter so they were probably together in their mother's womb. Their knowledge and understanding of the normal world as most dogs know it is minimal. The boys are learning though, and learning fast. As outdoor dogs they were not house trained, but for the last three nights we have had no accidents, so they are making great progress.

I guess the boys have never seen stairs let alone try to negotiate them. They follow me everywhere but not upstairs, this is WAAAAAAY to scary... Yet they want to follow me. Troy is the most adventurous of the two and each day he has ventured further and further up the stairs, then fear overcomes him and he backs down again. Yesterday I go upstairs and get to the landing, I turn around and there is Troy... "GOOD BOY" I praise. Roman though is in a panic, he must be with his brother but he is terrified to negotiate the stairs, but the love for his brother is overwhelming, in a semi panic and crying all the way, a step at a time he braves the stairs and makes it to the top by his brother's side. I give him a massive amount of praise. Now it gets really hard. Jo and I sleep in the attic so it's another flight of stairs, steeper, narrower, and it has a ninety degree bend at the bottom. Jo and I go to bed and we hear the commotion on the landing, after a while Troy appears but Roman can't make it, he is at the bottom crying, it's pitiful to hear. I try to help him but he backs

116

away, he is just too scared. We decide to go to bed and leave him to see if he can manage on his own. After what seems like and age of listening to Roman cry, we hear a determined THUMP... THUMP... THUMP... THUMP and he makes it to the top. "GOOD LAD". Reunited with his brother they settle down to sleep. In the morning neither of them can get down, but that's another story.

When I take the pack out for a walk they all sit at the front door quietly (apart from Saxon who is yelling at me to hurry up), I open the door and walk through, then invite the pack outside. They race to the front gate and wait, apart from Saxon who bounces around yelling at me to hurry up. I then go to my truck and lower the tail gate, extend the ramp, make sure no cats are around, and shout the pack to enter the truck. Saxon is always first in, he is not good at waiting. I know this all sounds a bit "dog whisperer" but while it works very well, occasionally one of them decides not to play ball, and it takes a few attempts to get them in properly.

Today it was Max's turn to be a pain, normally he is very good but today he refused to sit and stay. So it's back in the house for him until I get the rest in the car. I open the front door of the house and Max goes back inside but Troy also sneaks inside, not a problem I thought, as now I only have to get four in the car, I will get Max and Troy in afterwards. I go back to the front gate to begin the "get in the car ritual" and poor Roman is trembling, I mean massively shaking. All this stuff is so new to him, but now his brother is not by his side to reassure him.

At this point it struck me hard that people often treat these beautiful animals so badly, yet look at the capacity they have for love, loyalty, devotion and dependence on one another. With all of that goes intelligence.

Troy is let out the house to be with his brother and we head out for a lovely walk. See the pictures. Roman's ear is much better, we are off to see Uncle Jon tomorrow at the vets. They are adjusting very well, and mix well with other dogs when out and are generally AWESOME".

31 DECEMBER 2014

Uncle Jon was very happy with Roman's ear, it was all but sorted now. The boys were enjoying a raw diet and the change in their coats was starting to show already. No more dry, gritty, grimy feel, the fur was becoming softer and was starting to shine. Here they are enjoying breakfast with the pack. Being New Year's Eve, and living close to the city centre, as soon as night fell, the fireworks made the place sound like a war zone. So Saxon aka The Saxinator aka Big Guy aka the Dark Destroyer, decided that Mum needed a little reassurance so he plonked himself on her knee. To make HER feel better of course

3 JANUARY 2015

The boys were progressing well, I couldn't believe how attached they were to each other, it's like they were joined at the hip, or the spine, as they would often sleep back to back. Roman had discovered what the sofa was for and both boys were doing amazing at the "Stay" command. They were also progressing very well at getting in and out of the car when told. Troy sometimes needed a little reminder but all-in-all they were doing FANTASTIC. The pack were helping with the learning curve, apart from Saxon, bless him, who just couldn't understand why anyone should have to wait for anything, and got quite vocal about it.

Roman and Troy would wait at the back door to go to the toilet now, and aside from one little accident the night before, were just about home and dry on the house training front. Their recall was very decent now although it remained a bit shaky if they were in a state of high distraction, but then most dogs struggle with that. I had noticed no real vices, they were not destructive, they travelled well in the car, they were good at the vets, and they didn't bark much at all. They would make some family very happy I was sure.

Our walk schedule was a bit messed up as Monty was still on light duties, so we would all go out for a short one (Monty was good for two miles in one go, but I was not going to push him beyond his ability). Then it was back home to drop off Monty and the brothers (to keep him company), then I would be out again with Roxy, Max, and Saxon. Monty was more his old self now, he was alert and responsive, mobile around the house and keen to pinch anyone's dinner given half the chance.

The brothers were great on walks, Roman would just plod along by my side the whole time off lead. Troy was a bit more adventurous and would sometimes follow Roxy and roam a little further afield.

The thing that really struck me about the brothers was just how loving they were. Troy would often wander up to me, stick his head under my arm and nuzzle into me, and then Roman would follow him and do the same. It was almost like they were so grateful to have been taken from their previous existence into a home full of love. These two wonderful old gents, who I don't think had ever had much attention, finally were due a wonderful retirement that they so deserved. Jo and I did discuss adopting but as much as we were falling in love with them six dogs was just a little too much for us to handle on a permanent basis. I couldn't really take six dogs to work so they would have to be left alone more than I would want them to be. I was of the opinion that these two boys should never be left alone again. They craved human attention, and giving the neglect they had suffered, they had some catching up to do. The cost was also a consideration, the monthly breakdown was a bit scary:

£200	Petrol to drive to and from the park,
£350	Food
£150	Insurance (that's a rough figure for six dogs)
£100	Supplements
£100	The rest: treats, toys, vet bills etc.

Spending just short of a thousand pounds every month was significant. That said, we would keep them for as long as it took to find the right home, and if money became tight we would just have to find a way. We were under no illusion, we could have them for a while, it is uncommon to find someone that wanted an older dog, but to take two...

The rescue, rightly so, did not want the boys split up, and I did not want them to be passed around, their next home would be their forever home. As and when that time came it would break my heart but it would be best for them. I took solace in the fact they would have been comfortable, well cared for and loved, whereas they could have been put into kennels or worse. This would be the first time I have not failed as a foster but it had to be.

9 JANUARY 2015

We had a booking to take the brothers to our local groomer, Aunty Karen. This was not the best experience the boys had with me, but it was necessary. Troy marked the groomers' as his by having a massive wee up the wall as soon as he got inside and this distracted Karen long enough for Roman to nip through the back and have a huge poo.

Then Troy modified Karen's window display. Thankfully Aunty Karen takes everything in her stride and nothing is a trouble to her. Troy was up first, he tolerated the bath but when the dryer was turned on he went nuts so he had to come home a little damp. Roman hated the bath but tolerated the dryer. The water from them was BLACK. Karen remarked how thin they both were. "You should have seen them two weeks ago" I explained. Both boys came home smelling sweet and looking good. Troy is in the first picture and Roman in the second. The third picture is how the boys slept, sometimes they would top and tail, sometimes heads at the same end, but more often than not they had each other's backs.

The next job was for Uncle Jon to sort vaccinations as they had not been done for SIX years.

A VERY SAD BROTHER

Naughty boy Troy had been nibbling at his foot over the last couple of days and one of his pads looked a bit raw. After treating and dressing it, I had bought a special boot which we nicknamed "the welly of shame" Troy was not keen on his welly and Roman, sensing his brothers distaste for his new garment, decided to get involved in the welly fitting process, but not in a helpful way. This seemingly simple task became a two man job in the end.

The brothers would come to work with me this evening as Uncle Jon was coming to check out Troy's foot.

I am sure Uncle Jon LOVED my pack as they were going to help him pay off his mortgage and retire early. Or maybe even very early.

In the last two months we had fixed Roman's infected ear and sorted an ear infection for Roxy. Max, not wanting to be left out, started doing a weird snorting thing, so he had antibiotics for a possible nasal infection. Monty had been treated for a virus and had blood tests, with more tests to come. Also, Monty still had that lump on his foot that was getting a little bigger. We would have that removed- so that's a general aesthetic and an operation with a biopsy for the lump, and while he was out we would get some X-rays of his hips done as he seemed to be having a few problems in that area. Monty was on supplements for life and pain control for now. Finally we had to deal with Troy's foot which was a bit whiffy and so probably infected.

Saxon was not keen on Uncle Jon and so was not contributing to his wealth at all. Good lad Sax, keep it up.

On a more serious note, I was grateful to have such a vet as Jon. Not only was he damn good at his job but he was always there for us, even out of hours, and was very gentle on the fees. Financially, it just seemed bad at the time.

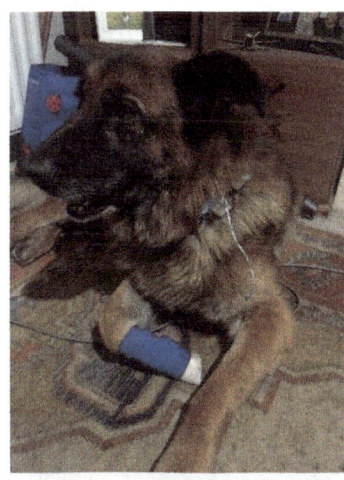

21 JANUARY 2015

The brothers had been with us for almost a month now with no interest coming their way regarding adoption. Given the time of year this was no real surprise to me, however I thought another little write up for Facebook would be a good thing to keep them in people's minds. I posted the following:

"COME ON PEOPLE... JUST LOOK AT THESE GUYS. I would love to keep these boys but I have to leave them on their own far more then I would like to. I fostered them knowing I could improve their lot in life and I am sure I have but these lovely old guys don't need to be left alone. Monday, Tuesday, Thursday and Friday they are left for a couple of hours in the afternoon then I pop home to feed them and let them out. Then they are left again for around three hours in the evening. These guys are just so loving all they want to do is to be with me. But left on their own I have to say they are as good as gold.

Out walking Roman glues himself to my left knee and that's where he stays for 90% of the time. Troy likes to run around a bit with the pack and both recall OK. They are totally house trained now and have been for some time.

They are both enjoying their food which is just as well as they still need to put on a little weight. All-in-all my crew, given their weight, age and exercise levels consume 7.2 kgs of fresh meat per day. If the boys stay with me for much longer I am going to have to make some domestic financial adjustments i.e. cut down on my beer consumption. Not a bad thing I suppose.

Troy in one picture is sporting a snazzy neoprene shoe as he managed to lose his expensive welly of shame. Oh well. His foot is sorted now and he should be out walking without his shoe in two days.

The two indoor pictures show Troy sleeping with his head on Roman's bum and the other picture shows our living GSD rug.

Roman and Troy are two lovely old vice-free boys, they are very affectionate and are so easy to have around".

4 FEBUARY 2015

Sweet and gentle, marvellous Monty was off to see Uncle Jon to have a lump removed from his foot. The lump has been getting bigger but it did feel self-contained so I was not too worried that it was anything nasty that may have spread. Nonetheless it would be sent off to the lab for a biopsy. While Monty was sedated I would get his hips and joints X-rayed just to see what was going on there as he wasn't strong on his back end at all. I hated leaving him to be sedated but at least he knew his Uncle Jon.

The operation went well with the vast majority of the mass being removed. Given its location, it was just not possible to remove every last trace but the lump was solid and Jon confirmed that it seemed to be self-contained. We could not be certain of things until the report came back from the lab and that would take a week or so. The X-rays confirmed what I thought, advanced arthritis in his hips and joints, so maybe we would have to look at some pain control for the future. It was becoming apparent that this young man was a great deal older than we thought.

Here is marvellous Monty at home following his operation, looking a bit unhappy but well nonetheless. In the second picture he is looking a LOT happier having had his dinner. Monty got to choose from the a la carte menu and went for some nice bland cooked chicken. I suggested that would be best on his stomach following his sedation; he would be back on his raw diet the next day.

7 FEBUARY 2015

My special boy Max was six on this day. Monty was able to accompany us on our morning walk as Jon was happy with how his foot was healing. Troy having lost the packs expensive welly of shame, now meant that Monty had to wear a fashionable supermarket bag to keep the bandage dry. It worked better than the expensive welly Troy lost.

Max got a squeaky duck and new tennis balls for his birthday. He wasn't keen on the duck so he buried it in the garden. Oh well, it only cost ten quid. Then it was time for the birthday liver cake. This was the brother's first experience of this doggie delicacy, surprisingly they didn't seem to know what to do with it. While Max was posing for his photograph and waiting like a good boy, Roxy quickly moved in for a cheeky nibble. Max got first bite after that, then it was cake for all, the frenzy lasted about fifteen seconds.

11 FEBUARY 2015

My office at work is located close to our reception desk and my door is always open so passing students can see inside. As needs be, the office is used to interview potential students and to conduct enrolments. So it's very important that the place is well maintained, clean, smelling nice and uncluttered. You may recall one of the reasons I couldn't keep the brothers was because I couldn't take six dogs to work. I posted these pictures on the rescue social page of my nice uncluttered office. The office is not huge so all it takes is one smelly fart and it's time to evacuate. I didn't make this a regular occurrence as it really couldn't have been good for business, but I wanted to reduce the time the brothers were left alone. As their confidence was building their characters started to show, Troy in particular was turning out to be quite a cheeky boy and a real love bug to boot.

12 FEBUARY 2015

MAXIMUM MERRIMENT FOR MARVELOUS MONTY

Monty's lab results revealed the lump was benign and nothing to worry about. It was similar to the lump that was removed from Kiera but Monty's lump had advanced to the next level. I can't recall its name but Jon said he had never diagnosed one before, and the lab said it is very rare, still... it wasn't a worry, that was the main thing. Although it was unlikely to have been bad news I couldn't help but have a nagging doubt while waiting for the results. Now I could breathe again. His wound was healing well and the stitches would be out in a few days.

In the picture I am giving Monty the good news. Just look at his face, he could be saying "Really Dad... really... so I am going to be OK am I?"

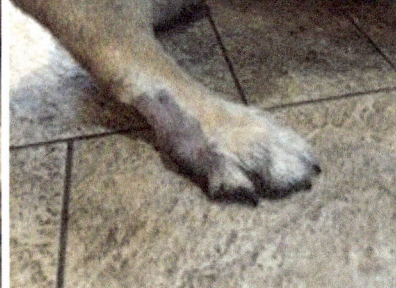

12 FEBUARY 2015

I got quite a response and a number of comments on the pictures I posted on Facebook of my office. In reply to the comments I posted the following:

"Lots of people seemed to like the pictures of my pooches at work, but for all you complainers that worry I don't provide enough sofas for my dogs, and made comments they were not pulling their weight. Then here is the gang again with PROOF that they DO actually have jobs and don't just sleep all day. The guys have responsibilities in my office, reception, reception lounge, staff room, and kitchen. Sometimes when I am not looking though they occasionally sneak off into the student lounge for tummy rubs and head scratches.

Here is Roxy the marketing manager, and she is sitting in the illuminated window at night attracting, err... customers!!! The brothers Roman and Troy are doormen, "If yer name's not down..." The big guy Saxon is just chilling out opposite the reception desk, he is head of security and here he can stare at his mum all day long and make sure no punters give her grief. Max as head of PR has monopolised the reception lounge sofa and he is just "keeping it warm for customers that may need it" Main Man of the Moment Monty is in charge of the maintenance department and is as close as he can get to the radiator behind the reception desk, this way he can monitor the heater to make sure it doesn't break down.

See... not one of them is asleep. The shots in my office I posted previously were taken when they were on a break. Also yes... they are on the payroll, they get paid in liver cake, which is waaaaaaaaaaaaaay better than money".

28 FEBUARY 2015

All the pooches got a rabbit for their late meal. I thought the brothers may struggle with this, they were good with raw food now, but they just didn't get the chewing thing, so I had to chop everything up for them. But Roman... my old boy... really showed everyone how it was done, he polished his rabbit off in no time and washed it down with a good swig of Mum's cider while she wasn't looking. Roman's face no longer had any trace of the droopiness when we first got him and he was looking younger. Troy was full of beans and loving his walks. Monty was still not back to where he was before his illness but he was on a new pain control protocol and was doing well. It seemed his initial age of seven when we got him was a guess, so it was very possible he was a deal older. He didn't come upstairs to sleep with the others in our bedroom any more, but he was comfortable on his bed in the living room. Standing up was becoming a little harder for him but the dear old gent was loved to bits and he knew it.

4 MARCH 2015

WORRIED ABOUT MONTY

Poor old Monty was struggling again, his mobility was deteriorating. I took him on a very short walk in the morning and it was clear it was hard for him. So we returned to the car and came home. All afternoon he just laid in one spot and didn't move. I tried to get him up to go for a wander in the garden and he couldn't stand unassisted. Once up he could walk, but he was unsteady and sitting back down seemed to be an effort. Given the state of his arthritis the vet said I had to keep him moving or he would stiffen up, but not to over-exercise him. It was so hard to get it right as old Mont was a bit of a trooper and he would just plod on regardless. He was back on stronger pain control as he clearly needed it but now his stools were soft and jelly like. This, I thought, could be a reaction to his change of meds. His latest blood tests came back good so I had no idea what to do next for him, I felt quite helpless and very worried. Monty had a bout of pancreatitis a while back; I wondered if it had returned. As a precaution I decided to reduce the fat in his diet until he could be tested again.

Roxy always came upstairs to our bedroom to sleep, her bed was right next to me. She would always sleep there. But since this recent decline in Monty she spent every night sleeping with him in the living room. Monty was on his bed and Roxy would sleep on the sofa next to him. I hoped this was not a case of her knowing something I didn't.

127

5 MARCH 2015

Monty was looking a little brighter this morning. He could just stand unaided and seemed a lot more alert. We went for a very short walk, on returning to the car he didn't want to get in, so we extended the walk a little for him. He wolfed down his dinner and pinched half of Troy's while he was at it. He remained a bit wobbly and shaky so we arranged for Jon to see him that evening. I felt encouraged at this improvement but I knew in my heart we had a long way to go. Here is Monty looking a lot happier than the day before.

6 MARCH 15

To aid with his mobility, Jon tried a little acupressure and Monty reacted well to it, so Jon thought he may respond well to acupuncture. Tests revealed Monty had colitis so he would be on antibiotics to clear that up. I would maintain his current pain control and supplements. Once the colitis had been sorted out, we would make a decision on whether to try acupuncture or not. Jon wanted to hold off on the stronger painkillers, as once they stop helping there is really nowhere else to go. Monty looked OK in himself but his gut problems would to be making him feel bad and would drain his strength. I was hopeful that in a week, with the colitis cleared up, he would be feeling much better.

18 MARCH 2015

Sansom Woods was lovely that morning. Monty's colitis seemed to have cleared up as his stools were back to normal. He was still weak though, so keeping things gentle for him we did a slow mile. He then waited at the car with Jo and Saxon (Saxon was a mummy's boy, if Mum was staying at the car then so was he). Then Roxy, Max, the brothers and me took off for a fast hike. This walk routine would become common.

Monty had been running a high temperature, at its maximum it hit 40C five days back- it should be 38.6c. At a temperature of 38.9 or above a dog would be considered to have a fever. A fever is not necessarily a bad thing as it is an indication that the immune system is fighting hard against whatever was going on inside him. His temperature had been dropping but was still 39.4c so he would naturally be feeling a bit washed out, bless him. We switched his antibiotics from gut specific to a good quality general drug to target whatever was giving him a high temperature. We had to keep him moving though, to prevent him getting too stiff from his arthritis. He was not that mobile at the moment but I would never leave him behind and I made sure he got to walk with his pack every day.

Roxy still slept downstairs with Monty which was really sweet of her. She came upstairs two nights previously and realised Monty was missing, so she turned right round and went back downstairs to keep him company.

25 MARCH 2015

MONTY – A PICTURE EMERGES

Monty was done with all his meds and treatments now, yet he remained weak. His temperature had dropped significantly but it was still a little on the high side. His hip and joint X-rays showed chronic arthritis, visually you could see that in his enlarged front joints, there must have been some discomfort there for him. His latest bloods came back fine, they were not perfect but there was nothing to be concerned about. His urine tests came back normal. His first set of antibiotics seemed to clear up a possible bowel problem but it didn't bring his temperature down, so another set of antibiotics were used with some better effect. On this day Monty had three chest X-rays and an abdomen X-ray. Thankfully all clear again and the spleen was normal, however there were images on the pictures that suggested Monty was an old boy, some arthritis of the spine was also discovered. All the evidence from the tests he had, pointed to the fact he was unlikely to be seven years old, probably more likely ten or eleven.

Yet just four months ago he was acting like a seven year old, a bit stiff maybe, but far stronger than he was now. So why the rapid decline? My guess was that when the whole pack contracted a virus four months ago, it hit poor Monty really hard. There were times when I thought he may not pull through, but he was a soldier was old Mont, and he did pull through, but he had never been the same since. Possibly due to his age, this bad illness hit him much harder than the others and maybe accelerated an age related decline.

Nonetheless, for the sake of completeness I would get a stool sample analysed even though the vet was not expecting anything to come back. Given his likely age, I was certainly not going to trouble him with further invasive or exotic tests. It was beginning to look like Monty was an old gent and he would be afforded the dignity he so deserved. I would still consider acupuncture to help with the joints, and I would certainly keep up with supplements and maintain his daily pain control. His exercise routine would be gentle, frequent, short walks, to help keep him mobile, I didn't want his arthritic joints stiffening up.

Here is my sweet old gent toddling along with the pack on his morning half mile. In the last picture he is waiting in the truck with Saxon and Mum before I head out with the others.

APRIL 2015

About three weeks ago Troy seemed to be off his food. I wasn't worried because dogs will often skip a meal or two, this can be for a number of reasons but then usually the appetite returns. But this was just not happening with Troy. The brothers had been with me for just under four months and their transition from kibble to raw food went well. Troy had been eating fine and even started putting on some much needed weight. Then, for no apparent reason, he went two straight days with no food at all. After that I did manage to coax him to eat some food but it was hard work. I tried all kinds of different meats, I tried cooking the food, and I even tried him back on kibble, but he remained reluctant to eat. One day he would show a little interest in cheese but then the next he wouldn't touch it, I even gave him a cooked sirloin steak, of which he ate a little but then left the rest. When he did eat, it was by hand feeding and he would take his food very gingerly, I did wonder if he had tooth or gum problems, but they both checked out OK. His food intake had dropped to about half of what it should have been. I had just managed to get some weight on his skinny frame and now he would lose it again.

After a lot of experimenting I found he would show some interest in raw chicken wings, cooked mackerel, cheese and sausages. This was not really a balanced diet for him but at least I could get some food inside him. His energy levels were good, his demeanour normal, and his stools were OK. Jon took a look at him and declared him to be a little underweight but otherwise in great shape. I consulted with the rescue and they agreed to have blood tests done. The results came back as normal.

I was not aware that anything had changed in his life, he wasn't being bullied by any of the others as that can sometimes cause appetite loss. I was completely stumped and had no idea what to do. Jon told me to just monitor his weight and energy levels. I asked for help and advice on the rescue volunteer group but nothing was really forthcoming that would help. Troy looked and was behaving absolutely fine, he just wasn't eating, and consequently was losing weight. I spoke to the rescue again and they were as puzzled as I was, but then suggested that maybe being in a pack of six just didn't suit him, his whole life it had just been him and his brother. All I could do was get what food in him I could and monitor him.

MAY 2015

While I remained concerned and puzzled by Troy's lack of appetite, his energy levels and activity within the pack were as they had always been. Monty, on the other hand, thankfully was causing me less worry. By early May he could crack a good three and a half mile walk with no problems. After his walk he would be alert and bright with no stiffness or ill effects. The light and shine were returning to his eyes. Only two months ago I thought it possible that his end was close, but my trooper Monty was a fighter and he just bounced back. He remained on daily pain control, supplements and Golden Paste. I was proud of how he had fought his way back to health, he had a good life now and he wasn't going to let it go. Here he is leading the pack, as bright as a button and as sharp as a knife.

Early in the month, the rescue contacted me to say a home had been found for the brothers. I had very mixed feelings about this. I was given the details of the person that was to adopt the boys and I called to make arrangements for the handover. A date was set and I waited in anticipation for this person to arrive and take the brothers away. The appointed time came and passed but nothing, I called to check if all was OK, only to be told that they had broken down about an hour away from me and had been waiting for a recovery vehicle for some time. I was told I would be kept updated. Time passed and still no news. I called again and left a voice mail saying I would drive out to meet them and help if I could. My call was not returned and despite leaving many voice messages and sending text messages I never heard from them again, nor was the rescue able to make contact again.

Later in the month when I received news again that another home had been found for the brothers, I thought "Here we go again". Julia and Peter lived on the Isle of Skye, they owned a croft with acres of land for the boys to roam in, there was even a stream running through their garden. They wanted to adopt a pair of older dogs as they felt the oldies were in less demand and would often be left on the shelf. Older dogs needed a nice loving retirement, and this is what was on offer now for my dear boys Roman and Troy. I was happy for them as this seemed the perfect home, but letting them go was going to hurt. Troy was still not eating well and if he was struggling in a pack environment, this change could be very good for him.

7 MAY 2015

This day would be the last time I would walk alone with my pack of six. It was a lovely day and I took my time over nearly four miles. It was a walk of reflection with the brothers being uppermost in my mind. It was lovely walking my pack with Jo alongside, but there was something special about walking them alone. I really LOVED walking with my pack, I felt privileged to be the only human in the company of these wonderful creatures. After this day a third of them would be gone, probably never to be seen again, Skye was not just around the corner so I would not be popping in for a quick visit. The following day would be Saxon's first birthday with us, and the brothers would be gone. (We later discovered we had made a mistake on the big lads' birthday, it was actually on the sixth). During the walk I took lots of pictures that included a very special shot shown below. From left to right we have Saxon, Roxy, Roman, Monty, Max and Troy. This picture would later be used on greeting cards to help raise funds for the rescue.

I had spoken with Julia and Peter who were driving down from Skye to stay in a hotel that evening, they would visit us in the morning and we would take a whole day to do the handover. They would come walking with us and I could demonstrate the work I had done with them. They could see for themselves how they reacted to other dogs on walks. We would discuss medical and feeding issues. This would be a good handover, much better than fifteen minutes at a service station. Sometimes that can't be avoided but you don't get to find out much in fifteen minutes. As well as this being an ideal handover, it was also going to be tough for me, I would spend the whole day in anticipation of the inevitable, and then my boys would be gone.

8 MAY 2015

We made sure Saxon had the usual birthday treatment before our guests arrived. He enjoyed a cake with his name on and he got a new bed which he seemed to like. Then we waited for the brothers' new Mum and Dad to arrive. I was mentally preparing myself not to get upset and look foolish.

Julia and Peter arrived at our house and we found them to be an absolute delight. I was so pleased I got to meet them, it could have been that the brothers would have been ferried to them as Saxon was to me. Having met them, I felt much better about the boys leaving as I knew they would be in very good hands. Roman and Troy were very well behaved, we had a lovely long walk in the woods and we got to meet other dogs. After the walk, Julia and Peter witnessed first-hand the trouble we were having feeding Troy. We sat in the garden for an age and talked about the boys, it felt I had known these people forever, it all felt right. I did fight back a lump in my throat a couple of times during the day but all in all I was doing well. At times though, I couldn't help but think to myself "What would Roman and Troy make of all this, maybe they don't want to go away with these two strangers?" It is easy to make sure that the humans are happy with the proceedings, but dogs have feelings and emotions as well, what would be going on in their heads?

Then the time came for them both to leave. I was stood in the middle of the street outside my house with the brothers by my side and I could keep it together no longer. I sobbed, I didn't just cry, I really sobbed-tears, snot, and snuffling; I did the complete package. I could only hope the neighbours weren't looking. Julia and Peter were very kind to me, they understood and offered me reassurances. They would write to me about the boys' progress and send me pictures. They drove off and that was it, my two sweet old boys that I took from that horrible existence, my two affection seeking love monsters were gone. I was not aware at the time, but I would meet Troy again.

I posted to the rescue Facebook community:

"*The six pack is no more... now it's just the fantastic four.*

The brothers have finally found the forever home they so deserve, they left me ten minutes ago so I am writing this with a lump in my throat. The house feels quiet and still... empty. But I am pleased for the old gents as they are off to a wonderful life on the Isle of Skye. New Mum and Dad spent the day with us, walking and finding out about the boys. They are a lovely couple with a six acre back garden with a stream at the bottom.

134

The brothers have the retirement they so deserve. Lots of love, lots of cuddles and lots of walks, spending quality time with quality people.

I will miss them so much, I am grateful to have been part of their lives if only for four and a half months, but in that short time they stole my heart.

Now... Where is that bloody bottle of Jack Daniels?"

There are many good, selfless people in rescues, that foster, time and time again, and each time a dog leaves, they are devastated. I don't know how they do it. I take my hat off to each and every one of them.

10 MAY 2015

As soon as Julia and Peter got home, they emailed me just to say all was well. The journey had been a bit of a slog, but Julia said the boys had been "a couple of dreamboats". The boys had been introduced to their new home and had been taken on a few walks. They had met the neighbours' dogs and all was well, except that Troy was still not eating - that remained a worry. Julia thanked me for the thorough handover and said she would send another update soon. She sent me the following pictures showing the boys in their new home. The boys, as always, lying back to back- their attachment to each other was remarkable.

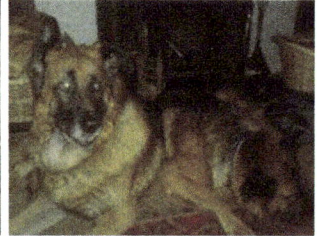

16 MAY 2015

As promised Julia sent me an email with pictures updating me on Roman and Troy. Here is a snippet:

Hi Ken and Gang,

The boys are doing very well, Troy slightly better than Roman. Troy has found his appetite, which is stunningly good news. Because I'm at home with them all day, I can afford the luxury of time and experimentation with their food. I am concentrating on calories and I swear we can feel the slightest hint of fat under his fur. Just a tissue paper's width, but the sharp angle between his last rib and hind quarters is softening and filling. We still have our two walks a day, sometimes three. Troy's personality is starting to come out now, he's cheeky and feisty and very loving, he head-butts you from underneath when he wants a love. He is the bolder one, always pushing and nosy as can be.

Roman tends to keep his distance a little more, though he is perfectly behaved on our walks, and attaches himself to my left leg. I think he is more the worrier and certainly more "conscientious" It is lovely seeing their characters and personalities coming through. We have a wood burner in the living room, and today for the first time I lit it. I laid the fire, firelighters, kindling, coal then wood and started trying to light it with matches. At that point, both boys went bonkers, barking and hopping around and squealing and shoving their nose into the (unlit) burner! And then as soon as it was lit, all was calm and tranquil, and they jostled for pole position in front of it, and haven't budged since.

I am taking the dogs into our vets at 08.30 on Wednesday for a good once over, I don't know when I will be picking them up, usually it would be the same afternoon, but this will be a bit more complicated and I have asked them not to split them up. Of course I will be giving you a full update

They are both sleeping quite well, we get used to hearing Troy moving around, but our only concern the last couple of nights has been getting Roman out at short notice. We have learned if he goes downstairs, he needs out, and sharpish! They are settling in very well and as time goes by it will get better and better. I have attached a couple of photos of them in front of the offending fire. We have to get up every half an hour and make sure they are not too warm, but they do enjoy the heat as you can see, especially on their bums.

Julia, Peter and the Boyz.

21 MAY 2015

For a while there had been talk of arranging a camping trip for the rescue volunteers, but finding a location was a challenge; obviously there would be a lot of dogs. Eventually a location was found in Wales. Chris and his team would conduct a little reconnaissance trip with me and my gang. As it was a quiet time of year for camping, we would be allocated a field to ourselves and if we could cordon it off from the residential caravans we could have all the dogs off lead. It would be perfect.

This would also be the amazing Monty's first camping trip. The location was everything we could have hoped for. Our hosts were perfect and the dogs had a fantastic time, especially old Monty. Walks were a bit limited as Wales is, of course, sheep land. We did have a choice of beaches which, although they did not offer a long walk, were good for the dogs to have a run around and swim. Monty even got his toes wet. On one occasion, with Monty stood right behind me, a wave came rushing towards my feet and I stepped back to avoid getting wet- falling on top of poor Monty who gave out a massive yelp. I felt so bad for him I took him straight to the beach café and bought him a lamb pasty. I swear from that point onwards he would walk so close to my heels, I was sure he was trying to get me to trip over him again, for another lamb pasty.

We also found a beautiful forest walk, it was fourteen miles away but well worth the drive. Had it not been for one of our volunteers that lived locally we would never have found it. In the first picture Roxy and Max stare at me as I disappear to get pasties all round from the café. Picture two is Monty looking really happy about camping, maybe we found something here that he enjoyed almost as much as food. Picture three shows what happened when I got up to go to the loo in the night.

  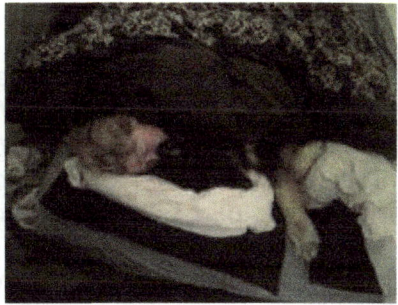

Following our recce mission I volunteered myself to write a report to go on the rescue volunteers' page to see if we could drum up support for a mass camping trip later in the year.

CAMPING WITH THE MAGNIFICENT 7 – REPORT

STARRING – Roxy, Max, Saxon, Monty, Wolf, Krystal, Summer, and some humans.

PURPOSE

The purpose of this report is to convey what an awesome time we had and to make you feel bad that you were not part of it. Also, we are looking to encourage you to join us on the next one.
https://www.facebook.com/brynawelonccp?pnref=story

ARRIVAL AND ERECTION PROCESS (meaning the tent)

Dead easy. This place takes dog friendly to a whole new planet. When I explained that I may be bringing six (at the time of booking I had the Brothers with me) and Chris had three, we were told if other site users didn't like it then tough. The attitude of the site owners has restored my faith in humanity. We were given the bottom field and were told if we could cordon it off with wind breaks then it would be secure enough for the dogs to not be tethered and have free run at all times – TOTAL BLISS. Did we have enough windbreaks? HA! With Chris's help, we could have cordoned off Wales if we wanted to. No stressing on where we put the tents, no one bothered to get out a tape measure and quote Health and Safety regulations. Power hook up points are everywhere which is great, especially for Chris, AKA Inspector Gadget, since he needed to power all his household appliances, entertainment suite, fairy lights etc. Chris is a great guy to go camping with because if you forget anything, then no worries, Chris will have two of whatever it is you have forgotten.

FACILITIES

Excellent, very clean, showers nice and hot. Tumble dryer washing machine, spin dryer, fridges and freezers, kettle, iron and ironing board (WHAT?... WE ARE CAMPING!), and, of course, a sauna. Tesco is about ten minutes out but a well-stocked shop is only one mile away. There is also a fantastic shop that sell lots of outdoor stuff, military surplus, gadgets etc. so Chris and I had a great time in the shop buying loads of stuff we didn't need. If you are a raw feeder there are local butchers that can supply you.

SHEEP

Tons of 'em

DOGGIE WALKS

If you want off lead then it's a drive of nine miles to the beach. It's a lovely place which can offer a two mile walk if the tide is out. I noticed the current out of the estuary looked a bit keen so we were wary to keep the dogs out of that bit of water. A nice café there that sells lamb pasties that Monty LOVES.

If you want woodlands then it's fourteen miles to Pengelli Forest, the sign says "dogs on lead" but no one does, in fact we never saw anyone there. MASSIVE thanks to Penny that met up with us and kindly escorted us to this lovely location. This is a very beautiful iron age forest, there is no litter at all, and I mean not even a sweet wrapper. The dogs loved it here. The long walk is just under three miles with lots of opportunities to cut it short for the oldies; the young guns could do two laps maybe.

THINGS THAT STICK IN MY MIND

I so love going camping with my four dogs, I love them so much.

This was Monty's first camping trip and he LOVED IT TO BITS bless him.

I don't know how Jo puts up with me sometimes. She thinks I love my dogs more than her but it's not true, I love them all the same.

Chris's doggie first aid kit is massive but unlike mine it does not have a thermometer.

If I get up to go to the loo there is a fair chance Roxy or Saxon will nick my bed.

Krystal is an amazing dog

This was Jo's daughter's first camping trip also, I am so pleased she joined us.

SO... WHAT ARE YOU WAITING FOR?

Enjoy the pictures. The first is the bottom field where we pitched, in the second Max whispers in Roxy's ear, and in the third-I don't think she liked what he said.

22 MAY 2015

We received another update on the brothers. They had been to the vets for a deluxe once over and all came back fine. Roman and Troy had both been neutered and so were feeling a bit sorry for themselves. Troy had a retained testicle, which was eventually found hiding behind his bladder. It had started turning cancerous but the vet was confident he had removed it all and explained that it was not the type that spread. There was another type of cancer where the likelihood of spreading was almost guaranteed, but he was certain this wasn't it.

Roman's hips were X-rayed and hip dysplasia was identified, as well as arthritis on the spine. He had a shallow joint on his hip, meaning the hip did not sit deeply enough; it would not be comfortable for him. Painkillers had been administered, the problem would slowly get worse and so there was no point keeping him in pain. Multiple short walks were in order to help build up the rear muscles; in the future there would be options for steroid jabs. Julia reassured me that they would manage Roman's back end problems for as long as it stayed pain free. The vet explained that over the months and years Roman would just struggle more and more to get up until the inevitable had to be faced, but he was confident that was a long way off.

I was not really surprised on the medical front, they were two older boys and Roman was obviously the less capable. Clearly the boys were in very goods hand with two people that loved them and cared for them. These two wonderful old gents had fallen on all four paws.

27 MAY 2015

I checked my emails first thing in the morning as was customary. I had two from Julia, the first was sent at 2:40am it read:

"Hi Ken

Just back from the vets where we have taken Roman. He woke us up at about half past one, vomiting and retching, with a hugely distended stomach. A full-on case of bloat.

Vet took one look at him, started scrubbing up for surgery, and gave us the usual warnings about his prognosis.

I'll let you know when the vet calls in the morning. From start to finish we got him there in about half an hour, but you know how quickly it can take hold.

Julia "

The next email was sent at 7:50am:

"Vet phoned at 5am this morning, I think they'd been working on him for nearly three hours.

Roman came through the operation OK .They had to remove his spleen and they have stapled his stomach to the wall so this won't happen again. However, Gareth said the stomach was bruised and he didn't like the look of it, and warned us the next 72 hours are critical. He added that it is depressingly high, the number of dogs who survive the op, only to die afterwards from damage to the organs during the episode.

Troy is lonely but still eating.

Julia"

I was in shock to hear this, more denial maybe, it just couldn't be right. After all the brothers had been through how could this be happening? I received another message later that day:

"The vet has just phoned with an update.

He is not happy with Roman's progress. Although Roman has "come to" his breathing is very laboured and he seems to be in distress. He also reiterated that the stomach, when they operated, did not look healthy. It's a bruised shade of black and Gareth is now wondering whether more damage was done than previously thought when the blood supply cut off.

He is also having arrthymia (irregular heartbeat) and Gareth is worried about that. He will be kept in tonight and possibly tomorrow night.

Troy is very quiet, although he has eaten. On his walk especially he kept turning around and looking for Roman. At home he just sits on his dog bed and does not interact.

Gareth will phone me should his condition deteriorate. We only live five minutes away, and Peter finishes work at 7pm.

Feeling very down".

Later that day I spoke to Peter and Julia on the phone. Roman, bless him, had lost his fight, he was gone. He did not go alone, the vet's wife had seen his distress in the dog recovery cage and held him in her arms as he slipped away. The diagnosis was a heart attack from major organ damage.

Julia and Peter were distraught as indeed were Jo and I. Roman was gone but now what about Troy, what would happen to him, how would he cope? The one constant in his life, his brother that always had his back, had died.

28 May 2015

I called Peter and Julia to see how Troy was coping. Troy was very subdued but was eating and had been out for his morning walk. Troy was present when his brother was lowered into a grave on the croft, alongside other Shepherds they had loved and lost, and where they planted clusters of daffodils and snowdrops.

Julia and Peter thought he was going to be OK, thankfully. Roman and Troy by now had accrued quite a following on the rescue Facebook page. Julia asked me to pass on thanks to those offering condolences. The first picture shows Troy at his brother's grave, the second he is sleeping when his brother was with him, in the last picture Troy is alone.

I really felt like I had lost one of my own. I asked Julia and Peter for permission to post a tribute to Roman.

"A TRIBUTE TO ROMAN

Each time I lose one of my dearly loved dogs I like to write a little tribute to them, if anything it helps me with closure, and for those who know or have followed my dogs on Facebook, it kind of brings the story to an end. Roman was my foster boy and was with me for five months, but he was Julia and Peter's dog at the end and they are happy for me to write this. So here is his story.

Early December 2014 I got this hankering to help another dog, I don't know why because we were maxed out with our four, so Jo and I thought to have another go at fostering. Whichever dog we took would have to be left at home from time to time as we can't really take more than four dogs to work. Looking on the Facebook page I saw an urgent fosterer was needed for two older dogs who were brothers. They were outdoor dogs, they were left to roam free on a very large plot of land around an old people's home. The business was going into receivership, so the brothers had to go. It looked like they did not have much human interaction but they had been together all their lives. This was just what we were looking for. The boys were not used to having humans around all the time and so could be left, and they would have each other for company... Perfect. Arrangements were made and very soon we were on the road to pick the boys up.

Jo and I arrived at the home in Northampton late afternoon 21st Dec. It was dark and cold. The owner didn't bother to show up, instead a relative was present with a grounds man. He led these two dogs out of the shadows, they looked quite big boys but it was hard to tell more as the area we were in was not well lit. We were introduced to Motu (meaning large or stocky) he would soon be renamed Roman, and his brother, Sheru (meaning tiger), who would soon be renamed Troy.

We were told the dogs had never been indoors, they were very close and they even ate out of the same bowl. I took this to mean food was chucked in a trough for them. I asked about their sleeping accommodation and was assured they had a blanket to lie on, and if the weather was really bad they were let into the foyer. Yes... right... I bet they were. They were rarely on lead but they were very friendly and the old folks in the home would pet them when they were sitting in the grounds. The volunteer who also did the dog assessment, suggested to me that reading between the lines he thought they had been used as guard dogs to patrol the grounds. Who knows?

It was time to load the boys into the truck, I lowered the ramp to let them in but no hope, not a chance. The grounds man, man-handled them in, it was clear they were very afraid. I had to help with Roman. By the time we had Roman in my hands were filthy and I had a black sticky residue where I had touched the side of his face. I took a closer look but in the dark couldn't see much but could feel that one side of his face was very matted. Mmmm would have a close look at that when we got home.

These two lovely old gents travelled in the car very well. We got home and tried to get them out of the truck, nope, no way... too afraid, we finally coaxed them out of my (now stinking to high heaven) truck. We would have to get these guys to the groomer's soon. Taking a close look at Roman it was obvious he had a serious problem with his left ear. It turned out that it was very badly infected. He carried his head like he had had a stroke, his face and left eye drooped; this poor old boy was in serious pain. A trip to the vet's first thing the next day was arranged. I could barely get my hand inside the collar so that had to be cut off. Both were underweight but no problems there... that would soon be sorted.

The boys adjusted to indoor life beautifully, mixed very well with my pack and were a dream to have around. Roman's ear was fixed, and he lost his droopy face, his eyes became bright and full of the wonders of this new life and his new experiences. Almost like "OMG Planet Earth is much bigger than we thought". Roman adjusted to a raw diet very well and soon started to put on weight, for his first indoor Christmas he enjoyed a dinner of surf and turf, cooked salmon and raw beef medallions... well... why not?

On another occasion shortly after the boys came to us I was leaving the house for our morning walk and Max decided to play up, so I ushered him into the house thinking I will get the other five in the car first then sort out Max. As Max slipped inside Troy followed him, OK no problems I will sort them out in a sec. I turn around and looked at Roman and he was shaking. He was with these other strange dogs and his brother was not with him.

144

Roman soon gained confidence though, it was not long before he was flying up and down stairs and jumping in and out of the truck. Groomed, well fed, exercised and loved, Roman flourished, he was truly LOVING his new life. Nine and a half years of neglect and now this. After a couple of months he even managed to be apart from his brother, he would sit by the door and wait for him but he wouldn't panic any more.

Roman just adored attention, I guess they had had so little. He would nuzzle into you, and if ever his brother was getting a cuddle he would wander over and join in... group hug.

April 2015 came, no one seemed interested in them and it looked like the boys were going to be staying, then I get a call from the rescue, a home had been found for them on the Isle of Skye with Julia and Peter. I was gutted... The boys were leaving. I was also very happy for them as this home was truly perfect for them. Julia and Peter could give them much more than I could, I was spread a bit thin with six dogs and work. This was the best retirement home for two wonderful old gents.

On the 8th May Julia and Peter arrived to meet the boys, we would spend the best part of the day together walking and chatting about them. I wanted to give the best handover I could. Also having spent time with Julia and Peter I was very happy, this union of humans and dogs was so meant to be. This was a perfect match. I lost it totally when the boys left but, hey, that's how it goes. Julia and Peter promised to keep in touch and they were good to their word. The boys were doing very well and Roman settled in beautifully- selecting Peter as his pet human.

On the 27th May I received an email from Julia to say there had been an emergency with Roman. He woke at about half past one in the morning, vomiting and retching, with a hugely distended stomach. A full-on case of bloat. The vet took one look at him then started scrubbing up for surgery, and gave warnings about his prognosis.

The operation went well and Roman made it through, but the vet was worried about damage that had been done to his internal organs. Later that day Roman was taken from this world. I don't know why the greater powers choose to take him. It was just not fair, not fair at all. This amazing lovely old boy had suffered a life of neglect, then finally he wins the jackpot, he learns about love and care, then he finds the lottery home... and three weeks later he is gone. Julia and Peter were devastated, as Jo and I were, it was like I lost one of my own.

Roman was a beautiful old boy. I feel honoured to have been a part of his life and to have been able to give him some joy and love in this life. I really felt for Julia and Peter, it was very tough on them and of course the

145

loving brother Troy. First week into June Troy is coping well and settled. Julia and Peter keep in touch which is lovely.

Roman my boy, you were loved dearly and you are sorely missed, you certainly have a piece of my heart and a few other hearts I know. Sleep well dear old boy, I will never forget you".

BIG MAX

(The Big Softie)

30 MAY 2015

One of the things I do as a volunteer for the rescue is home checks. Someone may apply to the rescue for a dog, but before the application can be accepted, a volunteer must visit them to check the property is safe and the family suitable. If I do a home check where there is no resident dog, I ask the applicant if they would like me to bring some of mine along for them to see. If they refuse, I would wonder why they want a dog in the first place and the chances are the home check may not go well, although that has not happened to me yet. I usually take Max and Roxy, but on the home check I did on this day, the lady, on finding out I had four dogs, asked if I would bring them all. Jo and I had a chat about this as Saxon can be a bit nervous around strangers. We called the family again to explain about Saxon, but she insisted we bring them all along.

We arrived at the home to find the house filled with children, I was not expecting this. However my pack behaved impeccably, including Saxon. Often if Saxon is in an enclosed space, where running away is not possible, and strangers are present, then he can get a little nervous. Maybe it was the presence of the children, but on this occasion he was fine. We were invited to let the dogs off lead and let them have the run of the house. Max, who loves doing home checks, ran upstairs to check out all the bedrooms with the children in pursuit, all giggling around him. The children reported that Max was checking the beds to see if they were comfortable enough for the new dog. The kids were delighted and Max seemed happy. Then it was outside to check the garden was safe and secure. While I was chatting with the family, Jo caught Max having a cheeky little nibble at the chicken wire on the guinea pig cage. I think he fancied the occupants could make a tasty snack. Fortunately Jo grabbed him before anyone else noticed. Monty was a firm favourite with the kids, they made a huge fuss of him.

The family were lovely and the home check was a pass. Soon another dog in need would be re-homed. Below we have Monty, Max (butter wouldn't melt) and Saxon, ambassadors of the breed, hard at work home checking.

JUNE 2015

Julia and Peter called me to explain they felt Troy needed some company after losing his brother. They had spoken to the rescue to ask if there was an older dog that would be suitable. They also asked if I could do the handover and assess if I thought the new dog would be a suitable match for Troy. They didn't want to make the twelve hour journey down from Skye to find the match didn't work. There could be no guarantees of course but I was delighted to help out.

The rescue contacted me to give details of Max who was an older boy that needed re-homing. He was currently with his original family but they were not able to look after him properly any more. I would go and pick up Max and foster him until Julia and Peter could get to me, assuming, that is, that I thought him a likely match for Troy. If he wasn't... I suppose he would be staying with me.

16 JUNE 2015

I contacted Max's owners to make arrangements to collect him, and we planned to meet at a service station on the motorway to do the handover. I arrived at the allotted time and didn't have to wait long before Max arrived. Max was with his owner's mother, apparently his owner couldn't come. It was a lovely warm day, and we got Max out of the car and took him for a walk around the grass verges of the service station. We chatted as we walked and I tried to get as much information about Max as I could. I didn't have much time as it seemed she was keen to be on her way as soon as possible. Max was a lovely old boy and a big lad to boot, a real gentle giant. He walked well on the lead and was really calm.

Of all the dogs I have transported, handed over, or collected to foster or adopt, this handover felt different, almost a little sordid. Max was given to me with no toys, possessions or paperwork. His owner wasn't present, and when the owner's mother left him with me, she walked away, seemingly without a care in the world and didn't look back. Max stood in the back of my truck and stared at her, his eyes were fixed on her for as long as she was in sight. The look on his face seemed to be a mix of disbelief, confusion and fear. Poor old gent had been dispensed with, and that's just how he looked. The family that he no doubt loved dearly, didn't want him anymore, and it was almost like Max realised this and you could see it in his face. I made a fuss of him and talked to him gently. I would give him my all to try to make up for what had just happened.

Max travelled very well in the car and was quiet for the whole journey. He was introduced to my pack with no issues at all, in fact he took a bit of a shine to my Max. Having two dogs with the same name was going to be confusing for humans and dogs alike. I was certain early on that he and Troy would get on well, so we would probably not have him for long. In the mean time we would call him Big Max. He settled in very well and the next day he was off lead on his walk with the gang. In the first picture Big Max is sat right in the middle of the pack, and in the next two he is making my Max look very small indeed.

20 JUNE 2015

Big Max was not with us for long. Julia, Peter and Troy popped down from Skye, a quick twelve hours' drive, to meet him and introduce him to Troy. The boys got on great as I thought they would. It was good to see Julia and Peter, and it was LOVELY to meet Troy again, he was looking in great shape. He behaved as though he had never been away, he just bundled into the house and said hello to his old pack, he certainly emembered. He spent a lot of time sitting with me, he would nuzzle into me and lean against me, maybe in his way he was trying to tell me that his brother was gone.

Julia and Peter spent the day with us again and this time we could go for a walk without the feeling of impending doom associated with passing on a beloved foster dog. Yes, Big Max would be leaving me, and although he was a real gent and a lovely boy, I had not yet got attached to him in the same way I had the brothers. I would miss him for sure, even after the short time he was with us, but I felt certain that I wouldn't be making a fool of myself again in the street for all to see. It felt good to be out with a six pack again.

The weather was lovely, so after our walk we all sat in the garden and had a drink or two and just relaxed. Julia and Peter were booked into a hotel with Troy and Big Max that evening so there was no rush to do anything as the afternoon rolled into the evening. While we were sat on the patio something really curious happened which made the hairs on the back of my neck stand up.

Every time Jo and I lose a dog we place a plant pot in the garden with the dog's name on it and we plant forget-me-not flower seeds. When Roman was alive, he and Troy would often lie back to back. They would even sleep that way. My garden was pretty big, it had to be with all the dogs we have, the dogs can choose to lie in a multitude of places. But Troy choose to sleep back to back with his brother for one last time. He lay with his back firmly against Roman's plant pot. Could this have been coincidence? Possibly of course, but given the size of the garden I felt it unlikely. I firmly believe that dogs know and understand things we don't. Maybe Troy's beloved brother was not that far away after all.

The time came for our guests to leave. Big Max jumped into the back of Peter's van with no hesitation. Troy had a new playmate and Big Max had an awesome home. Peter and Julia told us of their plans to move from Skye to Middlesbrough, where Peter had a house. That would make meeting up again much easier. I liked the idea of being able to see Troy and Big Max again.

25 JUNE 2015

Julia sent me an email just to let me know that the boys were getting on well together, she wrote:

"Thought you might like to see these photos, Max and Troy having fun at the beach.

In the background you can see the fisherman's float, the white marker buoy. Unbidden, Max decided that that was his "lost" ball and swam out to try and retrieve it. Unfortunately it is tethered and after a few hopeless bead butts he gave it up as a bad job and swam back. Troy and he are learning to settle down together now. The only issue is over pig's ears, which is their after walk treat.

Off to the vet this morning for his micro chipping and jabs".

In the second two pictures it would seem Troy and Max have been caught red-handed trying to nick Peter's van. In the last picture Troy could be explaining "We were going to bring it back, honest"

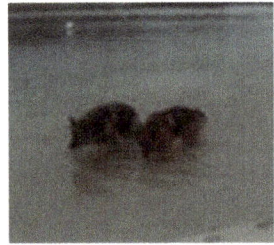

2 JULY 2015

It was time to saddle up and head out camping again, this time we were going back to Allensford, in County Durham, to see my sisters. The site used to be council owned and as a result it had become quite run down, especially the toilet block. Now it had been bought as a private venture and improvements were happening. In the long term there would only be residential and touring caravans, with no pitches for tents. On this occasion we were allowed to go one last time. We were the only tent on this lovely site, the toilet block unfortunately had received no attention. It wouldn't be needed by caravan users, so why spend money on it, I suppose.

Our walks took us mainly to Hamsterly Forest. It's a huge place, teeming with wildlife. Red kites were not uncommon and if you were lucky, you could catch a glimpse of red deer. We found a huge beach on the Northumberland coast that was all but deserted, it was truly stunning. Roxy and Saxon loved playing in the sea, Max, as usual didn't, and Monty, though still improving a little each month, just couldn't be bothered with getting wet, he would go in as far as his ankles and that would be it.

In the first picture we have Monty posing on the beach. In the second Roxy is giving Max a little love bite and in the third she gets a cuddle in return. Their relationship had come a long way since their first meeting at the RSPCA shelter.

The worst part of camping is packing up to go home. If you are lucky, which we were, then it will not be raining. It still takes ages and everything had to be packed carefully in the trailer. The dogs sense we are moving den, so they want to get in the car as soon as possible to ensure they don't get left behind. It takes us a good four hours from waking to ready to roll. The last job is to hook up the trailer and off we go home. Except on this occasion I couldn't hook up the trailer as I seemed to have mislaid the keys that unlock the coupling. I had no way of attaching the trailer to the truck. I thought I had left the keys on the grass just outside the tent, but since we had broken the tent down, a massive lawn mower cum tractor had rolled over our pitch and cut the grass. There was only one thing to do, and that was to unpack EVERYTHING in the hope the lawn mower hadn't eaten the keys. Some hours later, Ben saved the day, locating the keys, which were in the truck glove compartment, exactly where I had left them. The journey home felt quite lonely.

6 AUGUST 2015

Saxon had been with us for one year on this day. Lisa, who surrendered him to us, sent a message. Thankfully life was turning around for her but she still missed the big guy. I would message her from time to time and send pictures of Saxon just to reassure her that he was in good hands and enjoying life.

Shepherds tend to attach themselves to one person, all the dogs we have had attached themselves to me. I suppose as I always feed them and walk them that would make sense, but Saxon was a Mummy's boy through and through. On one occasion, Jo and Charlotte were heading out to attend a hen weekend. I was to take them to a friend's house early in the morning to drop them off. I packed the dogs in the car as well and planned to go straight to the woods after dropping the girls off. Saxon got quite excited when Jo got in the truck as he thought she was coming with us on the walk. When I dropped Jo and Charlotte off, they were in a hurry and didn't say goodbye to Sax, so he thought she was still in the truck. I arrived at the woods and got all the dogs out and we headed off up the trail. I looked back and Saxon stood at the truck staring at it, he just wouldn't move, nothing I could do would coax him away. Then I realised why he wasn't moving, he thought his Mum was still in the truck and he wasn't going anywhere without her. I had to open all the doors and lower the rear cabin tailgate and let Saxon have a good look around. When he realised Jo wasn't there he reluctantly set off to go on his walk with the rest of the pack.

9 AUGUST 2015

For the first time, we walked at Bevercotes, an old colliery. It was a GSD social walk and we got to meet up with Chris and Vicky and their pack of white GSD's. Krystal was not getting any younger and her treatment and lack of care before she came to Chris was beginning to tell on her. She had no end of ailments which had to be treated daily, asthma, bronchitis, diabetes and myasthenia (degeneration of the throat muscles). On top of which, now, she was struggling to walk any distance. Not wanting Krystal to miss out on her walks with her pack, Chris sourced a dog pushchair. At Bevercotes she was pushed around the walk, every now and again she would get out and have a little wander on her own, then it was back into the pushchair. This was the kind of commitment that Chris and Vicky gave to their dogs.

By now, Monty was off all pain control. He had been slowly improving over the months and the multitude of supplements he was taking seemed to be having an effect. I wanted to wean him off his medication so his body didn't become accustomed to it and in doing so reduce its effectiveness. Also the break from drugs would give his liver and kidneys a chance to rest so if the cold of winter caused his joints a problem, we could go back on the drugs again, hopefully without any adverse effects on his organs. On all matters of pain control I would consult with Jon. The wrong mix of medication, and especially the use of cheap over the counter human pain control can have serious adverse, even fatal effects on dogs. Self-medicating dogs is definitely not a good idea. Once the drugs could no longer help him, we would really have nowhere else to go. Yet here he was, drug free, my battling old Monty, who not so long ago couldn't stand unaided; I had thought it possible that we may even lose him.

In the first two pictures we have Lady Krystal in her buggy being chauffeured around, and in the last one Monty and I are enjoying a quick cuddle on our walk.

10 AUGUST 2015

Once again I was engaging in the life changing activity of scanning social media searching for souls in need. Having four dogs is more than plenty to be taking care of, but after the brothers and Big Max left, the house did seem roomy and a little quiet, apart from Saxon of course. I saw the following post from someone on the rescue social page:

"*Can we help, this is Tyson who is in the pound in Chertsey, he has until the end of this week to be claimed or he will be destroyed. This is what I know... the GSD is male, neutered, just under two years, very thin (see photo) but very happy and full of life! He was found yesterday but I have a feeling he will not be claimed. He is chipped but the chip is not registered, the company the chip was registered with did a back track on it, I have spoken to the vets' in Durham that chipped him but they have not heard from the client in eighteen months. The number listed for her does not connect. I will send a card to her address in Tyne and Wear. He is listed as being called Tyson! I have said I will let the dog warden know if we can assist*".

I misunderstood what was going on and thought Tyson was already in rescue care, this turned out not to be the case. However, this young lad only had four days to live so we had to act. I offered to foster and called the dog warden to make arrangements. I was told he was found as a stray on a deserted traveller's site, and had been wandering around loose for some days before he was apprehended. He was chipped in Durham but found in Chertsey, and the dog warden postulated that he had been "acquired" somehow by the travellers for breeding purposes. As it transpired, Tyson had not been neutered, so this was a plausible theory. The dog warden confirmed he was very thin and while he was a lovely boy, he was a handful. The original owner could not be traced so it was highly unlikely he would be claimed, and it was agreed Tyson would be surrendered to me. "So he's a bit of a handful" I thought, I mentioned to Jo he couldn't be as bad as Max was when we first got him... or could he? Life was about to get interesting.

BOLT

(White Lightning)

13 AUGUST 2015

I arrived at the pound after almost four hours' driving. I met the dog warden who did not require any identification from me, which I thought a bit worrying. She took me to her van to meet Tyson, she opened the rear door and this white whirling dervish shot out like a pinball, spinning and thrashing around on his lead. I thought to myself "Holy Shit, what have I done?"

"He's a lovely boy" the dog warden explained, "he just needs an experienced hand to do some work with him". Well, that was pretty obvious. While he was dancing around on the lead, I could see he was painfully thin, he reminded me of Max when I first collected him. This boy was going to need more than training, he would need time, patience, and lots of love and he would definitely need fattening up. Also, given how thin he was, I thought I had better get Uncle Jon to give him a good once over as soon as possible.

Tyson was handed over to me, I didn't have to sign for him, and no note was made of who I was. This event went totally unrecorded, I could have been anyone, with any motive. After some effort I managed to get him in the rear of the truck and the hatch closed before he jumped out again. My first task was to get to a garage and get him a load of cooked chicken. I thought he may start to attach importance to me and take notice of me if I gave him food, especially as he clearly needed it.

Seven hours on the road and our latest foster pup was home. The rest of the pack didn't know quite what had landed. The introductions were frantic as he moved around so fast, he was a constant blur. He displayed no manners at all, barging into the others as if they were not there. My guys were very tolerant, although that would not last. Once he bounced off all the walls a few times, he started to pay attention to the other dogs and had a go at mounting all of them. Things didn't really go his way but at least he found his position in the pack. He was at the very bottom.

His first feed was straight onto raw food and he devoured it. As I started to put the dog bowls down for each of the dogs he went into a panic. I am sure he thought he had to fight for food otherwise he wouldn't eat. Soon

156

he would learn this was not the case and he would wait, not too patiently, for his bowl that was placed down last. After his first meal it was time to pinball around the house again, he was all over the furniture and all but bouncing off the walls. Jo and I could barely believe what we were looking at. This was going to be a tough one.

We quickly discovered he could reach all the corners of the kitchen work tops and he could open doors inwards, as well as outwards. He could also turn door knobs with his mouth. This was certainly going to be a test. He didn't respond to his name, in fact he didn't really respond to anything, and given that he was white and skinny I thought Tyson didn't really work for him, so a rename would be on the cards. Eventually he wore himself out and threw himself on the sofa to recharge. I called the dog warden just to let her know we were home and the introductions to the other dogs went OK. I sent her the picture of him on the sofa. She replied to me saying that she had shown all the kennel staff the picture and they couldn't believe how calm and relaxed he looked. They had no idea.....

 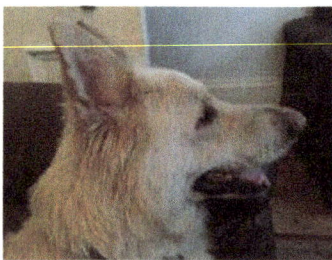 

14 AUGUST 2015

DAY 1 – WITH OUR WHITE FURBALL

We had a good night's sleep which came as a big surprise. Tyson was as good as gold, we were up a couple of times in the night to tend to Saxon which was a bit unusual. I think Saxon was feeling a disturbance in the force.

Jo and I discussed names and came up with Faolan which means little wolf. That didn't go down well with Charlotte, she thought it was too serious and boring and announced she would have a think. Having just passed her driving test she told me if she was allowed to name him then I wouldn't have to buy her a car (What!!... I NEVER agreed to that!) Soon the name Faolan was out and the more exciting, vibrant and fun name BOLT was in. It did seem fitting, as he was like a bolt of lightning. Also when a bolt of lightning strikes it can be devastating... well, that worked. And, he looked like the cute white dog called Bolt on the 2008 Disney movie of the same name. And, like the Olympian Bolt, he ran like the wind, and of course he would bolt his food. So that was it, Bolt it was, it was made official when we bought him his name tag with it on.

Bolt weighed in at 28 kilos which was more than I thought he looked, but as he was about the size of Saxon I considered we would need to put another eight or nine kilos on him. His front right paw was short of hair and it looked like he had a large worry spot there, although it was healed. One mystery presented itself though- his pads were very soft indeed and his front claws were long but his back claws were worn almost to the vein. I guessed that he had been tethered and spent a long time up on his back legs pulling, this may also have been why he was so frantic on the lead, as he may have had bad experiences being tied up.

On our morning walk the word chaos was woefully inadequate to describe events. He was like a wild animal, thrashing around so hard on the lead to get out of the house that one of the veins inside the claws on his rear foot, which were very short, opened. With his heart pumping with excitement, and with the vein exposed on his back claw, the amount of blood that spread over his white fur and up the walls of the hallway was alarming. His antics whipped the other dogs into a frenzy and it took an age to restore some order. I cleaned him up and thought he would still be good for his walk.

The plan was to let him settle in for a few days, then start any necessary training and correction. One mile into the walk and my shoulder was killing me. I am not a small guy and I am pretty strong but Bolt was going to have my arm out my socket. He even managed to snap a long lead. So I had to introduce some meaningful correction. By the time we got back to the car, which was another mile and a half, (as long as he could maintain his concentration), he was right by my side with only the lightest finger-tip control on the lead. Good lad. Later on he was sitting and giving paw on command. Bolt had started to listen to me, he was going to be fine.

After the walk we took him to the pet shop to get weighed and to buy him a comfy bed. More chaos. He was so excited his tail was wagging like mad, emptying pills, potions and products off all shelves that were at his bum height. Fortunately, the staff didn't seem to mind at all. Since then he has become a staff favourite at weigh in sessions.

Max started Bolt's education in dog etiquette and sharply kept him in check while Monty would just looked at him as if to say "STUPID BOY" like in Dad's Army. We met other dogs on our walk and he was fine.

Day one came to a close and proved to be a real physical and mental test for everyone, dogs included, but we had made progress and Bolt showed real promise. His interest in food and toys would make him easy to train, as long as I could get him to pay attention in the first place.

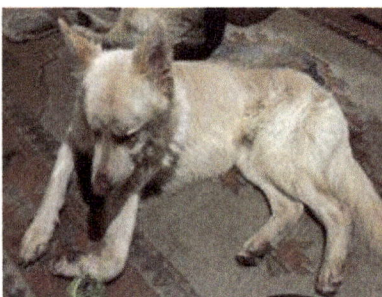

15 AUGUST 2015

Leaving the house for our morning walk improved from beyond chaos to just manic. We arrived at Watchwood and I got all the dogs out of the car. Bolt was on lead and didn't like the way the others could roam free but he couldn't, so it was whirling dervish time again, but this time he managed to slip his collar and he was off, running like the wind. I decided not to give chase, there was no point as I couldn't catch him. I would stay calm and just call his name. After the initial dash away from me he stopped to sniff the bushes and then he just wandered back to me. The change in him when off lead was unbelievable and I wondered what on earth this poor lad had been through. We started recall training and he did very well indeed. I would continue work on this to get him off lead as soon as possible.

18 AUGUST 2015

I had been updating people on the rescue social site on Bolt's progress. On this day I made a post that grabbed a lot of attention.

"WE HAVE FAILED BOLT

Something happened today, Bolt needs so much work, and he is so thin, I just can't do this anymore... I can't get him ready for adoption.

So we have no choice we will just have to keep him. Welcome to the pack, Bolt, my boy. He was off lead for most of today's walk, he is such a clever boy and he looks happy to have found his forever home".

Another failed foster and the pack was five.

21 AUGUST 2015

Bolt was going from strength to strength. He was a lot calmer, and by now off lead most of the time and recalling very well. He had met lots of other dogs and behaved himself. There was not a bad bone in Bolt's body, he just needed an education and boundaries.

He could sit, give paw and lie down, as well as recalling on the command "Here". He also knew "This way". The "This way" command has a very good use. Sometimes when in a state of excitement and the recall command "Here" is shaky, using the command "This way" often works better as it is more interesting. I will get back to these two commands and how I train "This way" a little later. Bolt was still totally crap at "Stay" and like Saxon made a hell of a noise when it was walkie time. He was still not good on lead and had a total temperament change as soon as he was tethered. If I held my hand over his heart, then clipped on a lead his heart rate instantly accelerated. He was worse on lead in the pack environment because he always wanted to be at the front, he was a little better if he was on his own. Next on the agenda was learning to leave the house quietly and get in and out of the truck calmly. Which now had a tailgate covered in Bolt claw marks. Oh well... I bought it for them I suppose.

This young lad was full of beans, he would play ball 24/7 and if I decided I was done playing ball, and then sat down to use the computer he would throw his soggy ball on my keyboard, or he would slip the ball between my back and the back of the chair, which is of course uncomfortable so I had to grab it and throw it away. He was training me well.

In one week in he had gained almost two kilos. He loved his food and would savagely attack the contents of his bowl, and anyone else's if I wasn't fast enough. On this day, he stole Saxon's full daily dosage of supplements and Yumove. Yumove is a premium joint supplement for dogs which soothes stiffness, safeguards long-term joint health and promotes mobility. This was just what Bolt didn't need. In fact if there had been a product called Yuslowdown he would have been on it.

Max was keeping him in check and Monty kept grumbling at him and showing his fangs if he got too close when charging around the house. In the first picture he is waiting nicely for his dinner, he is actually sitting still so this was a huge improvement. The second picture is what he was waiting for. The menu on this day was cow's heart with some fat trimmed off, with fresh tripe, liver and a chicken wing. After dinner he was learning to relax.

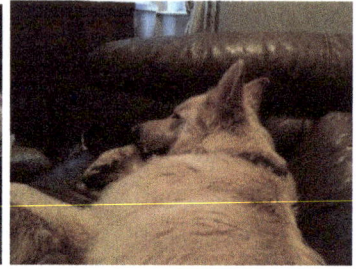

USE OF "HERE", AS USED FOR RECALL, AND "THIS WAY"

Recalling your dog is not always the most exciting thing from a dog's perspective. He may be engaged in something really interesting, then you call him using whatever word you have selected for the function, I use "Here". When he returns there is praise of course, but then something dull often happens, he is clipped on the lead, maybe because you saw another person approach with a dog, or maybe you have come to the end of the walk. Either way, from the dog's point of view, it's dull. I often recall my dogs just to give them praise to avoid this dull association, and I also use the command "This way". This command is much more fun and exciting and when used I I always try to avoid any chance the command could be associated with anything boring. This means the dog is more willing to respond.

So if your recall fails, "This way" is a nice little back up plan. I establish the "This way" command in two ways, this first is a game. I need an open space for this and all dogs off lead. Then, with them all around me, without warning I yell "THIS WAY" and sprint off away from them. They give chase, because that's fun, dogs love to chase, then without warning I change direction and yell the command again, then when they follow I roll around on the floor wrestle with them and just generally get all excited that they followed me. I can repeat this several times before the reward of play is given and it's clear to me this is fun for my pack, so a positive association is made. The other way I instil the command is when out walking and I come to a junction and I change direction I yell "THIS WAY" all heads snap towards me because they are wondering if I am going to run off, I point to the direction I want them to go, and they follow. The tone of voice I use is higher pitched and it's a fun tone. The number of words and commands a dog can remember is limited but they understand the pitch and tone of your voice, so "This way" is in a fun play tone. I find this command very useful.

22 AUGUST 2015

Today Bolt made progress on leaving the house quietly and entering and leaving the truck calmly and on command. On a scale of 1 to 10 where 10 = apocalyptic (that's where Bolt started) and 1 is angelic, in the pack environment Bolt hit a 5, and solo he did about a 3. I was very happy with the rate he was progressing. This earned him a private trip to the pet shop to pick himself a toy. All the staff remembered him, how could they forget him after our last visit? Bolt tried to pick all of the toys and then tried to help himself to the pick and mix, but in the end we settled for Mr Fox, which was soggy and frothy by the time we got to the check-out desk.

We got home, Roxy inspected Mr Fox, and promptly ripped off his left arm. Bolt didn't seem to mind but after being chastised, Roxy took off in the huff to hide in the bushes feeling hard done by. Naturally after doing that thing she does to me with her eyes (after that picture was taken of her in the bushes) she got lots of hugs and attention. She really knew how to play me.

26 AUGUST 2015

Roxy had always been an opportunist food thief but she had limits to places she could reach. There were places in the kitchen that I could reliably leave things to defrost. But now of course, things had changed...

WHODUNNIT?

The victim - Mr Bacon and Cheese Quiche

The suspects - Miss Scarlet AKA Roxy, Professor Plum AKA Saxon, Colonel Mustard AKA Monty, Reverend Green AKA Max (nothing holy going on there) and Mr White AKA Bolt.

The murder weapon - suspected canine teeth.

The rooms - The kitchen AND the study.

Circumstances - I vacated the premises to take my son to the cinema at approximately 13:00 hours. I left Mr Quiche sitting safely in a remote corner of the kitchen surface. I returned to the premises at approximately 17:45 hours to find Mr Quiche had been brutally murdered, only his clothing was left behind and scattered on Miss Scarlet's bed in the study. Mr Quiche's clothes displayed signs and indentations indicative of canine teeth.

So... Whodunit? Was this a solo effort by Miss Scarlet, or did Mr White have a part to play? Mr White is quite lanky and before he arrived, that corner had been safe. Or did everyone have a part to play since remains were found in the common room? Maybe it was time to invest in indoor cameras. Below we have the victim and the two primary suspects looking very guilty.

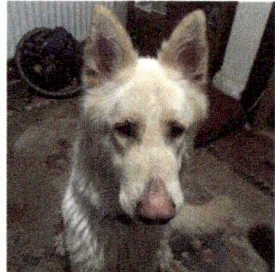

30 AUGUST 2015

Bolt continued to make great progress, I was still working on leaving the house calmly, on his own he had it nailed but he found it a little harder in the pack environment. This was largely because of Saxon, who always made a noise, so Bolt thought it was OK to join in. He still barged around when off lead and would often bump into the others; their patience with him was wearing thin. He was also a lot calmer on the lead, he still didn't like it, but a vast improvement from the Tasmanian devil of day one. The lad did so well walking on his lead it was back to the pet shop to replace Mr Fox. Mr Fox had an accident- all his limbs fell off, his tail fell off, his tummy exploded, then finally his head fell off, it was all just a big accident. So we bought a Tuff Toy called Mr Croc. Mr Croc was supposed to be for Bolt but Max took a shine to him, grabbed him and wouldn't put him down. Before Bolt came along Max didn't bother himself too much with toys, but whatever Bolt took an interest in, Max wanted. Almost as if to say "I don't really want this but you're not having it"

Bolt's new collar had arrived, it was brown leather with brass fittings and a paw print name tag. He looked really smart in it but I hadn't really thought it through, brass fittings and white fur do not mix well, as the brass tarnishes and discolours the fur. Bolt had not put any weight on recently which I found hard to believe as he was eating like a horse... no... two horses. Maybe the scales were wrong or his constant dashing around had put his calorie burn through the roof. So far, his wagging tail has accounted for three of my favourite beer glasses including a special edition glass, which was a gift from Charlotte.

As for the rest of the pack, Max's eyes had started to weep, he always had a redness in the corner of his eyes but now they were running more so than normal, so he was off to see an eye specialist in a couple of days. Roxy was still limping slightly from an injury she picked up three weeks ago. She had been on lead for seventeen days now and was very fed up with it, as was I. She wasn't really improving so maybe she would need X-rays. Saxon was just plain bullet proof, he never needed to visit Uncle Jon, and magnificent Monty, as always, just soldiered, on bless him.

1 SEPTEMBER 2015

Jon referred Max to West Midlands Referrals to have his eyes checked. He had an idea about the diagnosis, but wanted a specialist to check him out. Max had always had reddening in the corner of each eye but now they were weeping quite badly. I was told to arrive early and be prepared to leave him, if it was deemed necessary, to operate on him. This I was not expecting, no one mentioned anything about operations, so when we arrived I was feeling quite anxious. The reception and treatment we got was excellent, and I found the place to be very friendly and accommodating. The vet took Max and me into a consultation room to have a look at him and conduct some tests, after a while she confirmed that Max did have pannus.

Pannus is thought to be a hereditary condition that develops as the dog ages and although it can be found in any breed, it is more prevalent in German Shepherds. At first, a non-painful elevated pink mass appears on the cornea. As the condition progresses, the lesion will flatten out, spread and becomes dark in colour. Then scarring will spread over the cornea and vision becomes impaired due to an inability to see through the dark pigment. If left untreated, Max would become blind. Having being fed this information I felt my heart rate quicken.

The vet explained to me that treatment would not cure the condition, but it would halt the progression and may reverse some changes that had already happened. The right treatment for Max would have to be found, then he would need treatment for life.

Then came the good news. We had caught this condition in the early stages and treatment would prevent it from worsening. It would not affect Max in any way other than cosmetically, where he would have a red patch on his cornea. The vet knew the best treatment for him, and she was very confident about it, but it was an unlisted drug that could only be prescribed once the listed drug had been administered, and found to be ineffective. So I had to buy and use the listed drug, then I would have to go back when it had little effect to be prescribed the unlisted one, called protopic ointment. So double the cost for me but I didn't care one jot, my boy Max would keep his sight. That was a damn good call by my vet Jon, he potentially saved Max's sight. In the picture you can just see the reddening in the corner of his eye. Another bullet dodged.

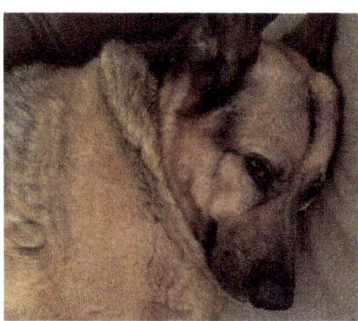

11 SEPTEMBER 2015

As my dogs spend most of their life off lead charging around the woodlands, it's very important I keep up to date with flea and tick treatment. I changed from my usual brand and after one week of using the new stuff, I had removed one tick from Bolt's face, another from Max's neck and found another fully bloated creature on the kitchen floor.

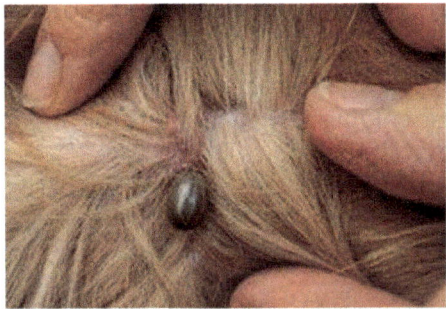

HOW TO REMOVE A TICK

STEP 1 Buy a tick remover from a pet shop and make sure it is always on hand. You can use tweezers but there is a greater chance of separating the tick's head from its body and leaving the head inside your dog to cause infection. Also there is a chance you could pop the disgusting bloated body if you are not careful.

STEP 2 Hook the tick remover around the body that's next to the dog's skin, then slowly and gently ease the monster directly away from the dog's flesh. It could be in quite firmly but take care not to twist or again, its head may come off.

STEP 3 Once you have the creature off, have a good look to make sure it still has its head on. Then gently wrap it in a bit of kitchen towel, carefully folding the paper over until the paper is about half the size of your palm. Then place the paper on the floor and stamp on the bloody thing repeatedly until your foot hurts, while yelling obscenities at the top of your voice. Scrape the vile, disgusting remains off the floor and flush it down the toilet.

STEP 4 Clean the dog's wound, wash your hands and put your tick remover away where you can find it again.

DO NOT cover the tick in petroleum jelly as some people suggest, believing it entices the tick to back out of the wound. This does not work and it will encourage the tick to put more disease-carrying saliva into the wound. Besides, entice sounds far too nice, these things need to be brutally murdered.

13 SEPTEMBER 2015

Bolt had been with us for one month, he had put on four kilos and had progressed very well. He was no longer frantic at meal times, he would sit and wait quietly for his turn to receive his bowl, and he waited until last so he was doing really well. He was even getting picky with his food. Sprats, kidneys and lung had to be finely chopped or he wouldn't eat them. Yesterday's morning walk was a bit of a nightmare though, Bolt was very excitable for some reason, a very high energy spread throughout the pack, which impacted Max who ended up having to have some naughty heel time on the walk. The afternoon walk was different again, it was our best yet. Leaving the house entering and exiting the car was calm and quiet, this set us up for a lovely walk. So ... bones all round.

Meanwhile Max's pannus seemed to be responding well to his medication. After developing a slowly worsening limp, my princess Roxy had X-rays which revealed a medium arthritic condition in her elbows. This would be potentially life changing for her as for now her walks had to be 50/50 on and off lead. She hated this as she couldn't tear around the woods any more. I was really very upset for her. She was currently on Yumove and Golden Paste. I was also going to try her on aloe vera gel. It worked for me and Jon was happy for me to give it a shot. Saxon remained bullet proof and my old soldier Monty just plodded along taking everything in his stride. Mont and Sax often walked side by side just behind me like two grumpy old men moaning about the silly youngsters tearing around, as in the first picture. In the second picture you can see Sax cooling himself down while Monty gets stuck in the mud and needs a little help to get out.

14 SEPTEMBER 2015

IT'S MY BALL....

Bolt had a ball that he dropped, so Saxon took it. Saxon didn't really want the ball, and as you can see below he was not doing anything with it. There were loads of balls lying around but Saxon wanted Bolt's ball. He only wanted it because he didn't want Bolt to have it. So there it was in his intimate space, lying dormant. Bolt wanted his ball back and so was staring at it intently. There were plenty of other balls he could have but he wanted that one. Bolt had learned some doggie manners (courtesy of Max), so he was not just wading in to get his ball, he was waiting for Saxon to abandon it or let him have it back... not happening. The stare off lasted ages.

Meanwhile Roxy and Monty didn't give a toss and were just chillaxing on the patio duvet (it's a hard life). The relationship between Max and Mr Croc had moved to a different level and had become quite intimate, yes... it was love. Max loved his Mr Croc. Or maybe he just didn't want Bolt to have it.

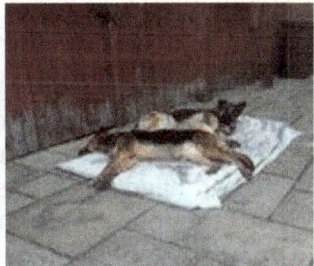

SEPTEMBER 2015

Following our reconnaissance trip to Wales earlier in the year, it was now time for the rescue volunteers' camping trip, arranged by Chris. There would be around eight pitches and fifteen or so Shepherds and one Chihuahua. As this was Bolt's first camping trip, we had all the ingredients for total chaos.

As it transpired, all went very well indeed. We had a few personality clashes, Bolt and Gumbo didn't really get on for some reason. Gumbo was a rescue from Romania and was aptly named as he had no teeth. Which is just as well because on one occasion when he and Bolt were having a little disagreement, Jo stepped in, got caught in the crossfire and Gumbo accidentally gummed her on the leg. She still had a bruise so it's a good job there were no teeth involved. The other clash was Max and Duke, both of them thought they were in charge of everything so of course they had frequent bark-offs, but nothing more serious. Outside of that, the dogs were a dream. To be fair to Bolt, given we had not had him long at all, he did very well indeed.

We enjoyed woodland walking at Pengelli Forest and beach walks at Poppit Sands. The weather for our beach walk was stunning, all the dogs had a fantastic time chasing each other in and out of the water. It was a real joy to see so many Shepherds playing together and having so much fun. Lots of seawater was consumed by the dogs so by the time we got back to the campsite I had to hose all the puke out of the rear of the truck, Chris had the same problem with his pack of Shepherds AKA the Mad Whites.

The day time was all about the dogs, and the evenings about the humans, probably the less said about that the better. Suffice to say some severe hangovers materialised. On the Saturday night we had planned BBQ and karaoke, the dress code was onesies, I found a wolf onesie to wear. Penny and Nick, the resident rescue volunteers provided quality entertainment around the drunken wailing. The Karaoke King by a long shot was Saxon. We managed to find a rendition of Amazing Grace, played on bagpipes, on an iPad. Saxon, bless him, didn't let anyone down, he sang along beautifully and enjoyed a massive round of applause and cheering afterwards. It was so cute to watch.

I wouldn't stretch the imagination as far to say this was a relaxing holiday, but it was great fun, and a real pleasure to meet other volunteers, that until then had been faceless social media friends. A date was set for the next trip for the following year. In the last picture Jo has borrowed little Mimi, who was not phased at all by all the massive German Shepherds running around.

3 OCTOBER 2015

FROM CALM TO CHAOS IN SECONDS

The reaction I get from people towards my pack when I am out walking often amazes me. This day was I was going to be more amazed than normal. I was out walking in Watchwood with the crew. It was a lovely day, and as usual the gang were all off lead. I walked here nearly every day and most of the people I met, I knew, and they knew my dogs. The woods have twisting and turning paths, and a few gentle hills so you can't always see what lies ahead. On this occasion we were walking towards the brow of a hill, Bolt was ahead of everyone as usual and the rest were close by. As I approached the brow I saw a lady ahead with two dogs I didn't recognise, so I started to get the dogs on lead, Bolt was already trotting towards her and she was putting one of her dogs on lead. I recalled Bolt but the recall failed, he was almost upon this lady. Normally Bolt's recall was very good, but nothing is 100% with dogs. Bolt was now almost upon her so I called to advise her that Bolt was friendly. I didn't want to scream and yell at Bolt to return as the lady may have thought I was panicking over my aggressive dog not returning.

Bolt slowed to stroll up to her dog that was off lead and had a sniff - a perfect greeting from both dogs- then Bolt moved to say hello to the other dog. I thought "OK, it must be really obvious that Bolt is not a problem". The lady raised what looked like a foam stick in the air and yelled loudly at Bolt "No". Bolt turned around looked at me then started to move back towards me. I praised him for his good behaviour and I think Bolt took that as my approval for him to return to the on-lead dog. So he turned to have another go at saying hello. At this point I recalled him again but he was too close to the lady, so I calmly started briskly walking towards him. I didn't want to run, again I was trying to manage the energy of the situation. This time the lady started screaming repeatedly at Bolt, raised her stick in the air and started whacking the floor next to him. Her dog on lead now totally freaked out, not because of Bolt, but because of what this woman was doing. Bolt in turn now got excited at a combination of the screaming woman, the barking dog, and the stick being whacked on the floor next to him.

Now Bolt was a good boy, but he was found abandoned on a traveller's site, so who knows what having a stick raised at him and striking with it means to him. Bolt now got very excited but just barked. Max, who I did not have time to put a lead on, was to heel by my side. All the commotion and excitement started to get to Max AKA Flash Gordon, self-appointed saviour of the universe, who felt it was time he sorted stuff out, so he left my side and ran towards the banshee with the flailing stick and panicking dog. Now I ran towards the woman and grabbed Max and Bolt, who were both well behaved throughout. The situation was contained and I ushered our gang along clipping a lead onto Bolt. The woman said something to me, I think trying to explain her actions, but I was so bloody angry I didn't hear.

One hundred yards later we ran into another person and my gang were perfect, apart from Bolt who was still on lead and still in a state of excitement. I apologised to the gentleman for his excitement and explained he had just been wound up. The gent had seen the whole episode and was amazed at the woman's reaction. Shortly after Bolt calmed down and was off lead, a few long range test recalls were done and all was back to normal. Apart from me. I spent the rest of the walk feeling very annoyed. Her insane actions could have resulted in a bite, for which Bolt would have had to pay the price.

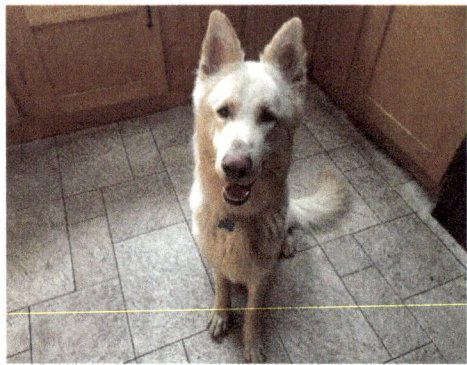

4 OCTOBER 2015

We had a lovely incident free walk in Harlow Woods. Bolt did a nice long range recall when he saw another dog, and started to run towards it to have a look. We met lots of other dogs and people and all was well. We stopped off at the pub on the way home for lunch and the dogs behaved perfectly. Even Bolt lay down for a bit. Lots of positive comments were offered to us about how well behaved they were and how good they looked. The landlady came out to offer the gang gravy bone treats. This was a much better experience than the drama of the previous day. Here are Max and Sax sitting nicely. Saxon is staring at the pub door waiting for Mum to return.

BACK TO DRAMA

On our morning walk Bolt, as usual, was living up to his name, charging around the woods and barging into the other dogs. About half a mile into the walk I looked at him and his head was red with blood. I grabbed hold of him and had a quick look and it seemed to be coming from his ear. I suspect one of the dogs got barged once too often, (my money was on Saxon or Max) and I guess they nipped him as he ran by, and caught his ear. Max was looking especially guilty. I yelled at them all "WHO DID THAT", but of course I didn't get an answer. I bundled the dogs back into the truck to go straight home so I could clean Bolt and have a closer look. I found a large one inch rip in his ear. So we were off to Uncle Jon's place to be sedated and stitched up, six hours and £300 later the young lad was home feeling very sorry for himself. He was slow to come round from the sedation, which worried me somewhat, and at home he was very groggy and sleepy. It was very weird to see my energy charged Bolt of lightning so quiet. Here is my little pup having some special Charlotte time having just been hand fed some cooked chicken.

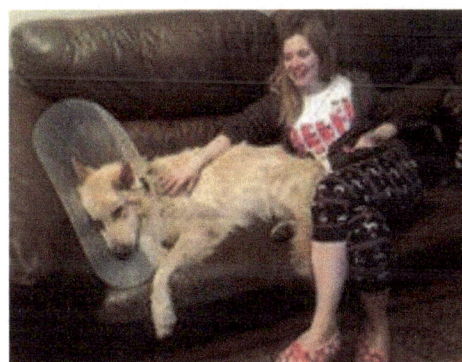 

18 OCTOBER 2015

Already one year had passed since Max and I jumped in the car to go pick up dear old Monty. As we didn't know his birthday or how old he was, we were going to make this his special day. His "Gotcha Day" would now be his birthday. This morning he had grilled black pudding from the butcher's for his breakfast, and he had friends Sansa and Lillie (These dogs belonged to Leigh, Jo's eldest daughter, they were also rescue dogs) round for a lovely walk in Harlow Woods. He got a nice warm coat ready for the winter, then it was liver cake and party time with the pack.

When Monty went into foster care he was 50 Kilos and could barely manage a walk, now he was a slim, trim 37 Kilos and could comfortably manage a four mile hike with his pack. He was getting a bit grumpy in his old age but hey... so was I. Monty had been through a lot in the short time he had been with us. He had surgery and an illness that almost took him from us, then a fight back to health. Possibly one of the main reasons he survived his illness was his stoic single mindedness and determination which he demonstrated frequently.

On one occasion when we were fostering the brothers, Monty decided he wanted to change the seating arrangements in the truck. Normally I would put four dogs, including Monty in the back cabin and Roxy and Max would go on the back seat in the front cabin. As they were the youngest dogs they could manage the jump in and out easier. One day Monty decided it was his turn to go on the back seat. I tried to gently coax him away but he was having none of it. Monty may have been a bit fragile at the time but he was as strong as an ox and there was no moving him, he had decided it was his turn on the back seat and that's how it was going to be. I had to help him get in and when we arrived at the woods and tried to get out, Monty saw why he didn't get to ride on the back seat. He was stuck and helping him out was hard work as I had little room to manoeuvre. After that day, he never tried to get on the back seat again.

The first picture is chunky monkey Monty doing time in the pound. In the next, he is recovering from his illness and is waiting at the car with Jo while I take off with the rest of the pack on a longer walk. He wanted to come bless him but he was just not up to it. In the last he is looking a lot leaner at 37 kilos sporting his birthday badge.

23 OCTOBER 2015

A PARODY

My son Ben always speaks on behalf of my dogs and has given each an accent. He has given Saxon a Scottish accent, as that is where he is from. He made this, I hope it makes you smile.

Both **Saxon** and **Shrek** have same scottish accents

28 OCTOBER 2015

WET, WET, WET

This was the wettest walk of the year. No problems for old soldier Monty though. Sporting his new birthday coat he ventured forth into the wild, wet wilderness undaunted. He looked very comfy, and his coat actually kept him dry. Unlike my coat. Even my waterproof socks let me down. Saxon, who had been to the groomers only three days ago, looked like he needed a return visit. Roxy and Max just got on with it but young Bolt danced. This young boy just danced in the rain, he LOVED it. He was the only one. On the plus side, given the weather, we had the woods to ourselves and saw no humans. When we got home, we got through nearly all the dog towels we have, getting everyone dry and clean. Then it was time for a hearty meal of tripe, liver, chicken wings, heart and lightly grilled sprats. I had to lightly cook the sprats as Bolt was the only one that would eat them raw. At first he wasn't keen on them but that had changed.

30 OCTOBER 2015

Over the last year or so Roxy had started to limp a little from time to time. X-rays revealed arthritic spurring on her elbow. The condition was more advanced than it should have been in a dog of her age. We had been doing all the usual stuff with Golden Paste, aloe vera gel, anti-inflammatory etc. and she had been doing well. However, this condition was not going to just go away, in fact it would only get worse. Eventually it would render her immobile, and when we could no longer control her pain, we would be out of options.

Once again, our vet Uncle Jon came up with the goods. He had read about Platelet Enhancement Treatment, (PET) and he discovered that West Midlands Referrals, the place Max went for his eye treatment, could carry out the procedure. After he described it to me I made this post on Facebook.

"Ground breaking arthritis treatment for my Princess Roxy - Does anyone have experience of this?

Basically it involves a procedure where blood is drawn from the patient and filtered. As platelets in the blood reach the filter they are selectively retained. When the filtration is complete, a harvest solution is back flushed through the filter to recover the platelets. This harvested product is the platelet therapy, and is ready to use. The solution is then injected into the joint. This treatment supports in a natural way the body's regeneration and promotes long-term pain relief and mobility. The whole procedure lasts about 30 minutes and is not very intrusive.

As this is so new, there are not many case studies and no information on long term effects, so I just wondered if anyone had come across this before. The treatment costs around £1000 and needs to be repeated annually. Hopefully her insurance will cover this. I have seen some very good testimonials so we are going to go for it. Looking after a princess is never cheap".

I was so excited we had a possible solution for her. The thing she loved more than anything was running free in the woods, It was heart breaking seeing her slow down.

1 November 2015

On this unusually warm day, Jo and I had a lovely walk in Harlow Woods with the pack. We tried to get some good pack pictures but it was very hard to get a picture of Bolt that was not blurred and harder still to get one of all five, but here are a few from this walk below. My old soldier Monty continued to improve and was going from strength to strength. He displayed another example of his single mindedness and determination yesterday. Normally Monty was last out the truck and I would support him walking down the ramp so he didn't come down too fast and jolt his arthritic joints, then my old fella just toddled around the walk on my heels. After the walk, when he needed to get back into the truck, he needed a hand on his bum and a little push to get him up the ramp. He was a very happy soul but I had to take great care with him as he was still a little fragile.

Yesterday we arrived at Hatfield Moor to meet up for a social walk and Monty had clearly decided in his head that today he was going to be first out the truck. Normally everyone has to wait until invited to leave but yesterday I dropped the tail gate and before I could do anything, Monty launched out of the truck like a missile. Fortunately I caught him mid-air before he hit the ground as that could have been bad news for him. Getting back in the truck after the walk, I dropped the tailgate and as I reached for the ramp I saw Monty was taking a run up to jump in without the ramp. He didn't have the slightest chance of making it, but bless him he was going to give it all he had. He has the heart of a lion and I love that old fella to bits.

Roxy's X-rays were at Litchfield for assessment to see if P.E.T. would be appropriate for her, hopefully we would get some good news the following week.

Max's pannus treatment was down to one application a day and his eyes were looking great.

Bolt had put on 6 kilos since we got him, God knows how, the boy never stopped, so we were about half way towards our weight goal.

Saxon, as always, remained bullet proof and very, very loud indeed.

12 NOVEMBER 2015

Every November I run a motivational event for the students at my Martial Arts School, then I put them to the test and invite them to walk on fire. It's a great fund raising event and this year I thought we could raise some much needed cash for the rescue. After we made the donation, the rescue posted a thank you on social media:

"It's been said many times that our volunteers will go to any lengths to raise funds for the rescue dogs- but WALKING THROUGH FIRE??? Well crazy as it may sound our very own Ken Robson got 45 students, friends and family from the Shudokan Black Belt Academy to do a sponsored walk on fire. A fire that burns around 1200 degrees.

Please, please join me in saying a huge well done as this event raised over £2,000 which is being split between the Wish upon a Star Foundation and the rescue.
Very proud of our team- and was pretty gobsmacked at this one!!!

18 NOVEMBER 2015

Saddled up and all aboard (Saxon, as always, had something to say), we were off on holiday to the Bed and Basket again. For another great, but this time, very short holiday. Thanks to Bolt living up to his name, doing everything at full speed, everything at full power, as if he is always running late. Bolt managed to hurt himself whilst hurtling around Cornwall at Mach 5, and started limping badly four days in. We took him to the vets who told us he had some kind of sprain so he had to have seven days' rest. This was not good news when you are on a walking holiday with the pack. So Jo and I had a chat, the lameness in itself we could deal with, but he was booked into our vets at home in seven days' time to have the snip. That would mean another seven days or so rest. In total that would mean Bolt would be facing fourteen days without a proper walk... NO WAY, that just couldn't be allowed to happen, the whole household would suffer. I gave Jon a call and asked if he could bring Bolt's operation forward a week. That way Bolt could recoup from both things at the same time. Uncle Jon gave the green light so in Bolt's best interests we decided to go home from our lovely holiday early.

We arrived home late at night and by the following morning of course, Bolt had no limp... Bah, it was too late to save his crown jewels though, and by midday that day, as arranged with our vet, Bolt was separated from his nuts. Poor soul was looking very sorry for himself, to be fair I would feel the same. I asked Jon to check out his foot while he was under and he confirmed Bolt had a slightly swollen toe. So... we binned our lovely holiday because Bolt stubbed his toe. GREAT.

24 NOVEMBER 2015

Ground breaking treatment for arthritis - for my princess Roxy

Platelet enhancement treatment (PET) youtu.be/nRU-5Enk9I8

A consultant from West Midlands Referrals, having studied the X-rays of Roxy's arthritic elbows, contacted us to say he thought Roxy would be a suitable candidate for treatment, and so we decided to go ahead as soon as possible. The treatment was not invasive, and the procedure only took about thirty minutes although she did need a general anaesthetic. Blood was extracted from her and a platelet concentrate was injected into both elbows. She was home the same day and looked quite bright. The surgeon said that if she responded she would not need her usual pain relief. The cost was over £1,000 per treatment and it would need to be repeated at least annually, sometimes more frequently depending on the dog. Thankfully the hospital was happy to claim directly from the insurance company so I didn't have to find the cash up front.

The success of the treatment would be dependent on many things.

Having caught Roxy in the early stages I was hopeful she would respond well. This would not be a cure but it should help the tissue regenerate and it might even protect the bone, slowing down any arthritic spread. All the fingers and paws in the house were crossed for her, we would just have to watch and hope. She was on light exercise for two weeks. After that, if she responded, her lameness should have gone. I was told to expect that the day after the treatment her elbows would inflame a little and look sore. If that happened, it would be a good sign that things were working.

Here is my beauty relaxing on the sofa after her treatment. It was a good job Roxy's boyfriend Max was not around to catch Bolt having a sneaky cuddle.

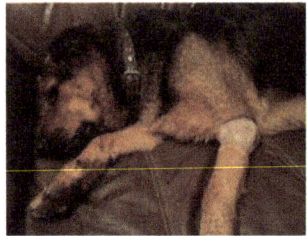 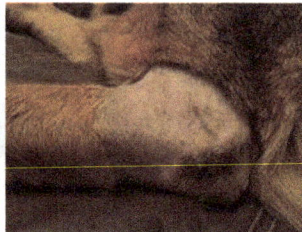 

5 DECEMBER 2015

Following the removal of Bolt's nuts, everyone in the household had a tough time enduring his barging around with a cone on his head for ten days. Backs of legs were bruised as he ran into you from behind, and paint was chipped from doors and skirting boards. Bolt had turned his cone into a bulldozing blade of mass destruction. Nothing and no one was safe.

Once the cone was off, he decided to give Jo a lap dog experience by jumping up on her knee, and for the first time, it seemed from his expression, he took a long look between his legs and noticed that a couple of things were missing. "Oh my God... MY BALLS HAVE GONE"

He was eating like a horse but remained a bit skinny and bony, hence the look of discomfort on Jo's face. He would put away two kilos of raw food a day over four feeds. He was gaining weight, but slowly, no doubt due to his incessant speeding around.

Roxy was two weeks post treatment following her platelet jabs. I could see nothing dramatic yet, but on our walk this morning, Charlotte, who doesn't walk with us often, thought there was a big change for the better. Maybe I was looking at Roxy so hard I was seeing things that were not there or vice versa. The three micro walks a day combined with giving the rest of the pack proper exercise was challenging time wise. We had an appointment to see her surgeon the following week, and I was hopeful we would get more of an idea regarding her progress then.

25 DECEMBER 2015

I posted the following message on the rescue Facebook page:

"On behalf of the Nottingham pack Saxon says

MERRY CHRISTMAS (well he actually said WOWWOW GRRR WOW WOOF) or something like that.

The pupsters have had a great time. Yesterday Bolt saw us hiding the doggie Christmas presents and he spent the whole day trying to get to them. He can open doors inwards and with some of the doors in our house he grabs the door knob and tries to turn it so it was a challenge keeping the prezzies away from him. Threats of Santa not visiting naughty dogs did absolutely nothing.

This morning we broke out the prezzies and even Monty who NEVER, NEVER bothers with toys had a little play and chew. That was truly heart-warming to watch bless his old soul. Then they all swapped presents and took the ones they wanted not the ones they were given, and largely that worked apart from Bolt who wanted all of them. Bolt is like the irritating little brother of the pack, he winds the others up, the rest demonstrate their displeasure with him but happy-go-lucky Bolt just sucks it up and doesn't care.

We tried to get a picture of them all to say Merry Christmas but everything was a bit energised this morning so here is Saxon on his own giving the message on our behalf. The highlight of the day was dinner, picture one is doggie dinner prepared, the next picture is dinner served, and the third is Saxon who, as always, has something to say. I pray this time next year I have the same crew, who knows maybe an addition.

To all you fellow volunteers out there, my rescue brothers and sisters, I give you respect for your tireless efforts, and for some of you the intense pain you have suffered this year. Next year with bring more hard work and for some of us more pain, but also incredible joy and satisfaction, that makes everything worthwhile. For everyone else in this group do what you can to help these truly amazing dogs

Today I got a t-shirt that reads "If God made anything better than a German Shepherd, he kept it for himself"

Here's to 2016 and all the challenges and joy it holds. BRING IT ON"

I was to regret making that last statement.

1 JANUARY 2016

THE DOGMOBILE IS DOWN

On New Year's Day, Jo and I bundled the gang into the truck and set off for our morning walk. One mile into the drive the engine cut out and died. I have no idea what had happened and we had no option other than to get the dogs out and lead walk them all home. This was a total nightmare as the dogs were not used to lead walking, especially five together and so they kept getting tangled up. Once I had the dog's home, I returned to the truck and spent a good chunk of the day waiting for the RAC. When they arrived the worst was confirmed, the engine had seized. I contacted the main dealer who quoted twelve hours of diagnostics at £120 per hour then a replacement engine costing between £5000 and £10000, depending on the damage. This was not an option so I explored other solutions.

The best option I found was a garage remote from Nottingham, who would pick up the car for me and fit a reconditioned engine for £2500 with the whole job taking a week. In the meantime, it looked like I would be lead walking the dogs on the streets for a while, the nearest park was just too far away.

The garage were a day late picking up the truck, then once they had it in their possession, it quickly became apparent I would not be getting my vehicle back in a week. The urban lead walking just wasn't working out, so I hired a van. The pack would fit in the back albeit with no windows or lighting. I rigged up a makeshift light for them so at least they wouldn't have to travel in pitch black darkness.

We were back walking in the woods again and the pack were a happy bunch. In the end it took me three weeks to get the truck back, but eventually the dogmobile was back, fully up and running, and all was how it should be.

11 JANUARY 2016

I took Roxy back to see the consultant that conducted her platelet enhancement treatment, he was delighted at her progress, giving her the green light to be off lead again. The damaged tissue around her arthritic elbows would continue to regenerate for the next month or two, maybe even three months, then things would stabilise. Then eventually the arthritis would take it's grip again, and then we would need to repeat the whole process. I would continue this procedure for as many years as it was effective for her. This was not a cure but it was going to make her life so much more comfortable and fun. The only cure as such would be elbow replacements, which is very much in it's infancy for dogs and the outcome is not certain. If things go wrong then you are looking at amputation or fusion. I had no plans to go down that road. So... squirrels of Watchwood, get your tin hats on, Roxy is back. (Picture one below)

My little lightning Bolt is in the second picture, or not so little by now as he had put on seven kilos in weight and was just loving life, as you can see from the mud on him in the picture. Monty in the third picture, it seems, was getting younger and stronger with each passing month. I needed this reverse ageing secret of his. When it was dinner time he would get very excited, jump up, and put his two front paws on the kitchen work surface. Yet only a year ago he did not have it in him to cock his leg for a wee.

Max continued to believe he was in control of everything in the pack, apart from the volume, that was Saxon's department. When these pictures were taken it was the first time Roxy had been off lead in six weeks.

JANUARY 2016

Roxy turned seven years' old this month, and so the usual birthday arrangements were made for her- special food, a big liver cake and toys. This month I managed to get her some very special food indeed. Every Saturday I would visit Uncle Tony, our dog friendly butcher, I would go just as the shop was about to shut and pick up a huge haul of leftovers. I would get it all home and separate it in containers for ease of use. On this occasion tucked away in the corner of one bag was a massive roll of veal and a big chunk of beef steak. The temptation was just too great, I cut a slither of steak and flash fried it. WOW... it was stunning. I looked down and saw Monty watching me, I had been caught. He had a very disdainful look in his eyes, I could imagine a speech bubble coming out of his head "YOU are eating MY dinner!" Having being caught red handed, all food tasting stopped.

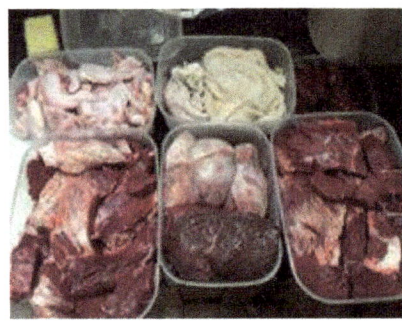

7 FEBUARY 2016

This was Max's seventh birthday and I made the following post on Facebook. I think the post epitomises what rescue is all about.

"HAPPY BIRTHDAY to a very special boy, my MAX

Have a great day Max you are loved so much and have a very special place in my heart.

Max is seven today, and of all the dogs Jo and I have rescued over the last five years Max has, without doubt, been the most challenging, the hardest work, and the one I have had the most doubts about along the way. There were times when I thought we would never get there with him. Day one he was seriously underweight because his EPI (the disorder with his pancreas) had taken a firm grip. He had little fur on his belly, his ribs looked like a piano keyboard and his hips stuck out like two sharp points. All of this and with some serious fear aggression thrown in. Max was the gateway to Jo and I getting involved with the rescue. Although Max was from the RSPCA who were very keen to get rid of him. "Yes he is good with other dogs, yes he is great with people" they told us. No, he was not, in fact not even close with either dogs or people. But with help, advice, lots of love, patience and perseverance we got there. Maybe this is why Max and I have such a special bond. He would have been a very easy dog to give up on and given the incidents surrounding him we could have justified it. We would never give up on him though EVER. Max is now an amazing loving cheeky boy with such a character. Max is a shining example of what can happen if you never quit on a difficult dog. It's not complicated, just give love and be patient. In Max's case our efforts were rewarded tenfold.

Max loves Roxy to bits, he really enjoys his long walks, and he loves to go camping and accompanies me on nearly all the home checks I do.

My boy Max has a nice big liver cake to share with his pack, his name is written in cheese. He also got lots of toys, the duck is his favourite".

13 FEBUARY 2016

BOLT DRAMA

This morning found us in Sansom Woods for our walk, and as it was a Saturday, Jo was with me. Bolt's recall was very good but if he got distracted and I wasn't watching him, he could be a good distance from me before I would recall, by which time he could be out of earshot. Bolt had been out of sight for a short while so I called him, then called again, and again, but nothing. Then I heard some barking from the direction I thought he was in, along with voices and some shouting, then silence. My immediate thought was that someone had taken him. We hooked all the dogs on lead and I left them with Jo while I took off running in the direction I thought he was in, shouting his name all the while. I came across other dog walkers and gave a description of Bolt but they had not seen him. Jo bumped into a couple we met early on in the walk and they said they had seen him, his head was covered in blood and they thought that maybe he had caught and killed a deer. Jo told me this over the phone while I was running around about one mile from her location. Jo was really upset at this point but we continued the search. I reached the opposite end of the woods where an archery group were meeting. Again I gave a description but no one had seen Bolt. At this point Jo called me again to say she had found him, he was stressed and filthy, but no blood, and very tired.

Clearly he had lost us, then was frantically running around trying to find us again. One of the archery people very kindly gave me a lift in his car to where Jo had found Bolt and we were all reunited after a very stressful hour. I have no idea why that woman told Jo that Bolt was covered in blood, but that really did add to the stress. My worst fear was that he had been taken, it was such a relief to have found him. I decided it was time to go shopping for a dog GPS system. There were a few devices on the market that attached to a dog's collar and when activated would show you their location on your smart phone. The better ones were not cheap but I had no intention of going through this again.

14 FEBUARY 2016

We had house guests for a week, Jo's daughter Leigh and her partner Emzy went on holiday leaving their two Collie cross breeds with us. They were also rescue dogs, Lillie was being advertised free on Gumtree, while

Sansa was rescued from Romania. We had a lovely stress free walk after the drama of the previous day. We went to Foxcovet Reserve which was a very large, quiet, enclosed area where Sansa, who had poor recall, could be off lead. It also gave me a chance after the previous day to confirm Bolt's recall. He was spot on. Bolt had become good friends with Lillie and they spent the walk becoming sprint buddies. In the first picture I managed to capture all seven dogs, the next is little Sansa, and the third is Bolt running with his new pal Lillie.

EMZY TELLS OF LILLIE AND SANSA

In July 2014, Leigh and I decided to have a dog. We searched all over the Internet, on Gumtree and on Preloved. We enquired about loads of dogs from Jack Russells to Border Collies. We set our hearts on having an active dog so we could share our love of the outdoors together. After searching high and low, I found an advert for a Border Collie in Stoke on Trent. She was black and white, 9 months old, named Lillie Bell-Bear and from her photos looked scared. Leigh wanted her, badly. I wasn't so sure.

The owners were selling her for £250 and I thought that was too much money for a dog to be sold on Gumtree. After I contacted the owner, we arranged to go see her. Leigh and I agreed that if we were going all that way to see her, we wouldn't be leaving without her. So, we made the trip to Stoke on Trent, roughly two hours, on a Friday evening after work to go meet Lillie.

When we arrived, we were welcomed into the home where right at the other end of the house, was the dog, on a blanket looking so sad. Immediately we were concerned. The owner had three children running all over the place and the house was a mess with a tiny courtyard as a garden. They told me the reason they were getting rid of Lillie was due to work commitments. I wasn't convinced this was the case at all, because out in the garden was another puppy that they were keeping!! We then pieced together that they were getting rid of her to make money as she was no longer a small cute puppy. She was this long-legged ball of energy that they couldn't cope with anymore. So sad.

We had been in the house for five minutes by this time and Lillie was still laying on her blanket staring up at us. The owner then proceeded to call Lillie and at this point, she came bounding up to us, jumping all over the place, super fussy. We loved her from that moment on and knew we had to have her and give her the life she truly deserved. After agreeing on a smaller fee, we bundled her in the car and off home we went with me on the back seat with Lillie on my lap and her head out the window...which led to her throwing up all down the side of Leigh's brand new car as we pulled up on our home drive.

Three years old now, she is an incredible, obedient, healthy happy dog. She loves her walks and the outdoors more than anything. Now she is raw fed, her coat is smooth and silky. As our vet would say, 'She is the perfect example of a healthy dog'. Although she is a super gentle, sweet loving dog, she has started to slip with her behaviour towards other dogs. We had no idea where this came from or why she was doing it so we took her to see a behaviourist. (I never thought I would ever have to take either of my dogs to naughty dog school!) At the moment, we can only put this down to her being unsociable and not interested in making new friends. She very rarely approaches other dogs or interacts with them, seemingly preferring her own company as she races in and out of the trees. Out on walks, she now has to wear a 'no dogs' harness so other dog owners are aware. This is such a hard subject for us as Lillie is an incredible dog who loves people so much. Hopefully, we can move forward from this and have our Lillie back the way she was when we first got her. We still love her endlessly...

We adopted Sansa in September 2014, after we had Lillie. Her background is truly heart-breaking but she has developed into such a loving and gentle dog.

Sansa is from the streets of Romania and was caught by heartless dog catchers who threw her into a tiny cage ready to be slaughtered (Common ways are to inject them with antifreeze or put them in a freezer alive). It is believed that in the cage, she was accompanied by a few puppies -they may even have been hers, but we will never know this for sure.

When she was collected, Sansa was in an awful state. She had no fur on her neck or ears, she had a massive hernia, and was incredibly underweight. She was operated on in Romania to remove her hernia and to be spayed, but this caused her so many problems. From the day we got her until about autumn 2016, she had a hole in her stomach that wouldn't heal. She had three more operations in Nottingham to close the wound, but nothing seemed to work. We eventually found out that she was allergic to internal stitches and the vet found a tiny strand of them left in her belly that was preventing the wound from healing. Now, apart from being a little on the chunky side, she is fit and healthy.

A few months before we got Sansa, Lillie was becoming very unsettled when we left her at home for a few hours and chewed everything and anything. That's when we made the decision to start looking for another dog and luckily for us, we spotted Sansa. She took our fancy for her Collie looking ways, and her tanned eyebrows. We had no idea how big she was going to be until we visited her in her foster home. We contacted One Paw and registered our interest in Sansa and within days, we were at her foster home with Lillie, waiting to meet her. The door opened and there was some tension between both dogs as we entered the house. My heart dropped. We decided to look past this and let the dogs loose in the garden to give them some space. Within minutes, they were smelling each other, Sansa bowing to Lillie to play and then following each other round, in between us having cuddles with Sansa of course. After the hour we spent there, we fell in love with her and wanted to bring her home there and then. After the meet and greet, Shaun and Shane arranged a home check just to make sure our house would be suitable for her as Romanian dogs are famously good escape artists. We passed the home check and a few days later on a Friday evening after work, we went and collected our newest family member.

She walked perfectly on the lead from the house to the car but was very cautious of her surroundings. On the way home we stopped at Pets at Home to get her a new collar and lead. At this point we knew she was desperate for some TLC. She was terrified of the automatic doors at the front of the shop and would not enter. We waited outside until she was ready to go in, which took around 5 minutes. This behaviour continued at home. She took her time with everything that was new to her. From walking in the front door, going in the garden or coming on the sofa. Everything was scary to her. There was a very heart-warming moment when Lillie was running from Sansa to the garden over and over again, trying to get her outside to play. The hardest thing at the beginning was getting her to come upstairs, fortunately Sansa is a food monster so a couple slices of ham did the trick.

Two years on and she's a different dog. She has such a cheeky character and is so gentle, although she still cowers her head and has her safe spot in the house when she is unsure. I don't think this will ever change.

Sansa loves nothing more than affection. She will nudge you, get vocal or do anything possible to get your attention. She is happy to just lay in the sun on warm days out in the garden or in the middle of the field on walks and somehow, has picked up the ability to forward roll. This is her new trick and loves making us laugh and smile. Sansa has turned into such a beautiful dog, with all the forgiveness in the world. Even two years on from her rescue in Romania, you can still see her sad story in her eyes. In picture one is Sansa in her cage waiting for destruction, in picture two she is still in Romania but has been rescued, picture three she is happy at her forever home with us.

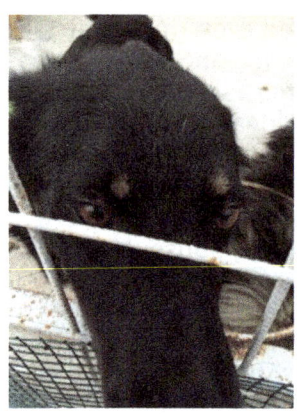 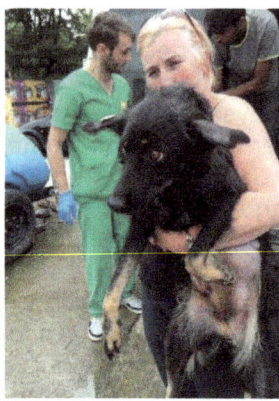 

A big thank you to One Paw at A Time Dog Rescue, for helping Sansa, and many more dogs who have now been given a second chance at life here in the UK. The rescue is run by two lovely guys called Shaun and Shane. Amongst having full time jobs, they manage to run this brilliant rescue, which I think is incredible. It shows how much dedication the guys have towards saving these dogs.

Nottingham based, they have been over to Romania many times, saving as many dogs as they possibly can. This isn't as easy as choosing the dog and then bringing it back to the UK. No! All dogs lucky enough to get out, get moved from the kill shelter to a local dog rescue where they stay until transport, vaccinations, foster homes, passport and a host of other things are sorted. A dog can remain in Romania for weeks and weeks. This could be due to lack of foster home or illness. Once all the important information is gathered, the dog is then brought over to the UK and placed in a foster home, where further checks are made on prospective adopters.

19 FEBUARY 2016

The tracking devices I was looking at for Bolt came down to a two horse race. One was a custom made dog tracker that looked very good indeed but was very expensive. The other option was a vehicle tracker that allowed me to locate it via SMS. This was a fraction of the price but seemed to be able to do what I wanted. So I went for the cheap option. It arrived and it was fine, I had to top up the SIM card in order for it to work. To find Bolt, all I had to do was call him on my phone, (yes, Bolt now had his own phone number), the call would go to answer machine, then Bolt would send me a text message with a link to Google maps which showed his position and the remaining battery life on the tracker. The tracker was not waterproof so it had to be placed inside a plastic pouch, then attached to the collar.

The first time I tried it I clicked on the link in Bolt's text message, Google maps opened on my phone and there he was, a red pin displayed Bolt's location. Hang on though... I didn't recognise the location? I zoomed out and discovered that Bolt was in Hong Kong. Now Bolty boy was fast for sure but Nottingham to Hong Kong in 10 minutes? I tried again and he was still in Hong Kong. On the third attempt I found Bolt was back in Nottingham, and it worked perfectly.

So off we went walkies and as usual Bolt was charging around doing his sprint thing and I gave him a bell. Within 10 to 20 seconds I had his location (as of 10 to 20 seconds ago) he was a red pin on the map. I was a blue circle with an arrow showing my direction of travel. I could easily see in which direction Bolt was in relation to me and I could see how far away he was. Job done, this would have saved a lot of grief the previous week.

After the walk, the fitting that zipped the plastic cover shut was missing. It wasn't Bolt proof, but then most things weren't Bolt proof. I couldn't get the tracker out the waterproof sleeve so I had to cut it out and find another way to waterproof it. The shape of the tracker was not too streamlined, so, unlike the sleek waterproof expensive option, it was possible it could snag on undergrowth and be ripped off the collar. Overall though, it seemed to do the job at a fraction of the price. (I later discovered the cost of topping up the SIM card actually made this the more expensive option).

Walking with the tracker made life relaxing once more. Bolt still got lost on occasion but I could easily find him. Finally things were coming together with the pack. Bolt had settled in and the pack dynamic was working really well. But something bad was coming, it would tear the pack dynamic apart, it would impact Max very badly and Bolt would be back to square one.

1 MARCH 2016

It was annual vaccination time for the dogs and I was in two minds whether I should do it or not. More and more evidence was coming to light suggesting that over-vaccination could cause serious problems. Already I had stopped worming, going instead for poop sample analysis, thereby reducing the amount of chemicals I put inside the dogs. I wasn't sure about vaccinating, so I asked for advice on the rescue group page using the style of Shakespeare to capture attention.

"To jab, or not to jab; that is the question:
Whether 'tis nobler in the mind to suffer
Distemper or Parvo of outrageous fortune,
Or to take chemicals against a sea of diseases,
And by opposing end them".

The consensus came back that most people still went for the jabs, so I decided to run with the crowd, at least for now.

11 MARCH 2016

ABOUT THAT BAD THING

What I am about to describe is something that happened to me, but I mention it here because of the impact it had on my pack and the pack dynamics.

It was getting quite late this Friday night, the dogs had been exercised, fed, watered, groomed and loved, now it was time to settle down and have a relaxing beer, it was after all, my birthday weekend. The security light illuminated on the front garden and we heard a loud knocking at the door, like thunder. The dogs, no doubt sensing the energy of the situation went nuts, especially Saxon. I went to the front door and cracked it open as I didn't want the dogs to get out, especially in their excited state. I saw a large young man in his mid-twenties and he was yelling at me. I couldn't hear a word because of the barking but the gist I got was that he thought I parked my car too close to his. Jo told me that she recognised him as a neighbour's son who visited the area from time to time. Through the barking I repeatedly heard him yell "I am not afraid of your dogs". Clearly this young man had no idea what a GSD or five could do. He was also yelling at me "What's your message?" I wondered if he was on drugs or something. This conversation was going nowhere so I apologised to him that I couldn't hear him because of the dogs, and I closed the door.

He didn't go away, he was bouncing around the street in a state of agitation. I decided to go out and see why he was so upset, I am pretty good at talking situations down and thought there should be no conflict between neighbours, I just wanted to make everything right. As I entered the street, he approached me with angry intent, I raised a hand and put it on his shoulder and calmly asked him not to come any closer. He told me not to touch him then BANG he hit me on the side of the head. I remember thinking "Shit... that rang my bell". I immediately responded with a powerful right punch that sent him reeling and staggering backwards. I would be taking no chances with him, he was big, fast, clearly strong, and less than half my age.

I forced him to the ground and while on top of him, in line with what I teach, I took control of the situation. In doing so he immediately went into a defensive posture and ceased trying to hurt me further, which was my aim. The plan now was to get an arrest hold on him and restrain him until the police arrived. (Jo was very quick to call 999 having witnessed all this). Throughout the struggle though I was having trouble gripping him, as everything was wet and slippery. The police finally arrived and took control of the situation.

At this point I realised why everything was wet and slippery. During the struggle, I had been stabbed in the chest. The knife punctured my lung which was slowly collapsing and filling with blood, my stomach lining and diaphragm had been pierced and I suffered a cracked rib where the knife entered my chest. The police took this fine example of modern day youth away to hospital to have his head looked at, which had become very swollen where I hit him. I waited for an ambulance, which took a very long time, and I started to feel sleepy.

In an almost dream state, I remembered the house being a hive of activity with police and paramedics, I heard someone shout at Jo to get the dogs out, which she did, but Bolt of course can open doors and he let all the dogs back in again, Saxon was going nuts, he doesn't like uniforms and hats at the best of times, but now he could smell his pack leaders blood and with all the excitement and energy, he just couldn't calm down. Bolt was whimpering and trying to clean my blood off me. Max was running around all the rooms not knowing what to do. Roxy took herself off to her mental private place where she goes when she can't cope, and Monty lay on the floor panting. The pack were very aware indeed that something very bad had happened to me. I don't remember how I left the house, it may have been on a stretcher but I am sure that once I was out of the den, the pack knew that their leader was gone, quite possibly dead.

I spent twelve days in hospital, having operations to repair the damage done by the knife. It was a very long twelve days and I often thought of my pack, wishing there was a way Jo could bring them to the hospital so they could at least see I was alive. At home, things were not going well. The pack dynamic was disintegrating.

My staff and a few of the students (that were aware of what happened) were solid, being there for Jo as she needed them. They made sure she was not alone and always had assistance to walk the dogs.

Monty, who never really had much to do with Jo, started following her everywhere, the way he did with me. It was almost as if he was saying "OK you are the pack leader now, you have to look after me and feed me".

This event hit Bolt very hard indeed, he went right back to square one. When out on walks he would run away and not come back and Jo was finding him very difficult to handle. While I was still in hospital she took him to a dog behaviourist. On her website, she stated she had worked with over 1500 dogs. She said that Bolt was the most unfocused dog she had ever seen. To be fair to the lad, he was in a bad place, and he just wanted me back. It got to the point though, in my absence, Bolt could not be off lead.

After I left the house to go to hospital. Jo let Max, Bolt and Saxon back in the house, Bolt and Saxon settled down somewhat, however Max continued to run around the house, he was looking for his Dad, and when he couldn't find him he went to the top of the stairs and sulked. Jo went to the top of the stairs to console him but he was having none of it, he buggered off in to the attic and there he stayed until the next morning. It was all Jo's fault! Mum had dragged him away from his Dad by the scruff of his neck and now Dad was gone.

My stay in hospital was prolonged because I had a chest infection when I was admitted, and they were not going to let me go home without that being sorted. Jo never missed a visiting slot and there were always friends or family around me, but I missed my pack. I couldn't help wonder what was going through their minds. I was desperate to be with them. Finally the day came, I could go home. I was still pretty fragile and having five dogs jumping all over me would do me no good. So we planned to put all the dogs in the back garden, sit me down on the sofa and pad me with cushions, then let the dogs in one at a time to see me. The greeting I got from each of them was truly unbelievable. Tails were wagging so hard it made their bodies wag, lots of yipping and yapping, HUGE wet kisses and it just went on. It was absolutely lovely to experience this. It was a good thing I was padded with cushions or I may well have been straight back to hospital.

I would be walking with my pack the next day but I would have hiking poles and the pace would be slow. I was under strict instructions not to hold a lead for six weeks, so I would need company walking every day. Jo was amazing, as was Matt, Andrew and many others. We would just make it work. Our first walk found us at Bestwood Quarry. We got to a spot where Bolt had been running off, there was a rabbit warren nearby I think. While I was in hospital he would just run from this spot and not come back. I saw him prick up his ears and he started to run, I called him three times (feeling the strain on my wound) but he stopped, thought about it, then he came back to me and got loads of praise. Very soon the pack dynamic was back to normal, and within six weeks I would be out with my wolves on my own again.

April 2016

I was intrigued about the dog behaviourist's comments on Bolt. As she came highly recommended, I didn't in any way doubt her judgement, but I thought it would be interesting to revisit her with the pack, and see what she made of them while I was around. I also needed some advice on using the "Stay" command on the pack as a whole, because up to that point Bolt would always jump the gun and the rest would follow. I also wondered what she would think of the role of each dog within the pack.

On the day of our appointment, knowing I had not been to work for a while, we were very generously asked only to pay what we could afford. A very nice gesture I thought. I offered to pay full price nonetheless. We were given her thoughts on the pack roles and it seemed to be, after me, there was no "Alpha" in place. Given what happened to the pack while I was in hospital that did make a lot of sense. Bolt was much better behaved and she did see a difference. Then I was shown some techniques I could put in place to enforce the pack "Stay" command. This was done by means of a very impressive demonstration with her own dogs. I thought to myself "Mmm Bolt... no way" As before with Max though, I would follow instructions to the letter and we would see. I would report the results back to our trainer.

11 April 2016

I have met some lovely knowledgeable people when out walking my dogs, I have also met some other people. A while back I found myself discussing scenting with Linda, one of the lovely knowledgeable people. Scenting is when a scent trail is laid for a dog and the dog is encouraged to follow the trail for a reward. Linda had a little Staffie called Dylan and she would hide treats around the house for Dylan to find, usually by scenting. I thought to try the same although I did think it may be a bit chaotic with five German Shepherds.

So the game "Hunt the Sausage" was on. A great game for the dogs and one we now play often. The dogs wait in the garden while I hide cocktail sausages all over the house, some would be easy to find and others very hard. The dogs are let in and off we go. I was really pleased with the gang because on our first attempt at this game everyone played nice and there was no falling out. Bolt's technique was to race through the house and snaffle up all the obvious ones as quickly as possible. I think this strategy earned him the most sausages. Roxy and Max took a bit more time to sniff out the more difficult ones while Saxon and Monty just couldn't BELIEVE I actually made then WORK for treats. They stayed pretty close to me because they knew I was a soft touch and I would give them both a little help. All sausages were gone after about two minutes but the pooches didn't know that, so they kept searching for another ten minutes or so.

17 April 2016

SUCCESS – GETTING IN THE CAR ON COMMAND AS A PACK

I never thought I would get back to this point with the current pack. Bolt was just too excitable and a bit scatty, and Saxon too competitive with Bolt. So I stopped trying. I worked diligently on the training techniques I was given only days ago and what a difference. I felt so proud of my gang, especially Bolt, bless him. Things were still a bit excitable while I was getting ready for the walk, but we would calmly and slowly walk to the front gate and the dogs would wait to be invited into the car. I used an old broom to gently hook around Bolt's and Saxon's chest just to slow them down if they got too excited or competitive. Soon the broom was not needed. The next step I wanted to achieve was to invite them into the truck individually by name, one at a time. That seemed a bit daunting at the time but then so did getting Bolt to sit and stay a few weeks ago.

The previous day Roxy and Bolt took off after a deer in the woods. On recall one, Roxy returned and Bolt slowed down. Recall two, Bolt stopped, recall three, four and five Bolt was staring into the woods where the deer disappeared. Recall six Bolt returned to my side. Good lad, he got lots and lots of praise and fuss. He had come a long way in the last six months, especially given his regression when I was in hospital.

Meanwhile, Uncle Jon gave the crew their annual once-over. He commented how clean all their teeth were, even the old guys. Thanks to prey model raw feeding, I am sure. He was also quite surprised at the low heart rate of Roxy and Bolt, suggesting a good level of fitness. That must have been all the off lead charging around they did. Monty and Max were doing great, but old Saxon was showing a few signs of age. His back end was not as strong as it was and he had been having a few issues with his back right leg so he was on a low dosage of pain relief for a while. There is no holding back the aging process I suppose. Saxon remained a very happy and noisy soul though, so that was fine.

19 April 2016

Well, that didn't last long! "That" was Bolt's hard wearing, heavy duty, durable pouch that I used to protect his GPS. It was two months old. To be fair it was a good bit of kit. It just had to endure the Bolt lifestyle and suffer the same treatment as Bolt's extremities. In picture two is Bolt's modified ear, all healed with just some bits of dissolvable stitching sticking out, it just needed his fur to grow back... again. It only cost £220 this time, better than the £300 last time it happened. So I bought the young lad another four GPS pouches in the hope that they would see him through the rest of the year. All I needed now was a doggie crash helmet and something to put his tongue in to stop him cutting it when running through the undergrowth. Picture three is the handsome energetic lad himself doing what he loves most and what he does best.

28 April 2016

What on earth was going on? We were a gnat's winkle away from May, and there were hail stones the size of peas and ice covered water. Check out the big lad in picture one, he had to break the ice to get a drink. Not that the gang minded at all. It was another three weeks before I could have a dog attached to me on a lead, so I still needed to have help when out walking the pack. So here I was with my six pack on my own. No one was able to help out today and the guys need their walk, so, when needs must... I had a six pack again as we had our little guest back to stay, Tag in picture three. He loved his time with us while his mum and dad were on holiday. He was not a fan of raw food and I was not a fan of commercial so he had gently stir fried chunks of meat every meal. I think I made a rod for his Dad's back with this, ah well... Before the walk was over, Bolt managed to snag his tongue on a bramble or something and put a small cut in it. Because he goes everywhere at Mach 1 his heart was normally racing and pumping blood rapidly around his body, making the smallest cut look like a mortal wound. Also because he was always running and his tongue was long it flapped in the wind stream often wrapping itself around his head and neck. All this combined meant that Bolt looked like he had killed a large animal, ripped its stomach open, stuck his head in the bloody gaping hole and wriggled it about. Needless to say I got some very interesting looks from other dog walkers. I tried to explain but one guy in particular was so horrified he just stared at Bolt, frozen on the spot, hoping this devil dog was not going to devour his pocket pooch on a string. We got back to the car and I cleaned him up fine, his tongue had stopped bleeding and drama was over. Until our next walk that is.

6 May 2016

HAPPY BIRTHDAY SAXON (AKA THE BIG GUY AKA THE DARK PRINCE AKA SAXOPHONE).

Our big handsome hunk was ten on this day. He would have been with us two years in August. We thought to do celebrations for him at the weekend. The weather was fantastic for him, to think it had been snowing just a couple of weeks back.

On Saturday morning we took off for a lovely walk at Bestwood Quarry. This is an old sandstone quarry that is very quiet. We stopped for a rest and Bolt quickly dug himself a hole to lie in between my feet for some reason only apparent to him. He truly was a wonder. In the afternoon it was time to give Sax his present. He got a big paddling pool which he absolutely loved. In one picture you can see Sax and Bolt willing the pool to fill faster. Having cooled down in the pool what better way to relax than with the bottom half of a pig's leg. As you can see, Monty did really well with his in picture three.

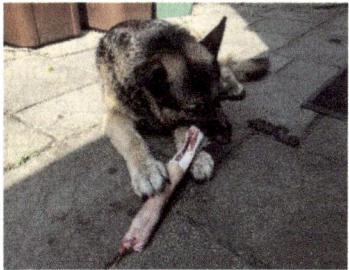

On Sunday we took off for another glorious walk at Watchwood and finished the hike by a big pond for a swim and cool down. I had not seen Bolt swim before, in fact this may well have been the first time he had. I was amazed at the way he cut cleanly and powerfully through the water. His swimming was as fast and efficient as his sprinting. THEN he realised he was out of his depth. He made a U-turn for dry land and he changed his swimming technique to something really quite interesting. No... interesting is not the right word, worrying is far more accurate. He slowly thrashed and splashed his way back to the shore with me chanting the mantra "Don't drown, don't drown, don't drown" while contemplating removing my boots and jumping in to get him. Drama over, it was time to go home and bake Saxon's cake and break out the party hats.

14 May 2016

SAXON'S VERSION OF SWAN LAKE

Chapter 1 - A new place.

We found a lovely new walk at Silverhill Woods, the car park post code is NG17 3JJ. It's next to Tattershall camping site which is a Caravan and Camping Club place and they often allow more than two dogs per pitch. We had not walked here before so the spider senses were on full alert. The walk was lovely, we only did half of the woodlands and still covered three and a half miles.

Early on in the walk we came across a pond that was full of small dogs swimming around, so we gave it a wide berth. This place was quite busy, so we had to lead up a few times but there were occasions when we couldn't as dogs met on blind corners, all off lead. My lot were perfectly behaved, I was so proud of them, even Bolt behaved impeccably. Our route took us back to the lake I mentioned earlier, which I assumed was okay for the dogs to enter since there were dogs swimming there before. This time it was quiet with no one else around. Which, as it transpired, was a good thing. I let the dogs run ahead to the water to get a drink as it was a bit warm. All five dogs disappeared from view as they crossed a rise in the ground and went into the pond.

Chapter 2 - Swan Lake meets Dodge City.

Jo and I crossed the rise and saw a lot of things at once. Monty and Max were on dry land, Roxy and Bolt were feet wet having a drink and Sax was in the pond up to his shoulders; the big lad was probably a bit warm. He was not far from the shore so the pond appeared to get deep quickly. At the same time I also saw two swans come around a corner and making a bee-line for Saxon. Sax was just chilling, cooling down and having a drink. Jo and I started yelling at the dogs to "Come here" and we started running to the pond. By now, the swans were almost upon Saxon, rearing up out of the water, honking and flapping like mad. Saxon responded by moving towards them. Bolt looked up, and in his head I suppose, he saw two great white water rabbits and got very excited. Bolt forgot his last swimming experience and shot straight into the water heading for these strange feathered rabbits. Maximus, the pack gladiator, had that look in his eye I had not seen for a long time and his tail was as straight as an arrow. Although he was not keen on water he was straight into the pond heading for Saxon's side.

Chapter 3 - Holy Shit.

Contact was seconds away. I grabbed Monty who, despite his multiple arthritic problems, was as strong as an ox, and determined to have a bit of the action. Bless him, I don't think he would fare well against a swan in the water but true to form he was up for it. As I grabbed Monty I yelled at Bolt and Max and they stopped still in the water. Jo was heading into the pond to get Sax. Sax took three left hooks from a swan's wing, causing him to blink and flinch, before he grabbed its wing in his mouth. Now Jo grabbed Sax by the collar and dragged him out the water. Bolt and Max recalled to my side and the swans retired. The swans I think had a lucky escape. We got everyone to shore and once again, the drama was over.

Chapter 4 - The aftermath.

When walking somewhere new with the pack it's always a bit tense as you don't always know what's around the corner. My guys were well behaved and all recalled in high distraction circumstances, apart from Sax who, to be fair, was being assaulted. Maybe the Queen wouldn't see it that way since the swans are hers, and killing one comes with a £5000 fine and 6 months in jail. Saxon could have got more bird than he bargained for, I could just see the big lad now in a pair of stripy prison overalls. I would have to sub his fine as he does not have that much in savings. I didn't take pictures of this incident because I was a bit busy at the time but the ones I have below capture the flavour.

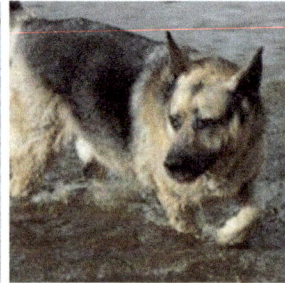

A CANINE PERSPECTIVE

Walking on a warm day, Saxon looks ahead and sees an inviting pond, he rushes in up to his shoulders in the cooling water. He yells to his pack in his deep booming voice "Hey guys the water is fine… come on in… cool down". The pack look at Saxon and they notice two shapes in the water behind him and moving his way. Bolt yells a warning "Hey Sax, there are some things in the water behind you, they are moving towards you". Saxon replies "Yeah, nice one Bolt, do you think I was born yesterday, we are not all as daft as you ha-ha". Max chips in "No really, Sax look behind you, I don't know what they are, but they are pretty big and they are getting close to you. "Ha Max… no way, you won't catch me out with that one… seriously guys". Then a lot happens at once, Roxy seeing what is about to unfold slinks away thinking to herself "Whatever they are I am sure the boys can handle them, I will just move back out of the way" Jo and I start yelling for the dogs to come to us, the pack yell at Saxon "BEHIND YOU". Saxon, who is now almost convinced takes a quick peek out of the corner of his eye "ARRRGGHHH WHAT THE HELL ARE THEY, OUCH, OUCH, OUCH. Snap, and Saxon grabs a wing and in a muffled voice calls to Max. "Hey Macsh, I got mmm one, I will mmm hold it while you mmm bite it mmm".

Max's eyes narrow and he takes a steely look at his adversaries while he assesses the threat. "Their necks are long, so easy to grab, they are also thin and my bite force is around 240 pounds of pressure. Yes, that's their weakness, right, this won't take long".

Bolt darts into the water seeing he has the support of Max "Yeah, come on Max, we can save Saxon, YOU FIRST". Simultaneously Monty addresses the pack "Stand back guys this is a job for me, I don't know what they are but this is nothing I can't handle". I grab hold of Monty, he protests "HEY let go of me, I need to sort this out".

Jo gets to Saxon's side and the swans retire. Saxon barks at their retreat" Yeah, that's right, run you stupid flappy honking things". Bolt confidently chimes in "Hey guys did you see that, they took one look at me and that was it, they were off, HA, I showed them... Didn't I Max?"

2 June 2016

It was time to saddle up and head out for the annual rescue volunteers' camping trip. Given how noisy Saxon was during the journey last time, we decided to let him have the back seat all to himself. He was happier there and hopefully would be quieter. Once we hit sheep country though, he had to let everyone know that this was Saxon's truck, and so the barking started. About two miles from our destination, Saxon was still making a noise but was looking a bit agitated. I mentioned to Jo that maybe he needed the toilet, although we had toilet stop half way through the trip so he should have been OK. As we were only two miles away from our destination we decided to press on. Saxon gave off a massive fart and squirted a very wet poop all over the back seat. Poor soul looked almost embarrassed as he is normally a very clean dog. We had to stop for a quick clean up as the big lad was now trying to climb into the front seats. It's a good job my seats were leather.

We arrived at the site to meet lots of friendly faces and started pitching. Poor old Saxon stayed in the car the whole time. He really was not happy about having done a poop on the back seat. Our stay was just for a long weekend on this occasion. Considering the number of dogs we had on site, the holiday was incident free. To a person though, everyone that had met Bolt on the last trip commented on how much progress he had made. That was good to hear. He was still not keen on Karen's dog Gumbo but he was far more restrained. He just had to tell Gumbo off a couple of times but you could almost see his thought process, "No I am not going to do it, Dad won't be happy... Oh but I really need to... No I mustn't ... Oh I just HAVE to... Oi Gumbo WOOF WOOF WOOF".

We had a few beach walks, which was good to keep track of where Bolt was, as he couldn't really get out of sight. We had one forest walk and he was as good as gold.

June 2016

Roxy had managed to hurt herself running around again, she was getting older but didn't seem to want to acknowledge that. A bit like me, really. This time she appeared to have inflamed one of the joints in her foot. So more vets bills and a bit of rest. When it was time to start exercising her again, it was to be on the long lead to restrict her activity. So you can just imagine how impressed I was when she managed to catch a rabbit while on the lead. Thankfully for the rabbit, things were over in the blink of an eye. Max took a keen interest in Roxy's kill and gently took it off her. Roxy, being the timid soul she is, just let him. I suppose in Max's mind, maybe he wanted to impress other dog walkers we met by pretending he caught it. Bolt I think thought it was a pull toy and wanted to play but Max would have none of it. Two miles later Max couldn't contain himself any longer and ate the rabbit whole, skin, feet, head and all. Monty and Saxon paid no heed at all to this little drama. They don't see the sense in wasting energy running around after a scrawny little rabbit when Dad feeds them cow's hearts and chicken wings after walks.

18 June 2016

Some months earlier, we had been contacted by Saxon's previous owner, Lisa. Her life had taken a huge change for the better, and she now had another dog called Ollie. We had kept in touch and I often sent her pictures of Saxon. The big guy wasn't getting any younger and one picture I sent her prompted her to contact us and see if she could come and visit him. I think she thought as he was looking a lot older and she needed to see him, possibly for one last time. She lived in Scotland but had family in the Midlands and was due to visit them. She was hoping she could combine visits, family and Saxon in the same trip. Jo and I didn't have a problem with this but we did wonder what effect it would have on Saxon. Sax had been with Lisa around seven years, we didn't want to confuse him or introduce him to Lisa, only for him to pine once the visit was over. We had done something like this before with Kiera and it went well, so we decided to give the green light for the visit. Lisa was delighted.

It was truly lovely meeting her. Saxon remembered her and gave her a lovely greeting but he knew where his home was now, so it worked perfectly. Ollie was a lovely boy and could have been Bolt's twin brother. We had a lovely walk together, then it was back to ours to chill out and relax on the patio in the sun. Having seen Saxon in the flesh Lisa thought that the picture I sent her didn't really do him justice; he didn't look as old as he appeared in the picture.

Lisa posted on social media. *"Lovely morning visiting the Dark Prince Saxon with his family. Ollie and I were made to feel so welcome, and what a lovely pack. Thank you Ken and Jo Robson for giving Sax the best home ever. Saxon is as handsome as ever and a happy boy. My heart is settled now"*.

26 June 2016

This morning found us at Watchwood again. I thought at the time it would be a great location for a social walk, which I should arrange some time. Bolt was very well behaved, he didn't run off at all and as such I didn't need to use his GPS. Maybe he was finally learning that it was his job to keep an eye on me and not the other way around. Regarding his GPS, I realised I had engaged in a false economy and was considering another product. Already I had spent £40 in topping up his SIM card, I spent a further £12 on protective pouches and the unit itself cost £35. In addition Bolt had managed to crack the plastic casing on the unit which could not be replaced. I thought that for not much more money I could have bought the POD from www.podtrackers.com , it did seem a better bit of kit. It was waterproof, streamlined to prevent snagging and it seemed to have more functions. I would invest in one and just hope it was Bolt proof.

Given the rain we had the previous night, Saxon found lots of muddy puddles to lie in. Max was moulting and it seemed this year he would be wearing stripes. His coat changed slightly every year, clearly Max like to keep abreast of fashion. I managed to get some rare shots of Bolt not moving and a few of old Mont sitting down having a rest. Roxy, as always, just looked a picture of health and beauty.

On our way home, we stopped off for a bite to eat at a pub called The Hut. We sat outside with the dogs all around us. It's a dog friendly place and we attracted a fair bit of attention. Lots of people came over to say hello and make a fuss of the dogs. The pack were very well behaved, although Saxon wouldn't stop chattering to himself. After lunch we were off home for pigs trotters all round and a nice glass of red for Jo and me.

POLICE ANIMAL WELFARE VOLUNTEER

For over a year now I have been a volunteer for the Nottinghamshire Police Animal Welfare Lay Visiting scheme. The purpose of the scheme is to enable members of the local community, with the assistance of the appropriate national animal welfare organisations to observe, comment and report on the welfare of animals engaged in police work. The scheme provides an independent check on police training methods and the conditions under which animals are housed and transported. This demonstrates that the methods employed are humane, ethical and open to public accountability.

The volunteer group I am associated with has a very good working relationship with the dog handlers and kennel staff. Certainly in the case of Nottingham, it is heartening to see that the inspector in charge of the dog unit really does care about the dogs and handlers in her charge, and readily makes herself available to the volunteers when making surprise visits to the kennels.

Most of my visits have been to the kennels (brand new and recently rebuilt) but on a couple of occasions I have been fortunate enough to observe police dog training sessions. My first visit was a general training session with several handlers and dogs present. Some dogs were conducting general training, while some were being licensed. A police dog and handler have to pass an annual check before they can conduct live operations, this test is called licensing. I was very impressed by the standards that were demanded of the dogs and handlers alike. The dogs performed very well indeed and were clearly enjoying themselves, while the humans displayed great team spirit and camaraderie, despite the pouring rain. There was a genuine feel of care and love between handlers and dogs that was lovely to see. I was particularly impressed by big, mean, terrifying police dog Ollie, who, at only eleven weeks old could, on command, sit, lie down, stand, speak, and bark at a suspect when stood still with hands above the head. Below you can see Ollie primed and ready to go.

One officer Chris told me of a story where his recently licensed dog Axo was out at work with him. For thirteen weeks the dog had been trained to bite a hessian sleeve. While on duty, Chris had cause to challenge a suspect. After the suspect failed to respond, Chris released Axo. However, Axo couldn't find the hessian sleeve to bite, so was happy just to run alongside the suspect. Chris said he felt his world collapse. Sometimes it can take some trial and error to transition from hessian sleeve to arm, but when the transition is made, and it always is, make no mistake, you would not want one of these dogs hanging onto your arm. Certainly Axo turned out to be a very good general purpose dog with a reputation for being a real hard hitter.

The second time I observed training, things were very specific, it was all about re-licensing three dogs and their handlers, ensuring, as always, SAFETY, EFFICIENCY and CONTROL. For the trainers, this is an excellent opportunity to get a good feel for where all the force dogs are, in regards to their capabilities. For the handlers, it's all about the annual MOT. Sometimes there can be some self-imposed pressure here by the handlers, as the idea of being TESTED fires deep seated feelings of uncertainty in people. This is not a bad thing as it demonstrates that they really do care about performance and want to do well.

Over a two day period, three teams would be put through their paces and would need to demonstrate acceptable performance in the following six areas.

1. Pattern tracking

2. Property searching a rural setting

3. Building searching for two persons, one accessible and one concealed

4. Conducting use of force exercises

5. Conducting heel work, long down, recall and speaking on command

6. Negotiating required obstacles on the agility course

I observed handler and dog teams perform and be assessed on the first three items.

For the pattern tracking, a trail is laid out over countryside that has at least seven legs, sometimes the leg taking a 90 degree turn, which may not be something a fleeing human would necessarily do, but it does test the dog. Along the trail three articles are placed, these could be a set of car keys or a mobile phone, and the dog has to locate them while following the trail. When the dog locates an article, it drops to the "down" position to indicate to the handler something has been found. Sometimes the trail will cross a gate or obstacle and the handler needs to observe the dog very carefully and read its body language to ensure the dog stays on track. If necessary, the team will stop, and the dog will be cast to regain the scent. For this test the trail is laid then left to go cold for 45 minutes, then the dogs are released. Under very difficult conditions all three dogs did very well and passed.

Jeff, one of the trainers, explained to me that, operationally, things can get quite complicated, for example a member of the public may report that the suspect went in one direction, because they may have genuinely thought that they did, but the dog will indicate the suspect went in a completely different direction. The handlers have to establish a solid bond with their dogs, get to know them inside out, and trust in them when they know they can. The human/dog bond and connection is critical for things to work. A dog may work very well indeed for its handler, that doesn't mean any dog handler could get the same result with that dog. Jeff was an absolute mine of information and clearly knew his stuff. He explained to me how the dogs work with scent, the things that affect scent and how the dog can differentiate between what it needs to focus on and what it needs to ignore. It was truly fascinating.

Task two took us to a different location where dogs and handlers had to conduct an area search to locate certain items, the items had fresh scent and could be hidden, and not only at ground level. To gain a pass, the teams had to locate a minimum of 75% of the hidden items, once again all three passed with flying colours.

During a break, Annie, the inspector in charge of the section, was talking about the possibility of re-introducing something called "duel". This is where a handler will have a general purpose (GP) dog, and a specialist dog. Specialist dogs could be drugs dogs or firearms dogs. Imagine a scenario where a car is stopped with four occupants and it has to be searched for drugs. Employing dual handling would allow the officer and GP dog to contain the occupants while the drugs dog located the hidden goods. I was surprised to learn that specialist dogs can include semen dogs. Semen dogs can be used at rape scenes to help direct where the forensic search should be focused. Wow, who would have thought, I didn't ask how you would go about training them.

For task three, we relocated yet again to a large, two storey, deserted building, containing a maze of corridors and lots of possible hiding places. For the building search, it is very important that the area is searched safely and systematically, there must be no possibility for missing an area where someone may be concealed, only for them to make an escape after the team has passed them by. The building we were in presented some real challenges to systematic searching with corridors branching off in different directions and a central stair case leading to more corridors. The dogs learn to scent under the doors or on door handles while keeping one nostril in the air, apparently some of the places people choose to hide when fleeing the police can be quite creative.

For this task the dog handlers were given a briefing on requirements, then the two handlers not being tested would pose as suspects and would disperse in the building with one of them finding a hiding place. The handler being tested offered a challenge on entering the building, allowing the suspect to reveal themselves. If there is no response the dog is released and the search begins. It really is clever how the dogs know who is in the game and who isn't. For example, I stood to one side with a trainer and the dog knew to ignore our scent and presence, yet focussed on the scent of a dog handler roleplaying a suspect. One of the handlers explained to me that at home his dog was the perfect family dog, great with young children and good with other dogs when out on walks, but when he went to work he knew, the switch was flipped and we had a working dog, not a pet. With this task complete, again I witnessed three good pass results.

Jeff told me of a building search story when he arrived at a scene that was to be his new dog's first job. A firearms team had cleared the building and assured Jeff that no one was inside. Jeff explained that as he was on scene he may as well conduct a search with his dog Tyler. As they searched the building they passed under a small attic hatch, Tyler detected nothing. As they passed back under the hatch for a second time Tyler's nose snapped into the air, he had something. Jeff was watching him intently and knew straight away they had found the suspect. Apparently this person had squeezed through the hatch and was sat on it. The second time Tyler passed under the hatch the scent filtered down, enough for him to locate the hidden person. It transpired that the suspect, for some reason, kicked a water tank over and flooded the attic, the ceiling became soft and he fell through and was apprehended. Without the dog team though, he could have escaped.

It was a real privilege to experience the expertise of the handlers and trainers, and to witness the dedication they have for their dogs. I spoke with Jeff at length and felt educated. Afterwards, one of the other trainers was kind enough to offer me some advice when I told him of Bolt's antics. You may recall earlier in the book I mentioned taking Max to a dog trainer that was ex-police, and I stopped taking him as I wasn't keen on some of his methods. Well, talking to Jeff, things have clearly changed, everything is positive re-enforcement, and the dog's welfare is paramount. Even when considering retirement, it is important to stop the dogs working soon enough so they can enjoy a happy healthy retirement. Below are some of our amazing working police dogs... that you really wouldn't want to mess with.

10 July 2016

Already Bolt had been with us for eleven months of madness and mayhem and on this day he was three years' old. He had come such a long way when you considered the semi-wild animal I took from the dog warden. Of late, I had been taking him to a local dog park on his own with a throw toy. I would launch the toy into the long grass and he would shoot in, chase, and find it. He would return the toy to me and drop it at my feet. He loved this game and was very good at it. I was working on the commands "Go left", "Go right", and "Away" if he needed help locating his toy in the grass, something I had seen demonstrated to me when I was working with Max some time ago.

We tried a new walk location at Netherfield that had quite a few streams. Zann, Tom and Elaine's GSD was with us, along with Lillie and Sansa. At one point we had seven dogs all in a stream cooling down (Monty didn't do streams) The banks were wet and slippery, consequently Zann and Saxon got stuck and had to be helped out of the water, and there I was expecting to stay dry, on this lovely clear day, after a night of rain. Zann, in picture two, came back to our house for the customary liver cake party and Bolt got a toy dinosaur as a present.

23 July 2016

The weather over the last few weeks had been very hot indeed. The dogs were really feeling the heat and could only be walked very early in the morning or early evening when things were cooling down a bit. Yet you would still see people out walking dogs on pavements in the mid-day sun. The weather was too nice to sit inside the house, yet our patio was scorching hot. So it was time to do some construction. I would need, 1 x paddling pool, 1 x large tent awning, 1 x comfy carpet for the dogs to lie on, 1 x extension lead, 1 x electric fan, and 1 x Saxon to demonstrate how it all came together.

24 July 2016

Finally I had found time to arrange a social walk at our favourite location, Watchwood. We had a pretty good turnout with around five humans, and a dozen or so dogs. Everything went really well for about the first five minutes then Bolt did his party piece, he took off in chase of something and didn't recall. I stood still and yelled his name for an age but nothing. I activated his GPS on my phone and I could see he was not far away in some bushes. My "guests" on the walk patiently stood by and waited. I headed towards the bushes where I thought Bolt was and I sent his GPS another locate. This time he was further away and a few locates later it seemed he was back on the main track and heading away from us. I don't think he had taken into account that we had been stood still for a while and he was now heading down the main track looking for us.

All I could do was hand the route over to Jo, and I took off down the track towards him with Jo's daughter, Charlotte. Each time I sent his GPS a locate request, he was further and further away from us. I was running at this point and took a quick look behind me to find poor old Monty trying to keep up with me. Bless him, the look on his face, as if he was saying to me "Dad I am trying to keep up, but I just can't, please don't leave me". My old soldier was doing his level best to keep up, he was giving it his all, but he was struggling. I stopped at this point and sent Charlotte ahead. The next few times I activated Bolt's GPS I could see he was running in circles at a T-junction. Then he took off in the wrong direction towards a main road. I called Charlotte on her phone to tell her where he was. A short while later Charlotte returned with an exhausted Bolt with blood all over his face. He had snagged his tongue again on a bramble. Monty had gotten his breath back by now and we back-tracked down the trail to meet up with everyone else.

Bolt had been gone for about 30 minutes and did a fine job embarrassing me on the first social walk I organised at Watchwood. It was my intention to keep Bolt on lead for the rest of the walk, but we got to the pond and all the dogs dashed in for a swim leaving Bolt by my side whimpering. "Oh let him go in for a swim, poor lad" I heard someone say, "No, there needs to be firm consequences if he misbehaves" I replied. As the discussion progressed it was clear I was outnumbered, in fact I was the only one on my side, so I caved in and let Bolt off lead to have his swim. He remained off lead for the rest of the walk and was as good as gold.

A BIT ABOUT BOLT GETTING LOST

Bolt's recall is excellent, he has the best recall of the pack. He gets lost because he just loves to run around the woods following scents and uncovering rabbits and the like, he absolutely LIVES for this. He can run fast and sometimes I think he gets so far away from me and so engaged in what he is doing that he just can't hear me, the recall just doesn't register with him. For me, I love to see him charging around and I want him to continue doing this thing that he loves so much but I can't have him getting lost, all manner of things could happen to him. The easy option would be just to keep him on a long lead but I don't want this, and I know Bolt doesn't, so I had to help him find a way.

At first, and for many months I would fix my eyes on him and if he got too far away or if I had not seen him for a minute or so I would recall, and for the majority of the time he would come back straight away. If he didn't come back, I would stand in the woods yelling and yelling, getting louder and louder while trying to locate him on his GPS, which to be honest didn't always work. Eventually he would come back looking exhausted. Clearly he had realised what he had done and was in a mad rush to get back to me.

Eventually I realised that I was teaching him to not pay attention to where I was, why should he? If I wanted him I would call him. If I didn't call him, he was free to do what he wanted. Well, this was not what I wanted. I needed him to pay attention to where I was and not get too far away from me.

So I changed my strategy. I started to not recall him and allow him to get a decent distance from me. Then I would give two or three loud recalls, if he didn't return I would give a very loud sharp recall that sounds like I am pissed off. If he returns before the pissed off recall he gets massive praise. If he returns during the pissed off recall he gets scolded and the head collar goes on, he hates this and I will explain what this is later. Then he is on lead for a while. If he is off running around and he pops out the woods to see where I am or he runs back to me of his own accord then he gets massive praise. Every time Bolt looks at me to check where I am he gets praise. He responds to it, and you can clearly see he is pleased that he has made me happy.

Now things have improved no end, Bolt knows it's his job to keep an eye on me, and when I call, he needs to get back sharpish, if he doesn't there is consequences and he knows what they are.

Every now and again though he gets it a bit wrong but these transgressions are becoming less frequent and less serious. But when it does go wrong, when he gets back to me the same sequence of events happens. First Bolt sees me running towards him reaching for the head collar, his ears go back he lies down and rolls on his side. Saxon runs up to him and gets right in his face and barks loudly. Monty just stares at him while Roxy and Max sit calmly and wait for his collar to be attached. Once the collar is attached, every time, without fail, Roxy and Max have a very noisy play fight. What on earth is all that about.

HOW THE PACK SEE IT

Bolt running around the woods, the cogs in his head are working overtime "WOW this is AWESOME, I can run so fast and I love the feel of how I can make the wind blow hard when I run, oh... wait... what's that smell, YES it's fresh, right the game is on, where is the little furry thing where is it, I think I am getting close, I must be getting close because I can run so fast, that smell is getting stronger. OH I so love being me, it's just the best thing ever". Then finally the sound of a faint recall seeps into his brain and Dad sounds a bit pissed off. "What... What's that noise, OHH

NO, it's Dad and he's not happy, oh no... This is really bad. I need to find him, where can he be, ahh... I can hear him again, he's in that direction, right, I need to run now as fast as I can".

Eventually Bolt gets back to me, he thinks to himself: "Oh no, he's really not happy, he's got that thing in his hand that goes around my nose, I know I will lie down and roll on my back and tell him how sorry I am". Bolt rolls on his side with his ears back, and I can see what he thinking from the look in his eyes. "Dad I am so so sorry I really didn't meant to, it's just there was this smell and the smell made me run after it, so it wasn't really my fault but I PROMISE it will never happen again, honest".

Saxon runs up to Bolt and has loud words. "YOU LITTLE SHIT... how many times have I told you? Every time you do this dad gets pissed off and angry. You know fine well how we have to manage his emotions, now he's not happy and we can all feel it, and it's ALL YOUR FAULT... YOU TOTAL ARSE.

Monty stares sternly at Bolt and adds to Saxon's scolding in a quiet, threatening tone. "When we get home young man, and when Dad is not around, we will be having words. I have been sat here with my ass on this cold wet ground waiting around for you, while you do your stupid running about thing... Make no mistake puppy, we will be having words later".

Roxy and Max sit by quietly and calmly, Roxy turns to Max "I don't know why he waits for him, if he runs off fine, just let him go", Max replies "Yeah, I know, if I was pack leader I wouldn't wait for him, if Bolt wasn't around we would have more room in the truck, more food, and all the toys would be mine, it's a no brainer really".

I get the head collar on Bolt then Roxy and Max start to play fight. Roxy sees I have Bolt restrained and turns to Max, "Right Max, let's have some fun, It my turn to be Dad and you pretend to be Bolt." Roxy pounces on Max and puts her mouth around his neck snarling "Roxy to Max, pretending to be me "Bolt I hate you... you make me so angry I AM GOING TO BEAT YOU UP NOW" Max replies to Roxy, pretending to be Bolt "Ha... you are not the boss, you tall hairless two legged thing, you can't even run fast, if I want to run around I will and you can't stop me" Roxy seeing my dark mood replies to Max. "I think that's all we can get away with now Max, that was fun". Max laughing "yes it was, can't wait for next time".

Bolt thinks to himself "I am never going to do this again, I am never going to do this again, I really hate this thing on my nose, I am never going to do this again".

THE HEAD COLLAR

A head collar somewhat resembles a halter worn by horses. It basically goes over the dog's head with a big loop going around the dog's neck and a small loop going over the dog's muzzle or nose. At times, people confuse the head collar with a dog muzzle; however, the two are very different and were built for different purposes.

The main purpose of a dog head collar is to provide better control. Horses are large animals that can be easily controlled by a halter wrapped around their heads, therefore, the dog head collar was crafted with the same idea in mind. Basically, the head collar works by controlling the dog's head, which makes it an ideal training tool for dog owners concerned about being dragged down the street.

The head halter was first crafted by Dr. Roger Mugford about 25 years ago. Dr. Mugford is a UK based trainer and animal behaviourist. Owning large dogs such as Irish Wolfhounds, and having back problems as well, Dr. Mugford understood the need for better control. Today, dog head collars can be found in any major pet store. Because head collars require some time for the dog to get accustomed to, it is best to consult with a reputable dog trainer for advice.

As with most training tools, there are pros and cons to keep in mind before investing in their use. As a dog owner, it is ultimately up to you to choose the most appropriate training tool for your dog. If you are uncertain, ask a dog trainer for advice.

4 August 2016

The rescue contacted me and asked me to do an urgent dog assessment in the Newark area. The dog's owner was moving into rented accommodation and dogs were not allowed. The dog had to be assessed and moved at the soonest opportunity so I arranged to go the Newark the following day.

COTTO

(The wrestler)

5 August 2016

Arrangements were made for me to visit and do an assessment on Cotto. When I arrived at the home I was ushered inside and told Cotto was in the back garden. The gentleman owner told me Cotto could be nervous around strangers and was giving me clear signs that he was a little worried as to how Cotto would react to me. I just remained nice and calm and avoided any eye contact with Cotto who by now was barking at me from outside open patio doors. I took a seat opposite the gentleman and his young son and we started to go through some paperwork. I came well-armed with sausages and nonchalantly waved one around by my side to see if Cotto was interested. He most certainly was, but remained very cautious indeed. Then the young boy opposite me chipped in "He's not allowed in the house, he probably thinks he is going to get into trouble". So... it seemed Cotto was an outdoor dog, I didn't know that, and it transpired he had been living outdoors since May. I explored this further and was shown the kennel where he slept outside. It was way too small for him. The gentleman then volunteered that Cotto actually slept under a bush where two empty bowls were placed. We had recently had some very wet weather and I really felt for this poor dog as I don't think that bush offered him much shelter at all.

I went outside to join Cotto and he was very happy to take the sausages off me. He may have been nervous in his back garden, but outside this environment he could possibly be a very different dog. I took him for a short walk on my own and he was very well behaved. I also gave him a good once over checking teeth, nails, ears etc.; he allowed me to do this without complaint and all looked fine. It appeared he could do with putting some weight on but he seemed calm enough away from his small back garden. I was told he was not good with other dogs but when I walked him past a couple he showed some interest but there was certainly no aggression.

I returned Cotto to his owner and set off home to file my report to the rescue. That night I couldn't stop thinking about the poor lad sleeping under his bush. The next morning I called the rescue and asked if they would like me to go and pick him up and foster him until a home could be found. I was certain it wouldn't take long as he was a lovely handsome boy, and quite young. People often prefer to adopt younger dogs.

Cotto had never been in a car at all. On the drive back to my home he travelled quietly but threw up twice. Luckily he was in the back cabin, so that was easy to swill out. Cotto was introduced to my pack and within five minutes he was starting to relax. He showed no dominance or aggression whatsoever, he did really well. Not bad for a boy that didn't like other dogs!

7 August 2016

We woke to a clean house which was very good, considering Cotto had been living outdoors.

On the drive to our walk he was still reluctant to get in the car but at least this time he wasn't sick. Eating wise, he was unsure about raw food but was very happy to have everything lightly stir fried.

I had arranged a social walk at Watchwood on this date so this would be Cotto's first pack walk, and quite a few people were present with lots of dogs. I was so proud of him, he behaved impeccably. He occasionally demonstrated a keenness to play with other dogs but most of the time he was calm and walked on the lead well. He was indeed a different dog away from his old environment. We met up with Ricky on this walk, with his two dogs Mindy and his foster boy Ross. Ricky worked for another rescue but recently had adopted a dog from the rescue I worked with. Sadly, he lost this dog to an illness and was open to the idea of having another GSD. Ricky was definitely taking a shine to Cotto but he had a cat at home and he had his foster boy Ross to look after, so he had a lot on his plate. After a chat, we decided to meet later that day to introduce Cotto to Ricky's cat, just to see how the dog reacted. It's always useful to know how a dog you are fostering reacts to cats.

This walk was also the maiden voyage of Bolt's new GPS tracker," The Pod". The old one he was using was proving expensive to keep topping up his SIM card and of course it wasn't waterproof. The new one was purpose built for dogs and cats, it had some great features and had a very solid build, ideal for Bolt. It was just as well he was wearing it, as about halfway through our walk Bolt took off after a deer. He came back soon enough after several recalls, and although he was seen by other dog walkers we met to be getting very close to the deer, venison would not be on the menu that day.

Cotto's introduction to Ricky's cat went well and sure enough later that evening Ricky contacted me to say he would like to adopt Cotto. Arrangements were made through the rescue and on the following day Ricky arrived at my home to take my foster boy away. Cotto had been with me for only two days but I still had a lump in my throat when he jumped up to give me a goodbye hug. At least I would see Cotto again on future social walks.

Below in the first picture you can see Cotto with his new pack. On the right is Mindy and in the middle is foster boy Ross. In the next picture is Cotto chilling out with his very best friend Ross. On 18th August Ricky decided to adopt Ross. So... the best friends would stay together.

ALEX

(My Best Friend)

Sometime in 1961.

I mentioned in the introduction that I could not write a book about dogs and not include something about the very best childhood friend I could ever have wished for. So this bit is about my first dog Alex, a black Labrador. Things were different in those days. People were a lot more tolerant and dogs could be afforded more freedom. Certainly Alex was able to lead a life that would not be possible for a dog to lead today.

My eldest sister Val and her fiancé Fred bought Alex as a puppy from a pet shop in Consett, County Durham for twenty shillings, when I was two years old. My sister left home to get married when I was six, leaving Alex with my parents. At the time we lived at Blackhill, an urban area on the outskirts of Consett. Alex was allowed out during the day to wander as he wished. He would often toddle off to visit my sister who lived about a mile away. He was street wise and no one seemed to bother him on his solo adventures. As a child I suffered with my health, largely due to pollution produced by the steel works at Consett, so my parents decided to relocate to the countryside when I was seven years old. I now lived on the outskirts of a small village called Medomsley. We were surrounded by open fields and had two trees in the back garden. It was perfect for a young boy, and away from the dust produced by the steel works, my health improved.

Alex and I would spend every waking hour together, the only time we were apart was when I went to school, but even then he sometimes found a way to be with me. The primary school I attended was only a short walk for Alex across three fields. During play time at lunch, he could often be found in the school playing field or playground, much to the delight of all the children. The school teachers would contact my parents and they would have to come and take him home. On one occasion he even came into the school looking for me. Alex had an uncanny way of finding his way around.

On another occasion while I was at school, my parents were worried as Alex had been missing for quite a while. He had decided to go and visit my grandparents, they lived a good three or four miles away and Alex would have had to cross fields, woodlands, and roads to get there. With no telephones it was purely by chance that my Dad thought to call in on my grandparents to see if Alex was there.

When not at school, things were idyllic for me and my very best pal. We would wander miles and miles, exploring and adventuring, Alex never on lead. Sometimes, if the weather was nice, I would find a phone box and call the operator and make a reverse charge phone call home, just to tell my Mum and Dad we would be sleeping out that night. Alex and I would then spend the evening huddled up together under the stars.

The secondary school I attended was in Consett which was a bus journey away. Alex could no longer visit me at school but he knew exactly when the bus was due to bring me home. He would leave the house and sit on the grass and wait for me to come home. As soon as I got off the bus he would dash to greet me and our adventures together for that day would begin.

Alex would, from time to time, come home with the odd cut which my dad would patch up. One day he ended up with more than just a scratch. There were two farm houses around where we lived. One farmer was very tolerant of Alex and had no trouble with him wandering through his fields, even when they contained livestock. The other farmer was not so tolerant. Alex was out wandering and was passing through a field that was full of cows. The farmer, on seeing him, took his shotgun and shot Alex. Apparently Alex was some distance from the farmer when he was shot so the buckshot had spread out. Alex made it home soaked in blood. Most of the pellets were in his neck and fortunately were not too deep. My Dad picked shot out of his neck, head and shoulders and patched Alex up as best he could. My Dad then went to visit the farmer, but he never told me what happened between them.

Alex made a full recovery, he would still go wandering when I was at school but there would be no more incidents with farmers. As my best pal got older, he slowed down somewhat. As he waited for me to come home from school, the distance he could see me approach got shorter and shorter, the greetings were a little less enthusiastic, but the love we had for each other just grew and grew.

When Alex was thirteen he was crossing a road while out wandering and got hit by a car. Again he made it home but he was in bad shape. With lots of love and care he made it through but after he recovered, he seemed to age very quickly. Walking was becoming very difficult for him. One day he took himself off and after searching for him we found him lying under a hedge not far from home. Alex was trying to tell us that his time had come. After some deliberation we decided to help him on his way. Dad and I took him to the vets. Alex lay on the table with my Dad at his head, I just couldn't bring myself to look him in the eye. At fifteen years old all I could do was cuddle him while my dad gently stroked his head. The vet inserted the needle and in moments my best friend, my childhood brother was gone. I was devastated, my life seemed suddenly very empty.

LIFE AFTER ALEX

Things were very quiet and lonely after Alex had gone. As a family we decided not to get another dog, our thinking at the time was it would seem we were trying to replace my pal, and in any event, no dog could live up to Alex. It was probably a good thing we didn't as two years later I left home to pursue a career in the Royal Air Force. My life became very busy and having a dog was just impractical. My ambition was to follow my father's footsteps and become aircrew. After an incredibly arduous selection and training process, I eventually earned my pilot's wings. I started my flying career on the Canberra which was an old twin engine jet bomber that was being used for electronic countermeasures and photographic reconnaissance. After some years I cross trained to fly the Tornado F3, which at the time was the RAF's state of the art fighter. My career took me around the globe. The highlights for me were Operation

Desert Shield, also known as the first Gulf war, Operation Deny Flight, which involved patrolling the skies over Bosnia, and being selected for the N.A.T.O. Tactical Leadership Programme. Very loosely, this was similar to the popular Tom Cruise movie Top Gun. When not flying, my secondary duties involved becoming qualified as a combat survival instructor and teaching escape and evasion from behind enemy lines. At this time of my life I didn't even have time to think about owning a dog, and that feeling of that magical connection that you have with man's best friend started to fade. My mind was elsewhere.

I left the RAF at age 38 and worked for a large retail chain. I moved on from there to work for a company that engaged in corporate team building and motivational events. This proved to be quite lucrative and so in 1999 I started to look for a way to run my own full time Martial Arts school. Martial arts had always been a part of my life and I thought it was time to run my own business. So the Shudokan Black Belt Academy was born, a school teaching the art of Aikido. Within a couple of years the school had grown to be one of the largest Aikido schools in the world with over 400 students at it's high point. Life was still very busy indeed and thoughts of dogs were far from my mind.

I met my wife Jo at my school; she joined as a student, so her daughter, who was also a student, would earn a "Join a friend badge". Jo's intention was to stay a few months and then quit. Years later, she earned her 3rd degree black belt, married me and became joint owner of the school. So her daughter got a badge and Jo got far more than she bargained for.

Jo was used to having dogs and we often discussed getting a rescue dog, but our working hours were long and we thought it would be unfair on the dog. The solution was obvious, it was our business and we were in charge, so we would take the dog to work with us. So it was in summer 2010 we went to meet Roxy. Now this tale has gone full circle.

Today.

I thought it would be worthwhile to wrap things up by telling you where things are today with the dogs that have passed through our lives, and certain other matters.

Starting with certain other matters, I thought it may be interesting to relate, that the neighbour's son that stabbed me has been charged with grievous bodily harm with intent, officially a section 18 which is the most serious assault charge. The court case will be some time in 2017. If found guilty, it is very likely he will go to prison.

KRYSTAL

This sweet old girl recently made her last journey to cross Rainbow Bridge. She had a wonderful life with Chris and Vicky, before which she had no life at all. Krystal is missed by all who were lucky enough to know her.

RICKY WRITES OF COTTO

Cotto is a typically inquisitive, attentive and alert young German Shepherd, having now reached his first birthday. He loves to chase toys, wrestle, eat all he can find and let the other dogs know he wants to be in charge. He has formed a brotherly partnership with Ross, a gangly and naive Pyrenees cross Great Dane of the same age. As a double act they enjoy chasing each other endlessly.

Cotto is particularly close to me, having taken on the role of protector almost immediately and is very classically aloof to others. His sole purpose is to follow his master, to interrupt trips to the bathroom, wake me up before my alarm and otherwise ensure my complete wellbeing at all times. His complex and deep range of emotions are simply fascinating. His strong attachment means he is the first on the scene to show concern at the slightest commotion, and the first to the door to protect me from dangerous couriers, postmen and passing dogs. Cotto is always keen to place his wet nose into my face and give as many licks as he can get away with. He has learnt a healthy respect for Mindy, our now seven year old, rather dainty, GSD bitch. She will be every dog's best friend until they want to chew one of the five or six bones accumulated in her bed. Cotto has learnt very quickly from her that sitting and giving a paw on command may result in a gravy bone or a sausage. He knows that her food goes down first and that she rules the pack, even if from afar.

After a walk, chasing each other through the undergrowth, a mock fight on the front lawn and a bowl of water, Cotto and Ross often end up entangled, one leaned upon the other as the warmth of a fire makes them drift off to a snooze. This is just a small part of the joyful reward of seeing rescue dogs flourish.

TROY, IN HIS OWN WORDS.

Mum has persuaded me to come out of retirement and say a few final words.

It has been hard to motivate myself, Dad recently bought me my own sofa and lined it with a soft plush fleece dressing gown, so I'm loathe to leave it's cosiness, but Mum has reminded me of my duties as a mascot for older rescue dogs.

Some of you who know my life story will know that life was, for the first nine years, mean and harsh and lonely. But thanks to the kindness and dedication of Uncle Ken and Aunty Jo, and my Mum and Dad, and GSD lovers everywhere, I am safe and warm and loved. I hardly dared dream of this, and my thoughts turn to Roman - I wish he could have been here to share this, but I know he is watching over us all, and one day I will meet him again.

So, even though my steps walk a little slower, my head bows a little lower, the silver on my muzzle grows a little more each day, and my eyesight dims, I have never been more content. And this is my fervent wish for all rescue dogs, to find peace and contentment, love and security in their final days. Just like I have.

BIG MAX, IN HIS OWN WORDS.

Hi, Big Max here.

Mum asked me to write a few words, so I've stopped exploring my bottom for a second and remembered the burning issues of the day.

Ball, food, stick, walks, treats, pigs ears, tummy rubs, gravy bones, kisses. Ball, food, stick, walks, treats, pigs ears, tummy rubs, gravy bones, kisses.

A quick bit of proofreading... yep everything important has been covered.

I know, I could go on about my stiff hips, my arthritic old bones, the marsh gas that seeps from my rear end, but I'm a positive soul and I've had a good life. (And the secret of a good life? Invest in some good quality balls and play with 'em all.) I know the time is coming when I'll close my eyes for the last time and run on to Rainbow Bridge. And Mum tells me my hips will be strong and my legs will run like the wind again and I will never be alone, nor passed around in a service station car park like a bag of sweets, for Mum will always hold me in her arms and heart.

Muuum, you said if I wrote something nice for Uncle Ken, I could have a treat! Can I have a pig's trotter? Pleeeease can I? Can I? Look what I've written...

MY GANG

Well... This story has been all about my gang so there is not that much more to add really, other than to bring matters up to date.

ROXY

Her arthritic elbows were starting to tell on her again, so she had a second platelet enhancement treatment in December 2016. She had done really well with her first treatment, it was supposed to give her relief for six to twelve months, and she had nearly fourteen months out of it. It is clear that the second treatment has helped her again, though possibly not to the same degree. She will be a subject for case studies as the treatment is still in it's infancy. That said, she has arthritis, which is a progressive condition and going forward, I will do all I can to manage her condition.

Roxy is still a bit of a loner, although having other dogs around her has definitely enhanced her life. She loves Max, who is really the only dog she plays and interacts with. It is a joy to see them romp around and play fight. Roxy will sometimes intervene if the others are picking on Bolt, she will nip them on the back and bum, trying to tell them to leave Bolt alone. Of all my dogs, she is the one that is most tolerant and protective towards the youngster.

My princess will be eight next year and she still runs around the woods like a two year old, running in the woods is what she loves more than anything. I hope her repeat treatment for her arthritis will give her many more years of joyful dashing about. Even after the love she has had with us, she still remains fearful. It is true to say the experiences dogs have in their early months will live with them forever. If I yell at one of the dogs she will always think I am yelling at her- the ears go back, her head down, and she drops to the floor. I dread to think what happened to her in her first eighteen months.

14 March 2017

While this book was with the publishing company, almost ready for print, on this day at 8:00pm, tragically, we lost our beautiful Roxy to cancer. This loss impacted Jo and I far more than any other, it was devastating for us. On social media I posted the following, the post received hundreds of responses.

A Dogs Purpose – A Tribute to Roxy

I believe the first 20 months of Roxy's life were not benevolent months, it was clear she had little experience of the outside world, she had not been exercised, she was underweight, and she was fearful and untrusting. In spite of this, when she came to us she was sweet and gentle, soon she became very affectionate towards people and good with other dogs.

Roxy was a GSD/Rotweiler cross with the most beautiful features. Her ears were soft and floppy and she loved it when I ran them through my fingers. If I sat at my computer, she would often give me a nudge for some attention. She loved it when I rubbed that spot between her eyes, she would stretch out her neck, close her eyes and pant away in pure joy. Or she would ask for a tummy rub, and if I rubbed in the wrong place she would move my hand to the right spot with her paw. Roxy loved her food and on special occasions would dine on the best steak and salmon. She adapted to raw feeding well and loved it. Although well fed she was still an opportunist food thief. If caught, she would do her thing on me, She would look at me with those doleful eyes, gently jump up at me and hook her front paws over my arm while nuzzling into my neck with her head. I just couldn't be cross with her when she did this, and bless her, she knew just how to play me.

Roxy loved to be outdoors, Often I would look out of our bedroom window and see her in the garden where she would find a stick and throw it in the air and just romp around. It was heart-warming to see the obvious joy in her. Jo and I abandoned holidays abroad, (we would never leave her), and went camping, which again, she loved. She enjoyed nothing more than charging around the woods, hunting squirrels and rabbits. Roxy has had many adventures, too numerous to mention here but they are all documented in my book "Tails of Shepherds".

Roxy's greetings were enthusiastic to say the least. If I was returning home I would see her at the front window waiting for me, her tail would be wagging so hard it would make her body and head sway from side to side. Jo and I run a full time martial arts school and we would always take Roxy to work with us, she was a firm favourite of all the students- adults, children and parents alike. As the pack grew, her visits to work became less frequent but on a Thursday evening I would often take just her and Max with me. Max would sit on the sofa in my office and Roxy on the sofa in reception. She would know exactly when the class finished and would greet me as I came down stairs from the training area. Sometimes she would jump the gun and come upstairs just as the students were lining up to give the closing bow. Roxy would sit by my side at the front of the class, much to the delight of all the students, who would then bow to her. She looked so pleased with herself every time she did this. Last night after I finished the class, I came downstairs to no greeting, and I felt the pain of losing my girl intensify.

Of all the dogs that have lived with us, Max was her favourite. She could be aloof at times but Max had a way to reach her. He was the only other dog she would play with, they had a very special relationship. She was under confident when she first came to us, but as the pack grew so did her confidence, even in her last few days. If the boys were causing trouble amongst themselves she would get between them and give the perpetrator a nip on the shoulder.

Since Roxy entered our lives I was determined she would get the exercise she needed, and so every day we would walk, rain or shine. Every month we would cover at least 100 miles with Roxy off lead. She was a good as gold off lead, I could take her anywhere. So, in the time she has graced my life, I have walked nearly 8000 miles with my beautiful girl by my side, which is an epic journey. However, our journey with Roxy can be measured in more than mere miles.

Roxy was put on this earth for a reason. Before Roxy, I had not had a dog since a child and I had forgotten many things. Roxy patiently re-taught me these things, and a lot more besides. She taught me the value of the unconditional love of dogs, she taught me to be patient and mindful of the vulnerabilities of all animals. She rekindled a love of the outdoors that has been life changing for me, and as a result I am a lot healthier than I would have been. I have made many mistakes in the education she gave me, but she was very patient, and always keen to remind me of her love. As a result, on a personal level, I believe myself to be a much better person for her influence. The joy she has brought into our lives cannot be measured, the impact she has had, has literally been life changing.

Above all, through her very nature, Roxy has inspired Jo and I to help more dogs. Because of her we have gone on to adopt Max, Kiera, Louie, Saxon, Monty and Bolt. Louie and Bolt were on death row, while Max was so ill and had so many issues it is likely he would not have had a long life. We have fostered Roman, Troy, Big Max, Cotto and Jack, all who found good loving homes. We have also re-homed Ben with a lovely family, who have in turn gone on to adopt and foster other dogs. Ben is now very happy in his very own pack of four dogs.

In addition people have told me that the tales of my pack on social media have inspired them to follow suit. To adopt, foster and get involved with rescue. For example, Tom and Elaine have adopted Zann and Marlow and they fostered Sasha. Roxy has been the inspiration behind my book which I plan to use as a fund raiser for dog rescues. The list goes on.

My son Ben had an intense fear of dogs, Roxy removed his fear. I saw one of our parents yesterday who offered her condolences and told me that it was Roxy that took away her sons fear of dogs as well. As a result, that family have now provided a wonderful home for their own dog. I wonder how many other families Roxy has helped in this way. Roxy has been the perfect ambassador for large breed dogs, she has changed many people's opinions and dispelled many negative misconceptions. The number of humans and dogs that Roxy has had a positive impact on cannot easily be counted, and so Roxy's purpose in life, which she achieved without question, was to be exactly what she is now, an ANGEL.

About a week ago Roxy developed a mystery lameness that presented itself in a confusing way. This led to blood tests, x-rays, a CT and MRI scan. The consultant took me through the images with Roxy still asleep from the anaesthetic next to me. Of all the possible things this could have been, we were presented with the worst case scenario. My girl had cancer in multiple locations in her spine. In places it was putting pressure on her spinal cord. My girl had clearly been in pain but she hid it well. The advice I was given was not to wake her, I called Jo who was at home at the time, (she thought I had just gone to bring Roxy home) and we agreed with the advice we were given. The consultant explained he would give her an overdose of anaesthetic, this would give her a feeling of euphoria before taking her pain away forever. It did not take long, I held her close and told her how much I loved her, I gave her a kiss and she took her last breath.

Max knows his girl is gone, we showed him her body at the vets to help him realise what had happened, he reacted with shock and recoiled away. The others know I am sure. Two days before she left us, Saxon stopped eating and started to be sick. Saxon is back on his food but I think he is pining. Jo is heartbroken and as for me, I miss my sweetheart with all my soul. I loved her with all my heart, she was special to us in so many ways. Run free my beautiful girl, be proud of what you have achieved on this earth, and look for me, one day we will be together again.

One last kiss

MAX

This boy has been the biggest challenge of all but is now possibly the most well behaved. The old Max is still just below the surface, you can see that in his body language when he approaches other dogs, his ears prick up and his posture is very upright, he wants everyone to know "I am Max, right?" If he is not sure if his behaviour is acceptable or not, he will look at me straight away to make sure I am not upset with him.

My gladiator will also be eight early next year, he is slowing down a bit for sure. He used to leap into the back of the truck with no problems but now he always needs the ramp. He still loves his walks as much as ever, though. He doesn't like to see people getting separated on our walks and he will always try to herd dogs and humans alike back together. If Jo is out walking with me and I get too far ahead he will stand in front of me to slow me down. He will even jump up at me as if to say "Dad... You have left Mum behind, you need to wait."

In the house Max is at constant loggerheads with Bolt over toys. Max is not really that bothered about toys, he just doesn't want to see Bolt have them, so whatever toy Bolt has, Max will try to steal it from him at the first opportunity.

Max is a very loving boy and enjoys sitting and interacting with me on evenings.

SAXON

The big lad is as noisy as ever, he remains unsure of strangers and lets them know by barking at them in a way that would make me nervous if I were in their shoes. At ten years' old he is in good health, although he has developed a bit of an issue with one of his back legs. Every now and again if he turns on it quickly, he will cry out and whine, holding his foot off the floor. After a minute or two it's fine and off he goes as if nothing happened. As he gets older, this is happening more frequently.

It's true to say Saxon is no fan of Bolt. He has never forgotten the day Bolt bowled him over when out on a walk. If Bolt is running (which is always) and it looks like he is going to get too close to him, he will try to nip him. Sometimes he ends up with white fur in his mouth, I look and yell at him while he tries to spit the fur out of his mouth to get rid of the evidence.

Saxon loves his Mum to bits and behind all of his fear and uncertainty he just wants his love to be returned. He gets that for sure, and more. If I am going on a walk without Jo, and Saxon thinks for whatever reason she is in the truck, he won't leave to walk until I have opened all the doors and proved to him she is not there. If Jo is getting ready in the house to come out walking Saxon displays his excitement by hopping around lifting his two front paws repeatedly off the floor.

MONTY

I have never met such a determined, single minded dog. Monty is an amazing character that deals with whatever life throws at him, he just gets on with it. Given the advancement of the arthritis in his spine and hips I don't know how I have not seen a more profound deterioration in his physical abilities. He has certainly slowed down, and will no longer attempt the attic stairs, but given his probable age that would be expected even without his ailments.

Monty could almost be described as a stoic character yet he does have emotions. He is very focused on me and is not really interested in interacting with other humans. Yet if I am not around for a period of time, he will switch his focus and attentions to the next human that he thinks will look after him. Every morning, as soon as he hears me moving around upstairs he will call to me in his deep voice "WUUH, WUUH, WUUH. I make my way downstairs for our bottom stair cuddle. I sit with my legs apart and he sticks his head between them for a back and neck massage, then he likes to nuzzle in under my chin for cuddles.

Monty prefers Bolt to stay away from him, he is possibly aware that Bolt's rampaging antics may cause him discomfort, so if Bolt gets too close to him, even in the house, Monty will show his teeth and growl at him. If Bolt is throwing a toy about and it lands too close to Monty, Bolt will just stand and stare at the toy, he won't approach Monty to retrieve it.

Monty gets really animated at dinner time. I get the "WUUH, WUUH, WUUH" again and he hops around lifting his front feet off the floor. As each dog bowl goes down he has to have a look in it to make sure the others aren't getting something he isn't.

BOLT

This young lad is such a different dog from when he first arrived. When out on walks now I rarely have to recall him, he has finally learned it is his job to keep an eye on me and not the other way around. We still have the odd lapse now and again but overall he has improved hugely.

Bolt is a very happy-go-lucky soul. Aside from Roxy the others in the pack really don't care for him but that doesn't trouble Bolt one bit. He has nice off lead walks at least twice a day, he has good food, lots of toys, lots of human love, to him, what is there about life not to like?

He tries to initiate play with Max, who never obliges, so he gets to play with me instead. Roxy will sometimes interact with him but Bolt mostly keeps away from Saxon and Monty. They don't bother him as such and he shows no fear or nervousness around them, he just knows they need their space.

Bolt just LOVES to run, and outside of our normal pack walks I will sometimes take him on his own to a local park to play fetch with his throw toy. That boy would run until his legs fell off. Bolt is still very young and he is very intelligent, I can't wait to see him flourish.

LATE 2016

Here our tale comes to an end, but the adventures will continue for many more years. For Jo and I, our experiences with rescue German Shepherds has been life changing. The love and joy these wonderful creatures have brought into our lives will be cherished forever. There has also been pain and sadness. This is the price you pay for love. It's been, and will continue to be, hard work, expensive, and time consuming. It will also continue to be rewarding beyond measure. At this point I can't imagine life without the unconditional love, the mischief, the playfulness, and the incredible character of a rescue German Shepherd.

RESCUE ORGANISATIONS AND VOLUNTEERS

If this tale has in some way inspired you to get involved with rescue, then I am delighted. If not, I am content with just raising awareness and knowing that funds raised by this book will be helping dogs of all breeds somewhere.

For anyone that may be interested in getting more involved at any level in a rescue, from foot soldier to general, my advice is go in with your eyes open. For the foot soldiers out there, take care when picking your rescue, make sure systems and especially insurance is in place to protect you. Ensure there is transparency. Also make sure that people in the organisation are prepared to support you when needed.

For the lieutenants and generals, don't forget your volunteers are your most valuable resource. Without them there is no organisation. Select them carefully, train them responsibly and then nurture and protect them.

At all times, don't lose sight that it's all about the animals.

To those of you already involved in rescue, at all levels, I salute you.

Lightning Source UK Ltd.
Milton Keynes UK
UKOW07f0132020817
306507UK00004B/12/P

9 783732 385638